East Timor

A Memoir of the Negotiations for Independence

by Jamsheed Marker

McFarland & Company, Inc., Publishers
Jefferson, North Carolina, and London

Library of Congress Cataloguing-in-Publication Data

Marker, Jamsheed.
   East Timor : a memoir of the negotiations for independence
/ by Jamsheed Marker.
      p.   cm.
   Includes index.

   ISBN 0-7864-1571-1 (softcover : 50# alkaline paper)

   1. East Timor—History—Autonomy and independence
movements.   2. United Nations—East Timor.   I. Title.
   DS649.6.M37   2003
   959.87'032—dc21   2003001315

British Library cataloguing data are available

Manufactured in the United States of America

Cover photograph by Mark Rhomberg/ETAN

*McFarland & Company, Inc., Publishers
   Box 611, Jefferson, North Carolina 28640
   www.mcfarlandpub.com*

For Kofi Annan,

The Secretary-General … in friendship and admiration.

"If a man be gracious and courteous to strangers, it shows that he is a citizen of the world, and that his heart is no island cut off from other lands, but a continent that joins them."
—Francis Bacon, *Essays*

Contents

Introduction: Why Me?   1

1. Why East Timor?   7

2. Getting Acquainted: People, Places and Perceptions,
   Part I *(Lisbon: March through July 1997)*   18

3. Getting Acquainted: People, Places and Perceptions,
   Part II *(Jakarta: March through July 1997)*   24

4. East Timor *(March through July 1997)*   37

5. The Negotiations Commence
   (March through August 1997)   46

6. The Consultations Widen *(Geneva, Pretoria, Vienna,
   and London: August through November 1997)*   56

7. Coming to Grips: The Negotiations Intensify
   *(Indonesia and East Timor: December 1997; Portugal:
   January 1998; London: April 1998)*   65

8. Negotiations Continue in the Shadow of Indonesia's
   Summer of Discontent *(New York and Washington:
   April and May 1998)*   78

9. The Second Innings: Indonesia in Transit and Tumult
   *(New York, Lisbon, Jakarta, and East Timor: June
   and July 1998)*   86

10. The Doctor's Dilemma: The Negotiations Intensify, but So Does the Conflict *(New York, Vienna, and Lisbon: October and November 1998)*   101

11. Sailing into the Squall *(Indonesia and East Timor: December 1998)*   108

12. A Dramatic Decision, and an Opportunity Seized *(New York: January and February 1999)*   121

13. Substantive Progress in Negotiations in New York; Ominous Signals from East Timor *(New York, Jakarta, and East Timor: February to April 1999)*   132

14. Agreement Between the Republic of Indonesia and the Portuguese Republic *(New York: April and May 1999)*   144

15. UNAMET and the Arduous Path to the Ballot *(New York, Jakarta, Dili, Sydney, and Canberra: May to July 1999)*   161

16. The Popular Consultation in East Timor: The Ballot *(New York, Jakarta, and Dili: July and August 1999)*   181

17. The Aftermath of the Ballot *(Dili, Jakarta, and New York: August 31 to October 31, 1999)*   192

18. A Review, and Some Reflections   202

Epilogue   211

Index   217

Introduction: Why Me?

The involvement of a Pakistani diplomat in the long-standing and conflict-ridden political dispute between Indonesia, Portugal, and East Timor may initially appear somewhat incongruous. But for the United Nations such a situation is by no means bizarre, and the induction of a neutral, distant national as a negotiator is, in fact, very much the norm. As background, therefore, it might be appropriate to give a brief account of the events in my life that led to my appointment as Personal Representative of the UN Secretary-General for East Timor.

I stumbled into diplomacy in the year 1965. Prior to that, following graduation from college, I had served as an officer in the Royal Indian Navy in World War II on convoy escort duties, mine sweeping, and combined operations. Even in those distant days of my brash youth, I was struck by the extreme moral complexities of war, with its manifestations of idealism and heroism, juxtaposed with revulsion and horror. This dichotomy has remained with me ever since, in its persistent, unresolved fashion, leaving me with the conviction that there must be a better way to resolve differences. It is surely an unmitigated paradox that one has to kill a man in order to convince him that you are right.

On leaving the Navy I went into a reasonably prosperous family business, until the government of Pakistan somewhat unexpectedly sought me out and proposed a diplomatic assignment. The 1960s was the heady decade of the decolonization process, with the emergence of a number of newly independent countries, each bringing its own hopes and aspirations, together with its difficulties and problems, and each being thrown up for grabs for the two super powers that vigorously conducted the then prevalent Cold War. For Pakistan, as for most other states, it became necessary to establish relations with these new entrants

1

Jamsheed Marker. Photograph: United Nations Department of Public Information.

to the international community, and to therefore expand its diplomatic service.

Pakistan possessed an excellent cadre of foreign service officers, but they were numerically insufficient, particularly in the senior grades, to cope with the requirements of this sudden expansion, and the government therefore appointed ambassadors from other departments, and from the political and private sectors.

I came under the latter category, and therefore started my diplomatic career as an ambassador, a convenience that obviated the necessity of hacking my way to the top, as is the fate of most diplomats everywhere. I also fully expected, at the time that I assumed my first assignment, that I would return to private life once the three-year term was over. This expectation proved to be erroneous—by about twenty-seven years.

Accordingly, I found myself in Accra, in April 1965, as Pakistan's High Commissioner to Ghana, with concurrent accreditation to Guinea and Mali. Those were the early days of independence, with "the winds of change," as Harold Macmillan so vividly described them, blowing in strong gusts all over Africa.

Those days revealed both the enthusiasms and the foibles of governments in emerging post-colonial situations, and they gave me my first lessons in the necessity of objectivity and the difficulties inherent in maintaining it. There was so much to admire and yet at the same time so much to deplore. And although a spirit of tolerance was always necessary, it was frequently hard to sustain.

From West Africa I was transferred to Romania, with concurrent accreditation to Bulgaria, and thereby commenced a ten-year tour of duty in the communist countries of Eastern Europe. The government of Pakistan decided to renew my contract each time that it expired, and I remained a "non-career head of mission" throughout my diplomatic service.

Naturally, I submitted my resignation whenever there was a change of government in Pakistan, but on each occasion I was ordered to stay on. My contract contained a clause to the effect that the President and I could each terminate the contract at will, "without assigning any reason whatsoever." But I was never unmindful of the fact that he was in a rather better position to exercise this option than I was.

Romania in 1968 was already well under the dictatorial rule of Nicolae Ceaușescu and his even more odious wife, Elena. Internally it was one of the most rigid, brutal Stalinist regimes in existence at the time, and the terrorization of its population was complete. Yet externally, Ceaușescu proclaimed a policy of "independence" from Moscow, established contacts with the West, sought to remain neutral in the Sino-Soviet dispute, and established diplomatic relations with the Federal German Republic and with Israel. This earned him far more diplomatic and economic advantages from the west than many of us thought he deserved.

For the diplomats stationed in Bucharest, who witnessed on a daily basis the ugly manifestations of Ceaușescu's extreme totalitarianism, the main preoccupation was to urge in their capitals a sense of balance and objectivity, and to point out the nature of the cynical and shrewd manipulation engineered by the Ceaușescu regime. In the end, fate decreed a just retribution on the Ceaușescus, although it need not have been quite as cruel and messy as it was. But in hindsight one wonders whether the imperatives of the Cold War justified the diplomatic and economic support for the Ceaușescu dictatorship, with the implicit acceptance of its gross human rights violations. It is questions of this kind that have haunted me ever since, and continued to pose a dilemma in my later negotiations.

I was next posted as Ambassador of Pakistan to the USSR (with concurrent accreditation to Finland) and spent three fascinating years in Moscow during the dark Brezhnev era. There was much to be learned from this assignment, but this is not the place to expound on it. Suffice it to say that it provided me with a new understanding and admiration for the human spirit, particularly in its capability for survival in conditions of the most profound adversity. Just as impressive was the unmistakable sense of patriotism, and sheer love of the Motherland, that pervaded the Russian soul.

After a brief spell in Canada (with concurrent accreditation to Guyana and Trinidad and Tobago), I was posted to East Berlin and opened Pakistan's first resident mission to the German Democratic Republic (with concurrent accreditation to Iceland). In Berlin the dichotomies and contrasts were particularly stark.

The glorious, inspirational joys and pleasures of Western civilization —three magnificent opera houses, two superb orchestras, and numerous museums and art galleries of the highest and richest quality—were interspersed in East and West Berlin. But in order to get to them one had to endure the grim, pervasive presence of the Berlin Wall, and the sickening process of transit through its oppressive checkpoints. Here again, there was the constant juxtaposition of the finest and the meanest in the human spirit, constantly demanding explanation, and persistently imposing choices in the thoughts and conduct of one's affairs.

From East Berlin I moved to Tokyo, where I got to live, work, and become friends with a people whom I had encountered under vastly different circumstances in a war thirty years before. In that war I had traded bullets with the Japanese, but now the time had come to trade yen credits. From Tokyo I was posted to the United Nations in Geneva, where my love for this organization blossomed from support to enthusiasm, as I became aware of the widespread opportunity for personal involvement and activity.

The multifarious specialized agencies provided the facilities for dealing with a plethora of important and interesting issues, varying from disarmament, human rights, trade, and development, to refugees and labor. The experience, despite innumerable frustrations, was both stimulating and satisfying, and Geneva became an admirable place for honing whatever multilateral negotiating skills I might have possessed.

My next assignments took me successively to Bonn, Paris, and Washington. The amount of diplomatic activity in each of these important capitals was, obviously, enormous, far too extensive to permit recapitulation. All that I can say is that the experience I gained was immeasurably supplemented by the friendships I formed with people whose wisdom and guidance, always generously extended, were to be so valuable in my future work over East Timor.

My last diplomatic assignment was as Permanent Representative of Pakistan to the United Nations in New York, where I had the privilege of working with colleagues from all over the world, and above all, with three distinguished Secretaries-General: Javier Perez de Cuellar, Boutros Boutros-Ghali, and Kofi Annan. A two-year stint on the Security Council and one year as Chairman of the Group of 77 provided valuable experience in multilateral negotiations.

This concluded a career in which I had served my country continually as Ambassador of Pakistan for thirty years, in eleven different capitals, with nine further concurrent accreditations. It had been a long and vastly interesting innings, and one that, I hoped, had justified the confi-

Secretary General Kofi Annan (left) and his Personal Representative for East Timor, the author. New York. Photograph: UN Department of Public Information.

dence that my country had reposed in me by honoring me with its representation for so many years.

During my tenure at the United Nations in New York I had developed a close relationship with Kofi Annan, both in personal and professional capacities, and in due course, after my retirement, Kofi offered me the post of Personal Representative of the Secretary-General for East Timor. I accepted it with alacrity and enthusiasm, coupled with a sense of honor and gratitude, convinced that nothing could be more worthwhile than to work with this dedicated, sensitive, modest, and decisive Secretary-General.

In the preparation of these memoirs, I have benefited greatly from the help and guidance so generously provided to me by Elie Wiesel, David Brown and Shashi Thardor. Their wise counsel has added immensely to the value of the contents of these memoirs. My thanks also to Rusty Fischer.

All imperfections and errors are mine alone.

Finally, a special word of deep gratitude and loving thanks to my beloved wife, Arnaz, whose affectionate companionship, lively encouragement, and astute perception formed an essential part of my voyages, and made this book possible. And also to my children, Niloufer, Feroza, and Sam, for their love, encouragement, understanding, and support for everything that I do.

For them, my feelings of affection and gratitude are boundless.

Independence for East Timor

"In 1999, the world watched as East Timor, a small island North of Australia, voted for and gained their freedom from Indonesian occupation in a UN-supervised referendum. As the referendum concluded with an overwhelming victory for independence, we watched on international television as Indonesian-trained militia and Indonesian armed forces were unleashed across the country—massacring civilians, cutting power and water lines, and burning 85 percent of the buildings in the country, including virtually all schools and nearly all businesses.

"Today, under UN protection, and with a UN Transitional Administration assisting in the peaceful transition to a new government, the East Timorese people are rebuilding their nation. They have held their first democratic election—an election so peaceful that families brought their children to the polling booths. They have drafted and adopted their country's first constitution, adopted their national flag and national anthem. They are even approaching their first-ever presidential election....

"On May 19 and 20, 2002, the world will again watch. This time, we will watch and celebrate with them, through two days of music, culture, and tradition, as the United Nations hands over the reins to this newly established democratic government, and East Timor stands on its feet as the first new, free country of the millennium."

—From www.easttimor.com

1

Why East Timor?

"When you start on your journey to Ithaki, pray that the road
you take will be a long one, full of adventure, full of things to
learn."
— *C.P. Cavafy*, Alexandrian Greek Poet

For most people, except those that live in the region and its proximity, East Timor is a distant place, not too easy to locate, even on a map.
Apart from its residents and immediate neighbors, its travails were known
to few, and since it possessed neither size, nor geopolitical significance,
nor vast natural resources or economic interest, it is no surprise that its
existence was largely overlooked.

But somewhere in that tiny, distant half island, a spark was flicker-
ing, and a small segment of humanity was not only struggling to assert
its rights, but more importantly was calling upon the United Nations to
act in fulfillment of its Charter. In February of 1997, when Secretary-
General Kofi Annan suggested that I attempt a mediation effort in East
Timor, I knew as little of the East Timor problem as most people did,
which was not very much.

I accepted the assignment essentially because, as I have indicated in
the preface, nothing could be more worthwhile than to work with Kofi as
his representative. But there was also, I think, the personal excitement of
an unknown challenge so famously expressed by James Elroy Flecker:

> We travel not for trafficking alone:
> By hotter winds our fiery hearts are fanned:
> For lust of knowing what should be unknown
> We take the Golden Journey to Samarkand.

What follows will, I hope, describe how this was done. For East
Timor *was* a United Nations success story.

Timor is a 32,000 square kilometer island, situated in the Indonesian archipelago, of which East Timor contains 19,000 square kilometers, populated by just under a million people. Timor was colonized in the early 17th century by the Dutch, who occupied the western part of the island, and by the Portuguese, who took over the eastern section. West Timor became a part of Indonesia when the country gained its independence from the Netherlands in 1949, but East Timor remained a Portuguese colony.

After the fall of the Salazar dictatorship and the establishment of democracy in Portugal in 1975, Lisbon embarked on a process of decolonization. But a failure to transfer power in orderly fashion led to civil war in East Timor, which triggered a military intervention and occupation by Indonesia. The United Nations condemned this occupation, and called for an exercise of the right of self-determination by the East Timorese.

The foregoing is a highly compressed genesis of the East Timor problem, and the purport of this book is to continue the story from the time that the United Nations assumed an active role in the problem of East Timor and brought about the international agreements which enabled the transformation of East Timor from a colony to an independent, democratic nation.

A new chapter has thus been opened in the history of a remarkable and lovable people, who have endured over three hundred years of a colonial occupation which was always neglectful and often violent, followed by twenty-five years of a powerful neighbor's domination, which was always exploitative and often brutal.

The East Timorese resistance movement has some unique features and well merits a case study. Unlike many other resistance movements (the Middle East, Kashmir, Angola, Mozambique, Afghanistan) it lacked any support in its immediate neighborhood, since the formal position of the ASEAN countries, as well as Australia, was a factual acceptance of the Indonesian contention that the integration of East Timor into the Indonesian Republic was final and complete.

Thus, lacking any contiguous hinterland for the purpose of retreat and regrouping, essential operational requirements for resistance movements, the East Timor resistance became a kind of hothouse flower which existed largely on its own intrinsic roots, fading and blooming as circumstances warranted, for over twenty-two years.

True, the United Nations had deplored the Indonesian military intervention from the moment that it occurred, and had steadfastly refused to acknowledge the integration, so that the "Question of East Timor" became a hardy perennial on the Agenda of the General Assembly. But in actual fact, for most of the international community this formal position was circumscribed by a de facto acceptance of Indonesian suzerainty. The support from abroad that fueled East Timorese resistance, though constant, was perfunctory and intermittent, conditioned as it was by Cold War imperatives.

There is a persistent view that a reluctant Suharto was pushed into military intervention in East Timor in 1975 by Washington, which was deeply concerned that the Soviet Union, taking advantage of the chaotic conditions that prevailed on the island following the precipitate Portuguese withdrawal, would establish a presence in support of an East Timorese communist regime.

The acquisition of Dili would supplement the existing Soviet facilities in Cam Ranh Bay and provide Moscow with a significant strategic naval presence in the region. Documentary evidence to support this theory is hard to find, but in the light of the tensions and hysteria of the Cold War period of the mid-seventies, it has an air of credibility and cannot be dismissed entirely. In my very first meeting with him in March 1997, Suharto sounded fairly plausible when he mentioned his initial reluctance to intervene in East Timor, and that he had been forced to do so by circumstances. His elaboration that the call emanated from the people of East Timor was, however, much less convincing.

While the general international response to East Timor was a grimace and a sad, helpless shrug of the shoulders, there were notable exceptions. Apart from the important symbolism of the United Nations' collective persistence in maintaining the issue on its Agenda, there were a number of Non Government Organizations (NGOs), which maintained a constant interest in East Timor, and the Nobel Committee made a contribution to this recognition at a crucial moment.

The most prominent activist was, of course, the Government of Portugal, in which country East Timor was the major foreign policy issue. Whatever the reasons, perhaps a combination of post colonial guilt and remorse from the past coupled with a contemporary emotional post revolutionary fervor, there was no doubt that on the subject of East Timor all the Portuguese political parties, from extreme left to extreme right, held the same vigorous, obsessional position. This was reflected in Portugal's diplomacy, which persistently raised the issue in all international fora, particularly in European councils, where the Portuguese skillfully and constantly thwarted attempts to advance Indonesian, and even ASEAN, interests.

The "Santa Cruz massacre" in Dili on November 12th, 1991, when

Indonesian troops fired upon and killed a large number of peaceful East Timorese demonstrators, raised considerable international concern. Furthermore, significant events such as the arrest and detention in December 1992 of the charismatic Xanana Gusmao, the universally acknowledged leader of the East Timorese resistance, and the award of the Nobel Peace Prize to Bishop Ximenes Belo and Jose Ramos Horta in October 1996, each in respective fashion, provided the impetus that turned the embers of East Timorese resistance into vivid flashes of flame.

On December 22, 1975 the United Nations Security Council called on Indonesia to withdraw its armed forces from East Timor, and repeated the call on April 26, 1976. The General Assembly on November 19, 1976, reacting to the Indonesian Government's legislation incorporating East Timor as a province of the Republic, rejected the move and called for an act of self determination.

The issue thus became a regular item on the Agenda of the General Assembly, and initiated, by way of General Assembly and Security Council resolutions, a process which required Portugal and Indonesia to hold negotiations, under the aegis of the Secretary-General, for a solution of the East Timor issue. The problem was also raised, in visible fashion, at the Human Rights Commission in February 1983, from which date it became a major focal point in the activities of the Commission, generating several heated debates that also found their way to the Third Committee of the General Assembly.

But despite the significance of the political process instituted by the General Assembly and Security Council resolutions, the practical effects did not go very far, proceeding in somewhat desultory fashion over a series of inconclusive biannual meetings between the Secretary-General and the two Foreign Ministers. The Secretary-General's annual report to the General Assembly reported this lack of progress, and the General Assembly in turn urged the continuation of the consultation process.

When Kofi Annan assumed the office of Secretary-General of the United Nations in January 1997, he decided that the East Timor issue needed a push, and a more vigorous approach than it had been hitherto accorded. In creating the post of Personal Representative of the Secretary-General (PRSG), he signaled his personal and active commitment to a solution of the East Timor problem.

We met in the office of the Secretary-General on a cold New York day in February 1997, when Kofi offered me the assignment for East Timor, subject to concurrence by the Governments of Portugal and Indonesia, which were received shortly thereafter. Our meeting was as brief and comprehensive as most meetings with Kofi Annan usually are.

His formula was quite straightforward: he entrusted me with the modus operandi of the negotiations, and assured me of his support. Few diplomats could have had it so good, and the start could not have been more propitious. I therefore reported directly to the Secretary-General at all times, even though during the later stages of the negotiations it obviously became necessary for me to report to the Security Council also. Naturally, as events progressed, the role of the Security Council increased from the important to the crucial, and the Secretary-General maintained, as was to be expected, the closest links with the Council, especially after the May 5, 1999 Agreements had been signed in New York.

The decision that I should report directly to the Secretary-General during the early stages of the negotiations was an admirable one as far as I was concerned. It provided for a measure of discretion, reticence, and flexibility, all of which are valuable elements in the initial stages of negotiations of this nature. Furthermore, the prevalent impression that East Timor was one of those almost forgotten, intractable issues that invoked frustration rather than optimism, generated an apathy and a comparative lack of public interest which I personally welcomed as conducive to our low key approach.

Also helpful, in those early days, was the collective decision taken with my collaborators to maintain as far as possible a public silence on the state of the negotiations. These Trappist vows provoked some irritation, but on the whole were accepted by the media in a generous gesture of understanding.

Kofi Annan's role in the East Timor negotiations was absolutely crucial, and its importance cannot be emphasized enough. It went far beyond the titular and involved an active, lively interest in the progress of the process, spurred when necessary by effective initiatives and interventions. Having once set the objectives and got the ball rolling, he chose a team and let it get on with the job, providing guidance when necessary, but scrupulously eschewing micromanagement in any form whatsoever.

Initiative and implementation are the principal amalgam of true leadership, and Kofi Annan demonstrated this in exemplary fashion. Having worked together before, when he was Under Secretary-General for Peacekeeping and I was Pakistan's representative on the Security Council, we had already developed a professional rapport. As time went on and as the East Timor negotiations went through the customary phases of setbacks and successes, my affection for Kofi and admiration of his skills grew exponentially.

The comforting feeling that I knew I had his trust and confidence was further enhanced by his ready availability for consultation, advice, and guidance. Despite the multifarious other issues that landed on the desk of the Secretary-General, Kofi always possessed an up-to-date knowledge of the current state of negotiations over East Timor. This enabled him to weigh in, whenever necessary, with the formidable combination of the strength and prestige of his office, coupled with his own immense personal dignity.

I can recall occasions when the two Foreign Ministers, each of whom severally entered the Secretary-General's office with grim expressions and knitted brows, emerged fifteen minutes later with smiles of satisfaction. When I complimented Kofi on the effectiveness of the West African spells that he had obviously cast on each of his visitors, the only response that I got from this most urbane and sophisticated of men was a quiet smile.

This, then, was Kofi Annan's method: (a) take bold and imaginative initiatives, (b) keep it low key, (c) maximum devolution of authority and responsibility, (d) zero micromanagement, (e) assume overall responsibility at all times, and (f) act decisively when circumstances so demand.

Next to the privilege of working closely with the Secretary-General was the stimulating satisfaction of working with his Chef de Cabinet. Iqbal Riza is a close friend and colleague with whom I have shared, over many years, not only a close friendship but also common understandings and values, the sort that binds friendship with companionship. We speak a common language in two languages. Iqbal possesses a sense of idealism which not only stokes his deep motivation but has remained unscathed despite vicissitudes and setbacks which could have turned most idealists into cynics.

Combined with this dedication is a fierce loyalty to the United Nations and, of course, his Chief. An able diplomat, with wide ranging experience of the United Nations system, both at headquarters and in the field, Iqbal's impressive professional competence is augmented by an equally impressive humane touch. In my work on East Timor, Iqbal was a true guide, philosopher, friend, and dogsbody, constantly providing political counsel while simultaneously guiding my incompetent navigation through the UN's bureaucratic shoals.

Iqbal effectively backed the Secretary-General in providing the encouragement and ready support, which was as reassuring as it was important to the work of the PRSG. Without this kind of involvement and support from the 38th floor, the story of East Timor could well have had a less positive outcome.

The Department of Political Affairs, which assumed overall responsibility for the East Timor negotiations, was headed by Under Secretary-General Sir Kieran Prendergast, a nimble minded Briton with 20/20 political vision, an incisive wit, and a decisive nature. Possessing an unfailing ability to identify, expose, and discard the superfluous, which he always did with devastating logic, Kieran's wisdom and counsel proved invaluable in crisis management. His attitude and approach remained at all times collegial in the extreme, and working with him was as intellectually stimulating as it was professionally agreeable.

The Assistant Secretary-General dealing with the East Timor dossier was Alvaro de Soto, a highly intelligent and competent Peruvian with a quiet demeanor and a subtle sense of humor. Alvaro's rich experience derived from a succession of diplomatic negotiations all over the world, to which was added an impressive institutional memory coupled with an extensive familiarity with the workings of the UN system. He was an invaluable colleague who handled a number of crises with his own inimitable competence and professionalism.

The two officers assigned to work with me on East Timor were Francesc Vendrell, the Director of the Asia Pacific Division of the Department of Political Affairs, and Tamrat Samuel, a Political Officer in the Division. The two could not have been more different in temperament and appearance, a disparity which was an asset in its own way, particularly as both officers were intelligent, deeply motivated, and had a thorough professional grasp of the issues.

Vendrell was from Spain, with a distinguished bearing (I thought that he looked like a grandee long before I ever knew him or his origins) and an extremely lively mind. Like many highly intelligent people, he was inclined to be temperamental, sometimes explosive, and had difficulty concealing his feelings, especially when confronted by acts of injustice or inhumanity. Since this was by no means infrequent in our line of business in East Timor, Francesc was subject to regular pangs of personal agony on this account.

His lively mind was also always full of ideas, and was on the constant search for new initiatives, which he would pull out of his hat with the proverbial magician's flourish. Not all of these were always appropriate, of course, and their acceptance, adaptation, or rejection became a regular feature of my work, adding to its burden and its fascination. Vendrell had a vast knowledge of the South East Asia region, and it was not acquired simply through the long experience of his duties.

An inveterate traveler, he had moved through the area not just as a modern day tourist but as an inquisitive explorer, rather like one of his 17th century forbears, and carried with him the observations of his keen eye. Above all, Vendrell was extremely conscientious, and either produced, or supervised the production of, working papers and reports of the highest quality. All these attributes, coupled with his intense loyalty to the cause and the institution, made him a very valuable member of our team.

Tamrat Samuel, a brilliant and highly competent young Eritrean, had joined the United Nations after a somewhat turbulent spell in Ethiopia. Tall, soft-spoken, and erudite, he had the unmistakable bearing of the nobility of his descent. He had worked on the East Timor dossier for many years, both in the field and at New York, and was thoroughly familiar not only with the issues but, more importantly, with the personalities involved, particularly the East Timorese.

As time went on, he increasingly developed this considerable relationship of trust and confidence with each of his interlocutors: the Indonesians, the Portuguese, and the East Timorese. Tamrat's long experience, coupled with his wide range of contacts, were invaluable assets to our work, often highlighting the dramatic elements in the contents of the extensive files and records in our archives.

For instance, Tamrat was present in Dili on the day that Xanana Gusmao was tried and sentenced to life imprisonment. His description of the sense of despair that pervaded the island on that occasion was unforgettable. It served to remind me, in my later negotiations with the Indonesians, of the political importance of Xanana to the settlement process. I owe much to Tamrat Samuel, for his expertise, his professionalism, and his devotion to our enterprise. But above all, I am grateful for his understanding and his friendship.

The early days of my mission were spent in New York, getting briefed by colleagues in the UN and meeting a number of diplomats, notably Antonio Monteiro, the lively and likable Portuguese Ambassador, and Makarim Wibisono, the less ebullient but equally likable Indonesian Ambassador. Our professional association quickly developed into warm personal friendships, which proved to be a most useful safety belt during the vicissitudes and moments of discomfort that inevitably occur during the course of long and complicated negotiations of this nature.

In addition, we were fortunate enough to have the invaluable help, advice, and support of a number of very able diplomats posted to missions to the UN. Most prominent of these were Ambassador Penny Wensley of Australia, Ambassador Nancy Soderberg of the United States, Ambassador Stewart Eldon of the United Kingdom, Ambassador Yukio Takasu of Japan, and Ambassador Michael Powles of New Zealand.

They met me shortly after I took over the assignment and conveyed their interest and support for the East Timor negotiations. They were true to their offer in word and deed, providing me with important information and intelligence obtained from their governments, the value of which was immeasurably bolstered by the supplementary advice rendered through the personal skills of the diplomats themselves.

Later on, these representatives were to form the "Core Group" of unofficial advisers on East Timor. This innovative idea emanated from the Secretary-General, and became an essential part of the negotiating process. We used the Core Group not only for advice and to keep them informed, but also for coordination with the Security Council (drafting of resolutions) and most importantly to prevail on their governments to lean on the Indonesian or Portuguese governments whenever we felt it necessary to do so.

My preliminary meetings in New York were rounded off by a session with Jose Ramos Horta, the East Timorese resistance leader who had remained in exile for a number of years, and had vigorously campaigned for independence. Ramos Horta called on the Secretary-General in March, and at our meeting he was informed of the renewed United Nations efforts for a solution, which he welcomed, and to which he promised full support.

The recent award of the Nobel Peace Prize had obviously been a boost to his morale, and had also added to his pugnacity. His denunciation of the Indonesians was forceful and scathing, and his distrust of their motives was as strong as his contempt for their policies. Years of exile, suffering, and struggle had left their mark on a basically assertive personality, and he had a tendency to indulge in wild outbursts (not to mention the occasional outlandish proposal, such as descending in East Timor with a planeload of film stars) both in private as well as public.

These were never very helpful. And yet, in his quieter moments, when he was not tub-thumping, Jose could be a very agreeable companion, prepared to share a joke and to discuss with animation his other passion, as Professor of Law at the University of New South Wales in Sydney, Australia. It was obvious that Ramos Horta would be an essential element in our negotiating process on the basis of his record and his status. His loyalty to Xanana was complete, and during the penultimate stages of the negotiations, when things got a little tricky, Ramos Horta curbed his impulsiveness and displayed cooperation, party discipline, and a sense of responsibility which was most impressive.

The dossiers on East Timor in the UN archives were voluminous in quantity and substantial in quality, but their perusal did not provide much ground for optimism. The Indonesian position that East Timor's integration was complete and final, and the Portuguese position that a valid act of self determination had not yet taken place, were the rocks of intransigence on which the negotiations had hitherto floundered.

A series of high-level as well as mid-level meetings over the course of the years provided glimpses of an occasional flicker of hope, but then seem to have concluded at the inevitable impasse. The process, it appeared to me, seemed to have survived only upon the oxygen of the General Assembly's acceptance of the Secretary-General's recommendation that the negotiations continue. The distrust on both sides was palpable and continued to permeate the atmosphere for a large part of the time that I conducted the negotiations.

Although this was awkward and frustrating, much of it was understandable and had to be accepted as standard. After all, we were dealing with a long standing problem which involved everything from the relics of colonialism to issues of international law and of human rights—and all of this against a background of a highly emotional public opinion in both countries. I reckoned therefore that our first small step would be to try and develop some understanding between the negotiators themselves, and to develop a sense of confidence between the negotiators and the United Nations mediators.

Another major problem was the East Timorese, the mention of whose existence provoked opposite but equally visceral reactions on both sides. The Portuguese regarded them as a people struggling for independence and worthy of support. For the Indonesians, such action amounted to interference in the internal affairs of a state, and that on its most vulnerable and sensitive issue, that of national unity in a multiracial, multiethnic, multi-religious society living in a far-flung archipelago.

It smacked of divide and rule, and of an attempt to re-impose the dark, murky policies of a past, hated colonialism. Previous attempts to involve representatives of East Timor in the negotiating process had been strongly rebuffed by Indonesia, and the most that had been achieved was the establishment of the All Inclusive East Timorese Dialogue (AIETD), an unofficial organization of East Timorese representatives from the diaspora as well as the island itself.

The AIETD was initially meant to be a forum for the East Timorese to get together and discuss cultural issues only. A ban on the discussion of political matters was enforced both by the rules of the AIETD and by the pro-integration East Timorese participants. A preliminary meeting was held in London, and two subsequent meetings were held in Austria, generously financed and efficiently organized by the Austrian Ministry of Foreign Affairs. The United Nations acted as a "facilitator" for the AIETD, a device which permitted Tamrat Samuel to widen his contacts and improve his expertise on the party groupings of the East Timorese. He was also able to persuasively prevent the breakup of the conference on one occasion.

Despite the creation of the AIETD, I felt that the existing process of trilateral consultations—UN, Portugal, and Indonesia—had in many ways marginalized the East Timorese, and that the time would soon come when we would have to stop playing *Hamlet* without the Prince. Clearly, attempts at a formal institutionalization of an UN/East Timorese dialogue would have wrecked the negotiations at the start, quite apart from the fact that it would have been impossible at the time to secure a credibly representative group of East Timorese. But the latitude and flexibility provided in the mandate of the PRSG enabled us to deal with the lacuna of the absence of their representation.

My colleagues and I maintained a regime of rigorous but unofficial contact with the East Timorese leaders on an individual basis, both in the island and from the diaspora. We kept them as fully informed as possible of our discussions with both governments, subject of course to the requirements of the confidentiality of the formal negotiation process. This device had the additional advantage of inducting the East Timorese viewpoint into the equation of our considerations, while simultaneously building their trust and confidence in the UN negotiating process. Of course, all this did not happen at once, but gradually evolved as events took their course.

In March 1997, however, after I had completed my study of the East Timor dossier and gone through a series of meetings with my UN colleagues and the diplomats posted in New York, the outlook appeared uncertain, to say the least. The many expressions of encouragement and support that I received were indeed reassuring, but seemed to me to reflect enthusiasm rather than optimism. Thus, with my backpack loaded with ideas, counsel, and advice, I started on my journey to Ithaki. The road promised "to be a long one, full of adventure, full of things to learn."

2

Getting Acquainted: People, Places and Perceptions, Part I

LISBON: MARCH THROUGH JULY 1997

> "Because your strength is unequal to the task, do not assume that it is beyond the powers of man; but if anything is within the powers and promise of man, believe it is within your compass also."
>
> —*Marcus Aurelius*

Tamrat Samuel and I made a brief visit to Lisbon in March of 1997. Our quest for a solution to the East Timor problem could not have started in more salubrious and congenial circumstances. The beautiful city, set amidst green hills with the Tagus rolling majestically into the Atlantic, the meandering roads bearing homes with walls of bright ochre, white and blue, topped by brilliant red roofs and decked with wondrous wrought iron windows and balconies, never fails to delight the eye.

The people matched the sunny disposition of the city and, since the local TV station had given our visit extensive coverage, we were greeted with courtesy, smiles, and greetings of encouragement when we visited the charming riverside restaurants and other public places during our infrequent leisure time.

Since our primary objective was the resumption of talks, the initial positive response of the Portuguese government was encouraging. I was kept busy during this short stay in Lisbon, meeting the President, Prime Minister, and Foreign Minister, as well as the Deputy Speaker and Mem-

18

bers of the Parliamentary Committee on East Timor. In addition, I also met a number of East Timorese exiles and the representatives of a number of NGOs, which were actively involved in the issue.

One was immediately struck by the immense and forceful unanimity of all shades of Portuguese opinion on the subject of East Timor. Far from being estranged from its former colony by time and distance, East Timor was a live issue of immense proportions. Despite the fact that Portugal was heavily involved at the time in augmenting its participation within the European Community, a worthwhile and practical project of obvious national political and economic benefit, distant East Timor continued to remain a subject of the highest priority in the Foreign Ministry. Self-determination for East Timor was a principle incorporated into the constitution of the country, and the dossier formed a special, and the only, political responsibility of an otherwise constitutional President.

I felt that the emotional attachment to East Timor was partly driven by a sense of guilt for Portugal's messy and precipitate withdrawal from the territory in 1975, before the completion of the decolonization process. Added to this was the crusading enthusiasm of a recently formed popular democratic administration, conscious of a guilty colonial past and anxious to provide moral compensation and redress.

For instance, President Sampaio told me that some of the East Timorese resistance leaders used to join him, in the old days, in the demonstrations against the Salazar dictatorship. Other contributory factors to the public feelings were the outflow of refugees from East Timor with horror stories of killings in their homeland, the Dili massacre of 1991 captured on film by the western media, the arrest and imprisonment of Xanana Gusmao in 1992, and the award of the Nobel Peace Prize to Bishop Belo and Ramos Horta. The diplomats whom I met in Lisbon were unanimous in their assessment that however bizarre it might appear to the outsider, East Timor was an emotionally explosive issue in Portuguese politics.

The United States Ambassador in Lisbon was Elizabeth Frawley, an old friend from my days in Washington, and she was most kind and helpful to me. Our conversations were a blend of pleasant Washington reminiscences and some very useful current Lisbon realities. Elizabeth, who completely fills the cliché of being as clever as she is beautiful, possesses an acute political perception, and her views on the current politics of Portugal provided me with invaluable background material.

The British Ambassador was Roger Westbrook, with whom I was privileged to enjoy a most productive and friendly relationship which was enriched over each of my successive visits to Lisbon. His knowledge of the Portuguese political scene was, of course, superb. Even more important, from my point of view, was his comprehension of the manner in which East Timor effected the politics of Lisbon and vice versa.

His calm, dispassionate appraisal of events was quite invaluable, and even more so was his willingness to respond to the ideas that I occasionally bounced off him. To top it all off, Roger is an elegant and hospitable host, and one was always assured of delectable nourishment for both mind and body each time that one accepted his gracious invitation. Alas, my inability to reciprocate, in either fashion, made these pleasant encounters very much a one-way affair, and left me with a feeling of inadequacy, which continues to linger.

Our first official meeting with the Portuguese took place at the Foreign Ministry, an edifice as historic and picturesque as the best of its counterparts in any part of the world. This was followed by a so-called working lunch, the quality and elegance of which gave an entirely new and highly sophisticated connotation to this otherwise rudimentary institution. It would certainly have smoothed out any wrinkles in the preceding talks, had they by any chance occurred.

Foreign Minister Jaime Gama, whom I met for the first time, and with whom I had a tête-à-tête before the formal discussions commenced, created an extremely favorable impression. Soft-spoken and courteous, he presented Portugal's case with the deliberation and clarity that reflected his legal training and background, and at the same time, with consummate diplomacy, expressed his readiness to be flexible in the search for a solution.

In due course, as our negotiations progressed over the months, I learned to appreciate and admire Jaime Gama's many qualities. Cool and temperate in his attitude, his highly analytical mind enabled him to quickly grasp the essentials of a problem, qualities which, when coupled with his assurance and decisiveness, made him an excellent negotiating partner. Apart from this, Jaime Gama and I developed a nice little side business in a commodity exchange of cigars.

President Jorge Sampaio, who was kind enough to receive me on the first and every subsequent occasion that I visited Lisbon, was a combination of courtesy, affability, and dynamism. A vigorous, activist political career had preceded his election to the office of President, and it was obvious that he was not going to be content with cutting ribbons and opening exhibitions. The constitutional provision that landed the East Timor dossier on his desk was, therefore, the ideal outlet for the exercise of his considerable skills, and he maintained a lively, energetic and compulsive interest in the subject.

Sampaio's dramatic participation at the Stockholm ceremony for the award of the Nobel Prize to Bishop Belo and Ramos Horta was a demonstration of his passionate attachment to the East Timorese cause. He brought to bear on the issue not only his considerable intelligence and political skills, but also the entire prestige of his office. He maintained frequent telephonic communication with the Secretary-General, and sometimes, in a gesture of disdain to protocol, even made calls to me—a particularly gracious one being a call to Dili, congratulating me on the success of the ballot.

In chronological order, the third member of the Portuguese leadership triumvirate that I met in Lisbon was Prime Minister Antonio Guterrez. His quiet, soft-spoken manner lent emphasis to the air of authority, which he carried with assured dignity. On East Timor he straddled the middle ground between the passionate contention of Sampaio and the clinical analysis of Gama, and absorbing a little bit from both these elements, Guterrez devised his own approach to the problem.

He was constantly seeking new avenues to explore, and was prepared to take initiatives, which were both bold and imaginative, even though they carried a large element of domestic political risk. Earlier, at an ASEAN/EU summit in Bangkok, Guterrez had buttonholed Suharto directly in an attempt to commence a direct dialogue on East Timor, but the exercise failed for a variety of reasons, resulting in mutual public recriminations and increased mistrust.

During my subsequent meetings with him, the Portuguese Prime Minister's approach maintained a boldly pragmatic line, motivated by a desire to obtain a genuinely political situation. He said to me that he would welcome it if the UN could arrange a meeting between the two leaders and added, with characteristic wry humor, that "a photo op with Suharto is not exactly the dream of any democratic politician," but that he was prepared for one if it would help toward a solution.

Finally, I had a round of meetings with the Parliamentary Group on East Timor, impressive in their unanimity and rhetoric on the subject, and with members of the East Timorese diaspora, disparate in their party affiliations and positions but similar in despair at their prevalent plight and in their determination to continue the struggle. The pattern of meetings held during my first visit to Lisbon, supplemented by the obligatory press conferences, became the format for my subsequent visits.

In this connection, I was tremendously aided by the help and advice provided to me by the resident Director of the UN Information Center, Carlos dos Santos. A cheerful go-getter from Cape Verde, Carlos had a wide range of contacts in Lisbon, which not only enabled him to provide me with shrewd political insight, but also ensured the smooth solution of administrative problems.

In my discussions with the Portuguese leaders, I said that the Secretary-General was fully aware of the lack of progress in the talks on East Timor, but that it was now our intention to conduct more structured and sustained negotiations. I suggested that these take place in New York, with the negotiating teams incorporating experts from the capitals in order to have more focused discussions of detailed ideas. Above all, I stressed that the negotiators be empowered with sufficient flexibility and room for maneuver in the discussions.

I suggested that these talks take place on a continuing basis, punctuated on occasion by a meeting between the Secretary-General and the two Foreign Ministers who would review the progress of the negotiations. The Portuguese were generally supportive of this approach, and we discussed the problem of balancing the need for quiet diplomacy with the need to inform the press and public of the progress of the negotiations. We talked about the kind of "package" formula for negotiations which the Portuguese might consider appropriate, given the difficulty in the past with Indonesia preferring to have a clear idea of what the negotiations would lead to before beginning to bargain on specific issues.

This item was clearly very important, and would prove to be quite vexatious in due course. All that we could do on this occasion was to flag it and give it some thought. The other important matter that we discussed was the East Timorese participation. Gama expressed dissatisfaction with the AIETD, but supported our decision to revive it. He warned, however, that if the East Timorese continued to be sidelined they would reject any "artificial solution" that may be imposed, and Portugal would do the same.

The Portuguese leaders emphasized, on several occasions, that their assistance to the East Timorese was essentially political and diplomatic, and that they had never supplied the East Timorese resistance with either arms or other military support. I was told, in the clearest terms, of the Portuguese principle that any solution would have to be based on the freely expressed wishes of the people through the exercise of democratic principles, although they were careful to avoid equating that with a referendum. At the same time, they insisted that Portugal had no "preconceived ideas" about a solution, and was prepared to be flexible.

At this stage Gama saw three alternative courses for talks with Indonesia: (a) to aim for a comprehensive settlement of the problem, (b) to adopt a stage by stage approach, first focusing on a transitional solution which could last up to ten years, or (c) to concentrate on an "Interim Package" that would include the improvement of conditions in the territory (human rights, protection of the identity of the people, self administration, etc.). He said it was possible to follow any of these three approaches, but did not hide his skepticism about the feasibility of the first option at the present stage.

In my report to the Secretary-General I said:

> The visit has enabled me to ascertain the position and views of the Portuguese Government at the highest level. Three points are of particular importance at this stage:
>
> (a) while the demand for a referendum is the formal position, it is my belief that the Portuguese Government would, under appropriate circumstances and at the appropriate time, be prepared to settle for some form of autonomy, particularly if the Timorese could be persuaded to accept it
>
> (b) the Government is in agreement with the view that more low-key discussions are needed to move the process forward (in the past there had been some concern about appearing to be negotiating "in secret")
>
> (c) it is prepared to discuss the long-term solution of the problem, although it clearly considers addressing short-term issues and seeking an interim solution to be the more feasible approach.
>
> The question will be if Jakarta would be willing to consider the step-by-step approach, which it has shunned in the past.
>
> I have so far seen only one side of the coin. My forthcoming visit to Indonesia and East Timor will enable me to see the other side, on which, I suspect, the engraving could be more intricate.

3

Getting Acquainted: People, Places and Perceptions, Part II

JAKARTA: MARCH THROUGH JULY 1997

A statesman ought to pay assiduous worship to Nemesis, to be most apprehensive of ruin when he is at the height of power and popularity, and to dread his enemy most when most prostrated.

—Macaulay

I arrived in Jakarta in the early hours of March 20 and almost immediately went into meetings with Foreign Minister Alatas and President Suharto, since both had to leave that evening to attend an Islamic Conference summit. This was my first visit to Jakarta, and the impression was quite vivid. Just before arrival, the aircraft's PA system informed us that we would be landing at "Jakarta's Soekarno Hatta international airport," an announcement that immediately triggered the thought that here was no de-Stalinization.

For thirty-two years Suharto had, with obviously perfect innocuity, retained his rival's name on a very symbolic piece of national real estate. Accustomed as I was from my East European experience to the reallocation of names in accordance with the changing requirements of an obsessive personality cult, I found the retention of the Sukarno name to be an agreeable piece of symbolism. The gesture seemed to be an interesting

24

reminder of the unique nature of Indonesian politics and society, with its subtle interplay of accommodation, shadow, and substance, a phenomenon which I found to be often bewildering but always fascinating.

Escorted by an efficient pair of outriders, our little motorcade whizzed along the highway past lush, green paddy fields, studded with tall palm trees, flaming hibiscus and oleander bushes, and clumps of wooded copses. Early dawn in the tropics is always a magical moment, partly because it is so brief, but also because the wisps of mist and smoke conceal much of the ugliness of the real poverty that is endemic in the third world. But here, in Jakarta's outskirts at any rate, this raggedness was noticeably absent, and the countryside presented an air of neat rustic simplicity.

This soon gave way, as we entered the outskirts of the city, to the quite different aspect created by the bustling prosperity that it exuded. The highways and intersections were choked with traffic, which our outriders sliced through with practiced ease, while the gleaming skyscrapers housing banks, insurance companies, national and multinational corporations, and glittering shopping malls seemed poised, in predator fashion, to swallow the few remaining old style wood and brick structures that cowered in their shadows.

It was a most impressive introduction to Indonesia. After all, this was early 1997, and the largest of the Asian tigers was feeling at the top of its unstoppable form, visibly flexing its muscles and audibly emitting deep belly growls. There were no outward signs, at that time, of the canker and bacteria that had already lodged in the system, viciously and rapidly gnawing at its vitals, and hurtling toward a devastation of the old order unforeseen in its rapidity and magnitude.

As we commenced our negotiations with the Indonesians, therefore, we did so under the circumstances of dealing with a powerful, dynamic nation surging toward greater glory and accomplishment. True, there were some indications that all did not appear as well and as solid as appeared on the surface, that there was dissatisfaction with the high degree of social and economic disparity, that centrifugal forces were becoming more manifest, and that political opposition to the regime was beginning to coalesce despite Suharto's ruthlessly efficient methods of repression and dispersion.

The question of Suharto's succession was beginning to be a matter of concern, but only in terms of personalities and consequent adaptations to the system, not to its total removal. The only ominous sign that I discerned at that time was the economic situation: it appeared as the proverbial distant dark cloud, the size of a hand. But even so, the general view at the time was that the robust Indonesian economy would be able to overcome it with nothing more than a hiccup.

Our first meeting was with Foreign Minister Ali Alatas in his office at the Ministry of Foreign Affairs (DEPLU), an imposing building, sumptuously appointed and furnished with artifacts of Indonesia's long and rich cultural tradition, as well as with souvenirs of its more recent achievements, notably its active and positive role in the Non-Aligned Movement, dating from its founding days in Bandung. Ali Alatas, universally known among his legion of friends as Alex, and universally respected and admired by his professional colleagues, is one of the ablest practitioners of the art of diplomacy.

Possessed of a razor-sharp mind, immense vitality and energy, a lively sense of humor, and a truly formidable negotiating technique, Alatas had a prodigious institutional memory as far as East Timor was concerned, having been an active and leading participant for years in the previous negotiations, an asset which contributed significantly to the formidable presence which he brought to bear on the current discussions.

In our earlier incarnations, Alex and I had served together as ambassadors, had been colleagues in the Non-Aligned as well as Group of 77, and had collaborated closely at a number of conferences. When negotiations drag on until two or three o'clock in the morning, one gets to know, at least, something of the caliber of one's interlocutors, either as partners or as adversaries. Alex and I had lived through some of these sessions, a positive result of which was a deep friendship between us, and my lifetime respect, admiration, and affection for Alex.

During the East Timor negotiations, Alatas constantly maintained a broad, constructive vision and proposed creative initiatives, while always vigorously endorsing his country's position. I am not sure which evokes the greater admiration, Alex's brilliant and forceful advocacy in early 1997, when the Indonesian position was so obviously dominant, or his assured and skillful equanimity in the spring of 1999, when he negotiated the final agreement under circumstances which were by then clearly much less favorable.

On this first visit to Indonesia I was accompanied by Francesc Vendrell, and we had three formal meetings with Alatas, as well as a number of informal discussions. In a wide ranging yet lucid presentation of the Indonesian case, Alatas raised a number of issues. He commenced by deploring the manner in which previous negotiations had been conducted by the UN, that although a dialogue had commenced in 1983 at the ambassadorial level, it had been both secretive and desultory, and that the Foreign Ministers had met only once between 1983 and 1991.

He accordingly welcomed the Secretary-General's initiative in appointing a full-time representative for these negotiations, and promised his support. I responded by putting forward my game plan, saying that the Secretary-General had accorded a high priority to East Timor, and that I accordingly proposed meetings on a regular if not continuous basis at the ambassadorial level. I added that these sessions might be reinforced from time to time by meetings of the two Foreign Ministers with the S.G.

I also stressed the necessity for two essentials that would make the ambassadorial meetings effective: secrecy of negotiations and flexibility of authority to the negotiators in order to permit the free flow of ideas and exploration of new avenues. With regard to the AIETD, I suggested that it proceed in parallel with the tripartite dialogue, with the UN participating only as a facilitator.

Alatas agreed with this approach, but said that it was important to find out if Portugal wanted a compromise solution at this stage. He expressed concern that Portugal's position might have become more inflexible as a result of "the latest developments" (he was referring to the current speculations over a post Suharto era), and that Lisbon was not interested in a compromise solution, one example being the Portuguese rejection of the Secretary-General's proposal for the establishment of interest sections.

Alatas had the feeling that Portugal and Ramos Horta believed that Suharto was soon going to die, and that they could get a solution totally in their favor in the ensuing chaos. This assessment was "dangerously wrong." A new generation of Indonesian leaders would not only not give up East Timor, but would not even want to talk about the issue. He reiterated his view that Portugal was not interested in an interim solution, and that I should ascertain if Lisbon was really serious, otherwise the Secretary-General and Indonesia would be wasting their time.

I agreed that this was the fundamental issue: each side was thinking that time might be on their side. I added that during my recent visit to Lisbon I was impressed by the immensity of the emotional attachment to East Timor, but at the same time I also noticed a willingness of the Portuguese to resume the dialogue. I accordingly suggested to Alatas that it might be a good idea for the Foreign Ministers to meet with the Secretary-General in the near future, so that we could get a substantive dialogue going. Alatas responded positively to this suggestion, and also to my proposal that we restart the AIETD. On the latter issue, however, he unleashed an outburst of objections at the way in which it had been constituted and insisted that there would have to be changes in its composition before resumption.

Alatas then gave me the Indonesian version of the origin of the East

Timor problem. He said that Portugal had "tried to forget certain things" in explaining the events of 1975 and 1976. It was not true that the decolonization process had ground to a halt after Portugal left. As a matter of fact, Jakarta had asked Portugal to come back to East Timor as late as November 1975. The Portuguese had a sense of guilt, and could not deny that the central government in Lisbon had no grip on the colonial government in East Timor.

The Governor, and especially his two lieutenants, politically leftist, had supported Fretilin, which had received weapons from the colonial government. That action nullified their alleged intention for a peaceful decolonization process. Fretilin had felt that they could do in East Timor what Frelimo and MPLA had done in Mozambique and Angola. Portugal, in its meetings with Indonesia in 1975, had recognized that, since the local population was 85 percent illiterate, the decolonization process in East Timor should not be done on the basis of one man one vote, but on a group basis through the liurais. But, in the event, the decolonization process had gone horribly wrong, and had led to 40,000 East Timorese streaming into West Timor.

Indonesia, which had never made any claims on East Timor, and had in fact been one of the promoters of Resolutions 1514 and 1541, found itself in an impossible situation. Having undergone a traumatic experience following the communist coup in 1965, Jakarta became concerned when Fretilin started appealing to the Soviet Union and China to intervene, and it was with the greatest reluctance that Suharto intervened in December 1975.

Alatas concluded this account with an anguished "we got embroiled and we have paid the price until now." He then went on to add how recent events, particularly the award of the Nobel Prize, had led the Portuguese to harden their position. There would be general elections in May 1997, followed by presidential elections in March 1998. "No one knows what will happen after that," he said. He added ominously that the United Nations might be saddled with this problem for years to come.

Alatas concluded his remarks by strongly reiterating that Indonesia was serious about the East Timor issue, but there was a line that they could not cross. They were willing to show flexibility, but one could not move forward unless it was through quiet diplomacy. He deplored the "trend that the Portuguese were saying that the UN could not succeed, and that the US and European Union should intervene." Alatas was firmly of the view that the UN was the best qualified to mediate, that the US and the EU were also of this opinion, and that what was really required was the political will on the part of Indonesia and Portugal.

My extensive discussions with Alatas, supplemented by consultations with other political observers in Jakarta, including especially a core group of able ambassadors, led me to a preliminary assessment which I duly conveyed to the Secretary-General.

I reported:

> Alatas is an old friend and colleague who is no stranger to either the East Timor issue or to the UN, and whose ability and diplomatic skills are universally known and admired. He is waging a campaign on two fronts, externally with the Portuguese, and internally with the hard-liners, notably some within the military hierarchy.
>
> He enjoys the confidence and support of the President and this, together with his innate talents and ability, constitute the elements of his political power base. He is obviously going to be the prime interlocutor in our future negotiations, which, in my view, is a positive element. While I am satisfied that he genuinely wants a settlement, I am a little disturbed by his frankly dubious view of Portuguese intentions.

In my own notes, I maintained a basically optimistic view, as I summed up in seven points the gist of my discussions with Alatas:

> 1. How sure are we that the Portuguese genuinely want a settlement at this time?
> 2. Suharto is fully in charge, and political stability is secure in Indonesia. Any ideas to the contrary are illusory, and possibly dangerous to the peace process.
> 3. The present is the most opportune moment for a settlement because nobody would be able to take the hard political decisions necessary for the purpose in a post Suharto era.
> 4. Negotiations should be meaningful and conducted in a purposeful step-by-step manner. Above all, they should be conducted in the confidential manner requisite for quiet diplomacy.
> 5. Indonesia wants a settlement of the East Timor issue, but not at an exorbitant price; they could live with things as they are.
> 6. Once there is a clear and definite indication of progress on substance in the negotiations, Indonesia could activate a number of confidence-building measures, including the release of political prisoners.
> 7. Alatas is eager and willing to restart a meaningful dialogue under UN auspices and would be available for discussions in New York immediately after the May elections in Indonesia.

Our next meeting that busy morning was with President Suharto. It took place shortly after the meeting with Alatas who was, of course, also present with the President. Judged by the standard of opulence of the living quarters of dictators (and I have seen quite a few in my time) I thought that Suharto would rate a low four, on a scale of one to ten, from utility to luxury. Situated in a quiet, shady section of one of Jakarta's central residential areas, the house did not appear to be noticeably different from the others in the neighborhood, and even the security arrangements did not appear to be excessive.

The President received us in a modest sized living room, rendered even more so by the excess of paintings and artifacts that adorned it. The first impression was that of being surrounded by kitsch in an antique store, but this was soon dispelled on closer scrutiny. The decor was entirely Indonesian and represented, some in breathtaking magnificence and beauty, the rich and diverse cultural, social, and historic tradition of a remarkable people and civilization.

Suharto had traveled all over the world and must obviously have received many valuable gifts, but in this room there was almost nothing of foreign origin on display. It was as though to reflect the contentment, pride, and satisfaction that its occupant derived from the rich and vivid nature of his cultural isolationism.

Suharto's greeting was warm and gentle. He spoke in a soft baritone, without undue emotion or excitability, during the entire course of our meeting. An interpreter translated for me from Bahasa into English, and only provided the occasional clarification to Suharto, whose comprehension of English seemed to be perfectly adequate. There was no question that Suharto radiated an impressive presence. A refined and courteous demeanor did nothing to conceal the aura of power and authority that exuded from a personality that had exercised these functions for thirty-two years.

Of medium height and an upright soldier's bearing, he seemed no less diminished by the absence of the phalanx of military brass that surrounds him in photographs. His eyes were a steely dark gray, and never lost their intensity despite the fact that he smiled a great deal during our conversation. Suharto spoke softly, with cool assurance, and without ever raising his voice or gesticulating with his hands, yet his words were anything but a monotone, compelling attention through the magnetism of his personality.

After all, it should be remembered that at that particular point in time Suharto was still at the height of his power: he had been acknowledged as one of the leading heads of state in the world, a powerful representative of the Non Aligned Movement, and a distinguished elder statesman whose accomplishments evoked applause and whose counsels were regarded with respect. And, as we met on that March morning in Jakarta, Suharto's manner and attitude clearly indicated that we both knew this.

Suharto said that East Timor had been a long-standing issue, but "apparently it had not been possible to achieve a meeting of minds." For Indonesia the situation was fine, and it considered the issue as already settled, especially as Indonesia had "from the start insisted on basing its position on the wishes of the people." Suharto recounted the history of Indonesia's struggle for independence and went on to explain its present political philosophy of Pancasila: "defend our sovereignty and assist those countries not yet independent."

He asserted that in East Timor the Portuguese had failed to put into effect the right of self-determination and had allowed a minority to take over the decolonization movement, although the majority had wanted integration with Indonesia. It was a "heavy burden" for Indonesia to accept the integration of East Timor, because the other twenty-six provinces in Indonesia had to "sacrifice some of their development plans" in order to assist East Timor. Suharto remarked wryly that after four hundred years of colonial occupation, the Portuguese had left East Timor with 20 kilometers of paved road—and one doctor.

He went on to describe the development projects that had been undertaken by his government in East Timor, and stressed that the people of East Timor enjoyed the same rights and duties as all other citizens of Indonesia. Suharto then enumerated the economic successes of Indonesia and said that the poverty rate had been reduced from 60 percent to 11 percent. This was still too high, and he was hopeful of eliminating it much further in the near future.

Reverting to the issue of East Timor, the President said that the presence of the Indonesian armed forces in the territory was for the purpose of national self defense, countering subversion, and assisting in the economic development of the region. He felt that the disturbances in East Timor "were a minor irritant" which would be readily contained. However, since there was a view held abroad by Portugal and some other countries that the right of self-determination had not been carried out in East Timor, he welcomed the Secretary-General's initiative in this respect, and reiterated that he would personally give the UN effort "the highest priority" toward solving this issue.

Macaulay's words were very much in my thoughts after we had concluded our meeting with Suharto and left his comfortable home as the flash bulbs, TV cameras, and reporters' shouted questions sent us on our way. Suharto was obviously the key to the whole issue. His authority was at that time supreme and unquestioned, and he appeared to be entirely unaffected by the incipient political opposition which had just begun a tentative manifestation in Indonesia.

As far as East Timor was concerned, I believed that while Suharto continued to declare it as an irritant, the pebble had been in the shoe for too long, had developed from irritation into discomfort, and was now causing an embarrassing limp, particularly in terms of Indonesia's external relations and international image. I had a feeling that Suharto realized this, notwithstanding the Panglossian nature of his recent presentation to me, and that this realization, based in terms that were pragmatic rather than morally compulsive, was that the situation was now becoming an impediment to his justifiable ambitions for enlarging Indonesia's position and stature in the international sphere. This, coupled with his repeated assurances that he would accord the UN effort "the highest priority," were encouraging signs, and left me with feelings of cautious optimism.

My next meeting was with Major General Prabowo Subianto, the charismatic and controversial commander of the Special Forces (KOPAS-SUS), and reportedly the favorite son-in-law of President Suharto. Shortly before the formal announcement of my appointment as PRSG, I had received a message from a friend in Pakistan who was also a friend of Prabowo, that the latter wished to meet me "in a social capacity."

I was informed that Prabowo would be entrusted with the overall coordination of the East Timor negotiations from the Indonesian side, and that he wished to meet me in secret for some preliminary discussions. I conveyed my acceptance in principle to meet in either New York or London, but this could not be arranged, and our first meeting therefore took place in Jakarta, also under conditions of strict secrecy, although I could not quite understand why.

Prabowo Subianto was at that time considered to be one of the rising stars of the Indonesian establishment. He had the reputation of being an outstanding army officer, socially urbane and charming, but professionally highly intelligent, dynamic, efficient, and ruthless. He possessed two other assets which enabled him to be one of the most powerful men in the country at the time: the first was political acumen of a high order, and the second was a closeness to President Suharto, who reportedly regarded Prabowo as his favorite son-in-law.

The KOPASSUS was a corps d'elite of the Indonesian armed forces, a combination of Praetorian Guard and SS, which was equipped with the choicest men and weapons, and whose duties included a great deal of internal surveillance and repression. It also spearheaded the Indonesian military presence in East Timor, which it tended to guard jealously as a special preserve, and gained the dubious reputation of being the most hated and feared of the occupation forces on the island.

Above all, KOPASSUS had been organized, trained, and fashioned by Prabowo, whose name was linked to it in an ominous and indelible manner. As so often happens, power and the personality cult, when they get enmeshed in such visible form, attract not only the hatred of the victims but also the enmity of erstwhile allies. Major General Prabowo Subianto was no exception to this rule, and with the fall of Suharto was obliged to flee the country, partly to escape the wrath of the people and partly because his exit was expedited by elements in the armed forces which had clearly been inimical to him.

My first meeting with Prabowo took place in secret at a working lunch organized by him in the presidential suite of the hotel where I was staying. Prabowo's perfect English enabled both of us to make it a very useful tête-à-tête, and our subsequent meetings were also to take place in the same manner and at the same venue. Prabowo was polite, charming, and articulate, without a trace of arrogance or military swagger, and our discussions took place under the most cordial circumstances.

He considered that a solution to the problem of East Timor was essential, that he was actively working for it, but that there were powerful elements which were opposed to any change in the status quo. The President was not yet convinced of the need for a settlement but was veering toward it, and "we have to carry him." Prabowo said that Alatas had been under severe attack and criticism during recent meetings of the inner circle of policy makers, but that the President had defended him strongly.

Prabowo confided to me that he was working "quietly but closely in alliance with Alex," that they envisaged some broad form of autonomy for East Timor, but that a referendum was definitely out. He said that there were very few who could influence the President, especially on the subject of East Timor, but that one person for whom Suharto had tremendous respect was Chancellor Helmut Kohl of Germany. At the appropriate time it may be necessary to enlist his support.

I said that I was sure that this could be arranged, but first we needed to do some important groundwork. In this connection I raised with Prabowo my current problem of getting to meet Xanana Gusmao. I said that my request for a meeting had been passed from one Ministry to another, and that I was getting the run around because obviously none of them seemed to have the authority to decide. In requesting Prabowo's intercession (I did not specify how, but we both obviously knew it) I was guided by two major considerations.

Xanana was clearly the most important East Timorese political leader, and could not be ignored. I said that I was willing to meet him in secret, and that when I did meet him I did not need to believe everything that he said. But a contact with Xanana at this stage was essential to the credibility of my mission: if my request was denied then we would be obliged to review the Indonesian government's assertion that they were serious about negotiations over East Timor.

As far as the press was concerned, I would merely announce at my farewell press conference that I was very grateful for the facilities provided by the Indonesian government to meet Xanana, and that I would report our discussions to the Secretary-General. If, on the other hand, I was not permitted to meet Xanana, then I would be obliged to express my grave disappointment that my several requests to meet him had been turned down by the Indonesian government, and the international media would then draw the obvious conclusions—and have a field day doing it.

At about midnight I received a call from the Foreign Ministry informing me that a meeting with Xanana had been arranged for the next day at 1100 hours. The conditions were that I was to go alone, that there should be no previous intimation to the media, and that I would be taken to the Cipinang prison not in my official car, but would be driven there by an official of the Foreign Ministry in his personal car.

After receiving this call, I knew that the clearance could only have come from Suharto, and I thought to myself that although it could not have been very easy for him, old Prabowo had delivered. This was encouraging, and confirmed my earlier view that we could do business with him.

My first meeting with Xanana Gusmao took place at Jakarta's Cipinang prison, where he had been detained for a number of years. As previously arranged, I was picked up at my hotel early in the morning by Rezlan Ishar Jenie, a senior official of the Indonesian Foreign Ministry, and driven slowly through the rush hour traffic to our destination.

Cipinang, which I was to get to know quite well in course of time, was situated in a central part of the city, bustling with traffic, and possessed none of the forbidding aspect of most prisons, such as ramparts, armed watch towers, or fierce security patrols. On arrival, we were taken to the office of the Governor of the prison, a comfortably furnished room, decorated with the obligatory portraits of the President and the Vice President, some leather chairs and sofas, and bookshelves in which impressive leather bound volumes shared space with a large number of sporting trophies.

After the usual courtesies were exchanged, Xanana was brought in, escorted almost respectfully by two police officers in plain clothes. The greetings exchanged between him and the Governor appeared to be as friendly as they were courteous, and preceded my introduction to him. Xanana was simply but impeccably dressed in trousers, shirt, and tie, and appeared to be physically fit and well. Of medium build, trim and alert, he radiated a quiet magnetism that was unmistakable: his eyes possessed a deep intensity and yet displayed great gentleness.

Our discussion was obviously constricted, partly because Xanana's English was rudimentary at that time (it was to improve tremendously within a remarkably short period of months), but mostly because we had three officials listening in on our conversation and making notes. Xanana thanked me for visiting him, and said that he and his followers had now taken a decision to abandon military confrontation in favor of political action and peaceful resistance.

He stressed that he was now prepared "for a dialogue without pre-conditions." After twenty years of resistance and over 200,000 deaths the problem still remained, and was, in his view, not one between Portugal and Indonesia but between Indonesia and the East Timorese people. His movement was similar to the PLO, and no solution was possible without Timorese participation: under his CNRM plan there was a political will-ingness to accommodate all the partners.

Xanana welcomed the initiative of the Secretary-General and assured me that he would work closely with the UN. In response to my query, he said that the AIETD was a "manipulated" institution, and that genuine reconciliation could only take place on the basis of the UN resolutions, which respected decolonization norms, leading to a referendum.

Xanana presented Timorese scarves for the Secretary-General, Ven-drell, and myself, and to my embarrassed observation that it was me who should have been bringing gifts to him, responded with a gracious dignity that my presence was the greatest gift that he could receive. An interview conducted under such closely monitored conditions had obvious limita-tions, but there was little doubt in my mind about Xanana's character, lead-ership, and commitment, and I remember thinking as I left Cipinang that we have the good fortune to deal with a junior Nelson Mandela.

The remaining days in Jakarta were spent in meetings with a num-ber of Indonesian ministers and senior officials. This was essentially an exercise in establishing friends and widening contacts, since the views that they expressed were basically those that had already been communi-cated by Suharto and Alatas. It was difficult to form a distinction between the military and political leadership, since most of my civilian interlocu-tors were either retired or seconded generals, while those few who were not voiced the view of the establishment anyway. There was clearly a core of hard-liners somewhere, but their precise influence in the decision mak-ing process was hard to estimate.

I also established preliminary contact with some of the leading oppo-sition figures, notably Megawati Sukarnoputri, Abdurrahman Wahid (Gus Dur), and Amien Raies, a relationship which I developed on my subse-quent visits to Indonesia. Most important and useful of all were my meet-

The Senior Officials' meeting. At this one in Jakarta, left to right, Francesc Vendrell of the Department of Political Affairs, Ambassador Nugroho Wisnumurti (Indonesia), Jamsheed Marker, behind Marker is Joachim Hunter, Brigadier Mohinder Bhagat of the UN Department of Peacekeeping and Ambassador Fernando Neves (Portugal), all were in a cordial mood at the start of a session. Although invariably businesslike, all encounters were not always as convivial. Photograph: Tamrat Samuel, author's collection.

ings with members of the diplomatic corps in Jakarta, notably Ambassadors Stapleton Roy of the United States, Robin Christopher of the United Kingdom, and John McCarthy of Australia. These superb diplomats—immensely wise, well informed, and experienced—were lavish in their hospitality, and generously shared their advice and counsel, both individually and collectively. In course of time they constituted an informal core group with whom I met regularly.

Last but not least was Ravi Rajan, the UNDP Resident Representative. A highly competent and capable professional, Ravi provided everything from logistical support and organizational arrangements to highly instructive background briefings on political and economic conditions in Indonesia. And he did it all with the utmost amiability and cheerfulness.

4

East Timor
MARCH THROUGH JULY 1997

Upon the king! Let us our lives, our souls, Our debts, our careful wives, our children and Our sins lay on the king! We must
bear all.
> —Shakespeare, *Henry V*

On March 21 we left for Dili, stopping for a day in Bali for a useful meeting with General Rivai, Military Commander of the Udayana Region, which included the territory of East Timor. This was the first of several visits to Bali, and the beautiful island, together with its amiable people, cast its magical and indelible spell upon us, as it has done on so many others. The nature of my work over the next two years, combined with the structure of airline schedules, made these stopovers in Denpasar a most agreeable necessity, permitting the restoration of equilibrium from the frenetic activities in Jakarta and Dili.

As time went on, the contrast between the serendipity of Bali and the oppressiveness of Dili became increasingly stark, often causing one to wonder whether the two islands were really part of the same country.

General Rivai was a compact little man who looked like a soldier even when he was kitted out for golf. Intelligent and soft-spoken, he gave the impression of genuinely wishing to find a solution to the problem of East Timor. But despite his spirit of accommodation, his mind set, alas, was patterned on what I was soon to mentally docket as the "military missionary" approach to East Timor.

On my subsequent visit to Bali I discovered that Rivai had been "transferred" to the National Assembly in Jakarta, as part of the military representation in that august body. While regretting his absence from

Bali, I felt sure that his balanced views would be of benefit to the legislature. Rivai's successors, notably General Damiri, were hard-liners and were more difficult to deal with.

General Rivai briefed me on the situation in East Timor. He estimated that there were about "100 anti-integrationists and a further 3,000 clandestines." (Later I discovered that the figures were as inaccurate as the nomenclatures were misleading.) Rivai thought that much of the unrest in the island could be attributed to the fact that East Timor was subject to international attention, which in turn encouraged local agitators.

He was sure that there would be demonstrations during my visit (in this, at least, he could not have been more right), but he assured me that the overwhelming majority of the people were happy as citizens of Indonesia. He felt that Bishops Belo and Nasciemento were not being as helpful as they should, and could do much to counter the "manipulation in East Timor by outsiders."

When I asked whether he viewed the situation in East Timor as one of low intensity guerrilla warfare or one of sporadic incidents, Rivai was evasive in his reply and said that the resistance could easily be eliminated but that ABRI was exercising considerable restraint. We discussed human rights issues, and Rivai said that the Indonesian constitution did not permit human rights violations.

The Army thus faced a dilemma: restraint was regarded by the East Timorese as weakness and triggered further provocative actions, which in turn compelled the army to use force to restore order. Rivai preferred to use the police for enforcement of law and order, adding that the army was only used under exceptional conditions, and even in such cases the units had been "given special training in human rights" and were obliged to exercise restraint.

Expanding on the theme of the wholly beneficent role played by the army, Rivai said that the five territorial battalions, which possessed a significant East Timorese component, were engaged essentially in development work, and thereby gained popular support. This detracted from the influence of the "clandestines" and consequently incurred the latter's opposition. While Rivai was obviously giving me the party line, the undeniable evidence of material infrastructural development in the territory clearly supported his assertion, but like everything else in East Timor it was only the partial truth. Our subsequent discussions gave me the impression that Rivai believed, as an intelligent and observant administrator, that clearly more was needed in East Timor than roads and buildings.

We arrived in Dili on a hot and sticky morning on March 22 and were greeted at the airport by senior members of the regional administration, as well as a traditional welcome ceremony performed by a charming pair of young East Timorese girls. We drove into town past ochre hills covered in scrub plant and bush, which descended abruptly onto beaches of pristine white sand bordering the ocean, whose deep blue waters and foaming white waves sparkled in the bright midday sun.

The sights of human habitation were, unfortunately, much less engaging. Most houses were primitive, the exceptions being the homes on the sea front, which clearly belonged to the small but opulent elite of the island. On entering the town we saw the Governor's office, a relic of the colonial days with its distinctive Portuguese style architecture, and proceeded to our lodgings at the nearby Makhota Hotel, which we would get to know well in the coming months (Everything in this hostelry was rudimentary, except the rates, which always seemed to keep at least two steps ahead of inflation.)

Our first official engagement in Dili was a meeting with Colonel Simbolon, the local military commander, and his staff of eight officers. A military-style briefing, complete with maps and slide show, was presented and a vast array of statistics was reeled off. My notes recorded, inter alia, that according to Colonel Simbolon, 94 percent of the population was native Timorese, 4 1/2 percent was Indonesian, 1 percent Chinese, 0.4 percent Indo-Portuguese, and 0.2 percent Arab.

In 1975, 93 percent of the population was illiterate, and in 1996 only 25 percent. There were 765,000 Catholics, 30,000 Protestants, 25,000 Muslims, 5,500 Hindus, and 2,787 Buddhists. There were a total of six East Timorese lieutenants, three captains, and three majors in the army and police force. The number of guerrillas was 183 and of clandestines 3,000, plus an unknown number of what Simbolon curiously named as "political diplomats," which included "intellectuals, students, youths, and religious followers who tried to internationalize the issue."

In the somewhat sterile discussions that followed, my concerns regarding the welfare of the East Timorese population remained largely unaddressed, and I was assured that, barring the occasional incident caused by a few disgruntled agents provocateurs, everything was in order. I left the slick and polished headquarters building to the cracking of salutes and the somber impression that the local military elite were in a self-satisfied mood, believing that everything was under control and determined to keep it that way.

We had two meetings with the "Governor" of East Timor, Abilio Osorio Soares, one at his office and the other at a dinner in our honor at his opulent official residence. The ever-protective Francesc Vendrell had

advised me, in his usual meticulous fashion, that I should not address
Soares as Governor, since the United Nations did not formally recognize
his authority in the territory.

But I decided to ignore Francesc's well-intentioned advice, because
the preening "Governor" was so obviously conscious of his status, and
seemed to be so much enjoying the perks of his office, that I thought it
would add to the pleasantness of our relationship and our work if I allowed
a little expediency to bend the requirements of protocol. A highly controversial personality, Soares was a former truck driver, imposed by a distant government in Jakarta in a gesture that most East Timorese, with
good reason, resented as one of contempt.

A big, burly man, with a bearing that was pugnacious, arrogant, and
abrasive, Soares had the reputation of being both brutal and corrupt. But
he was obviously an able manipulator and managed to hold on to his office
till the very end, surviving both the dislike of his own people as well as
Jakarta's frequent impatience with many of his actions and statements.
Declaring that the people of East Timor were incapable of managing
their own affairs, Soares strongly encouraged migration from the other
provinces. However, he felt that a degree of autonomy for East Timor was
desirable and assured me of his cooperation if the United Nations were
to work toward that end.

This came as no surprise to me, since it implied an augmentation of
his powers. A negotiator does not possess the convenience of selecting his
interlocutors and must deal with the prevalent incumbents. In the case of
Soares, I felt that his role would never be a major one in the decision making process, but that he could become an effective and unwelcome spoiler.
I accordingly decided to handle him with a distant politeness, fortified by
Bismarck's observation that "when I estimate the danger that is likely to
accrue to me from my adversary, I first of all subtract the man's vanity
from his other qualities."

We met with a series of East Timorese personalities, including Bishops Belo and Nasciemento, as well as members of the different political
parties, teachers, students, and a very few distraught women's representatives. These were emotionally charged, powerful encounters, which left
a profound and sobering impression. Bishop Belo invited us to dinner at
his residence, where the food was simple but the discussion rich and varied—the exact opposite of the lavish but vacuous reception at the Governor's the previous evening. Belo had invited some priests from his
diocese, both East Timorese and foreigners, from whom we gained disturbing and largely accurate information about the state of affairs on the
island.

In 1983, the Vatican had appointed Bishop Belo as the Apostolic Administrator of Dili. The diocese had served the whole of East Timor until January 1997, when the Pope, in response to the growing number of Catholics in East Timor, ordained a second Bishop, Monsignor Basilio de Nascimento, for the eastern part of the island. This noticeable increase in the Catholic population was a tribute to the tolerant form of Islam practiced in Indonesia, the significance of which was not lost on the Vatican, which in turn adopted a policy of moderation on the East Timor issue.

Bishop Belo had replaced an outspoken critic of Indonesian rule in East Timor, but he had not been expected to follow the policies of his predecessor. Belo was in Portugal pursuing his studies at the time of the invasion of East Timor and its aftermath of violence and repression. However, intense exposure to conditions in the island, and the channeling of grievances through the widespread church network, compelled Belo to become increasingly outspoken in his criticism of the Indonesian armed forces and the denial of rights in East Timor.

In 1989 he addressed the UN Secretary-General, calling for a UN supervised referendum in the territory, and added that "we are dying as a people and as a nation." Nevertheless, Belo exercised a moderating influence, and had a sobering influence on the youth as well as the more radical elements of the clergy. He discouraged the holding of anti-Indonesian demonstrations because of the dire consequences on the general population, and constantly maintained a link with the authorities with a view to easing the pressures on his flock.

Belo's role was a delicate and difficult one, and became increasingly burdensome over the years: the anguish that this caused him was apparent in his demeanor from the first time that I met him. During our conversation, Bishop Belo said that he constantly traveled all over the island, and therefore knew that the East Timorese did not like Indonesia and that the only group that supported integration were those who were working for the government, estimated to be about twenty-five percent of the population.

Many of the APODETI were disillusioned, while the youth wanted independence even if it meant living in poverty. There were others, mainly from "chiefly families," who wanted the Portuguese to return and conduct a referendum. There were informers everywhere. In order to go to university, students had to pass a selection test showing that they were in favor of integration and not supporters of Fretilin.

Bishop Belo thought that a solution to the problem lay in having a referendum, but this could only be done if it was preceded by troop withdrawals and a considerable reduction of the military presence on the island, particularly the Special Forces. He thought that the guerrillas had developed a new strategy, working in small groups and relying on ambushes. They had also considerably strengthened their contacts with local groups in the villages and mountains.

Belo said that General Prabowo had also set up militias, and that Colonel Simbolon, who had local command of operations, reported directly to Prabowo, often bypassing General Rivai, with whom Belo had a good relationship. I pointed out to Belo that the idea of a referendum was so fiercely opposed by Jakarta that its pursuit was unrealistic at the present time. We discussed the possibility of a wide ranging autonomy, and the Bishop thought that it could be acceptable if it were an "open" and not "closed" proposal, meaning a review after a period of time. But he reiterated the necessity for a reduction of oppression, and the withdrawal of a substantial number of troops.

We made a quick visit by helicopter to Bacau for a brief meeting with Bishop Basilio de Nascimento, who told us more or less the same things as Bishop Belo, adding however that in his diocese of Bacau the repression was perhaps less harsh than in other parts of the island. Nascimento is a most impressive personality, tall, well built, and possessed of a quiet self-assurance.

His bearing, and particularly his voice, which is a basso profundo, made me readily visualize him as playing the title role of Boris Godunov in Rimsky-Korsakov's opera. Nascimento's prolonged stay in Europe and not just in Portugal, as in the case of Belo, had expanded his vision, and he brought to bear on our discussions a wholly welcome degree of sophistication and flexibility. His cool, analytical mind did nothing to detract from the compassion that filled the soul of this admirable cleric.

Bishop Nascimento had been in East Timor for two years, having spent the previous twenty-five years in Europe. He said that tension in the territory was sporadic and not continuous, partly because the army needed it "as a pretext" to justify its massive presence. The people suffered from despair and disillusion, and the Bishop thought it would be difficult to find a definitive solution under the present circumstances. The overwhelming military presence made the people feel asphyxiated. It was necessary to lower the tension in the territory, and this could only be done by reducing the military.

When discussing the Indonesian-Portuguese dialogue, Nascimento said that the two Governments talked past each other. Referring to the incident in Bangkok, when Prime Minister Guterrez met Suharto, the Bishop made a most perceptive and interesting observation. He thought that it had been a mistake for the Portuguese to publicize their proposal.

It was a clash between the Oriental concept of "talk in the shadows" and the Cartesian mentality of open discussion. The impasse that followed was the result. What was now needed was a thaw in the situation, and the United Nations could urge the parties to "a path toward a solution."

I felt that my meetings with the two bishops had been most productive, and found that both were extremely impressive personalities, imbued with a sense of understanding, tolerance, and sympathy. There was no doubt about their knowledge, contacts, and influence over an overwhelming majority of the East Timorese people. From their pained reports we learned of the repression that continued on the island, and by the terror tactics—some subtle, others less so—employed by the Indonesian army against the population.

The Bishops had admirably steered their way through the difficult and dangerous minefield of constant repression and equally constant resistance that had for so long characterized life in East Timor. It was also evident that after over twenty years there was a feeling that some form of compromise was necessary. While a referendum was still the desired and expressed goal, I thought that it might be possible to persuade the Bishops to consider using their extensive influence toward working out an appropriate package agreement.

Our meetings with the representatives of the different political parties and groups took place in my room at the Makhota Hotel on two successive days. They began in the evenings and worked their way through smoke-filled hours into the early mornings. These were highly charged, emotional sessions wherein reports of atrocity, repression, arbitrary imprisonment, torture, and rape were mingled with political demands and discussions regarding the future status of East Timor.

I felt myself looked upon as a Merlin who had descended into their midst, ready with a wave of the blue UN flag to remove their oppression and restore their freedom. Their faith in the United Nations, and their expectations, were as great as they were touching, and left me feeling both humbled and troubled. Most groups wanted independence, coupled with the release of Xanana Gusmao, while a few of the moderates were prepared to accept an interim period of autonomy.

A very few representatives were pro-integration, and were happy to leave things as they were. They had clearly been inducted into this process of consultations with the UN mediator by the local authorities. Their sleek, smug, and assured appearance was in stark contrast to that of the other groups, shabbily dressed and carrying gaunt looks and expressions of desperate hope in their eyes.

On our last day in Dili there was an early morning demonstration outside my hotel, with some of the protesters breaking into the premises and causing some damage to the property. I was much later informed that they wished to present me with a petition, but saw no signs of that at the time and would most certainly have accepted it if there had been one. More likely, the purpose of the demonstration was politically motivated, designed to call attention to the East Timor issue, an action that I viewed as entirely legitimate.

The demonstration was put down firmly and quickly, fortunately without any serious casualty. Despite my pleas to the authorities for clemency, harsh sentences were imposed on some of the demonstrators. My subsequent but equally futile attempts with the authorities for a mitigation of the sentences added considerably to my mortification.

My first visit to East Timor left me with two firm convictions. The first was, as the Secretary-General had rightly anticipated, that the United Nations would need to play a strong, proactive role in the quest for a solution. Both the Indonesian and Portuguese Governments were prepared to support this and participate in serious, constructive negotiations. But the initiative would need to emanate from, and be constantly maintained and pursued by, the United Nations.

The second conclusion was that the desperate people of East Timor had now pinned all their hopes and anticipation on the United Nations, and appeared pathetically certain that we would have the answers to their problems. Their faith in the United Nations was absolute, and was exhibited in awesome intensity and simplicity. "Upon the king! Let us our lives, our souls, our debts, our careful wives, our children and our sins lay on the king!" I did not wish to get melodramatic, but I confess that on the flight from Dili to Jakarta I found myself crossing oceans and centuries in empathy with *Henry V* at Agincourt. By going before the people of East Timor, we had triggered a manifestation of trust, faith, and hope which we would now have to justify. It was a sobering thought.

On our return to Jakarta we had some less than productive meetings with two of the Indonesian Army's top brass, Generals Feisal Tanjung and Eddy Sudrajat. Their position on East Timor was of the largely dismissive, "whiff of grapeshot" variety, tempered by a pro forma acceptance of the United Nations efforts. By contrast, my closing meeting with Alatas was most useful, and I was able to frankly convey to him the kaleidoscope of impressions that I had gained from my first visit to Indonesia and East Timor.

As far as the latter was concerned, I said that I was impressed by the economic and infrastructural investments made in the island by the central government, but that Jakarta was a long way away from winning the hearts and minds of the people of East Timor. We agreed that negotiations needed to be intensified, and that every effort made to reach an equitable solution. Alatas agreed to come to New York shortly for a joint meeting with the Secretary-General and the Portuguese Foreign Minister. This was very satisfactory, and my final discussion with Alex, who was positive and determined, as always, left me with a sense of cautious optimism.

We left Indonesia at the end of March 1997, vividly impressed by the sights and sounds of that vast and colorful nation, of the dynamism of its people and leaders, and with a fuller notion of the challenges that now confronted us.

Arnaz, my wife, had accompanied me on this first visit, and would do so on the succeeding ones. Ably as she fulfilled both roles, she was always far more than my personal caretaker and traveling companion. Her beauty and vivacious personality, combined with an admirable intuition and a sharp sense of perception, made her an instinctive and effective diplomat. Possessing a resourceful capability for networking, she was quick to make friends, gaining their confidence with irresistible enthusiasm. Her obvious delight and relish in the assignment, coupled with a shrewd and perceptive observation of persons and events, made her the most invaluable of advisers and companions.

5

The Negotiations Commence

MARCH THROUGH AUGUST 1977

Heed not the blind eye, the echoing ear, nor yet the tongue,
but bring to this great debate the test of reason.
— *Parmenides*

Kofi Annan's meetings on June 19, and 20, 1997, with the Foreign
Ministers of Indonesia and Portugal, formed the beginning of the meaningful negotiations on East Timor. Both Foreign Ministers were accompanied by high-level delegations which, combined with the publicity
evoked by the news media, gave a powerful start to the talks. The Secretary-General first met individually with each of the Foreign Ministers,
succeeded by a tripartite meeting with the full delegations, and this in
turn was followed by a working lunch hosted by the Secretary-General.

I chaired the afternoon session with the Foreign Ministers, as well
as the morning session on June 20. On the afternoon of the second day,
the Ministers and their delegations had a final formal session with the
Secretary-General, followed by a press conference.

The atmosphere and the circumstances under which the talks commenced were not exactly propitious. Tension had risen rather sharply in
East Timor in the preceding weeks. The long dormant guerrillas had
recently launched a series of coordinated attacks, and it was not clear
whether this was haphazard or deliberately timed to coincide with the
commencement of negotiations in New York.

In any case, the Indonesian authorities responded vigorously, and
there was a large number of arrests. On the diplomatic front, also, a res-

olution just passed by the Commission on Human Rights in Geneva came as a serious setback for Jakarta, causing the Indonesians to volubly question Portugal's commitment to conduct serious negotiations. Portugal, for its part, had expressed frustration at what it considered to be Indonesian intransigence, and seemed to be all set to shift its focus to the mobilization of greater international pressure on Indonesia.

The only element that was common to both Indonesia and Portugal seemed to be a profound and surly distrust of each other. I was obliged to send identical letters to the two Foreign Ministers, and a separate one to Ramos Horta, calling for restraint. A statement was also issued through the Secretary-General's spokesman to the same effect. I felt that we would need to take care that the forthcoming meeting of the two Foreign Ministers did not become sidetracked into polemics on this and other similar issues

The Indonesians had the uneasy feeling that Ramos Horta may be pressing Portugal to take the East Timor issue back to the General Assembly, or possibly even to the Security Council, of which Portugal was a member. While the Portuguese had said that they had no intention of going to either the General Assembly or to the Security Council unless something very serious were to occur in East Timor, the Indonesians suspected that the Timorese resistance could provoke incidents inside East Timor precisely for that purpose. Ramos Horta's recent vigorous campaign in New York, where he met several Security Council members, further darkened Indonesian suspicions.

In expressing its frustration at Indonesian intransigence, Portugal was beginning to feel that the issue could not be resolved so long as Suharto was in power, an assumption that Alatas had described as a serious mistake. Gama argued that Jakarta's failure to carry out its undertaking on a number of confidence building measures, and its unwillingness to make a serious effort to improve the situation in East Timor (Bishop Belo had just spoken of a worsening human rights situation since the award of the Nobel Prize) was an indication that the only solution that Indonesia was seeking was an acceptance of the status quo, which Gama declared would never happen.

Alatas, on the other hand, rejected the confidence building measures approach, which he considered to be no more than a disguised Portuguese maneuver to extract endless concessions from Indonesia ("salami tactics," as he called it), while giving little or nothing in return. Mutual distrust and suspicion could hardly have been more profound.

Although both sides had given me their agreement to hold low-key but sustained negotiations, as it seemed obvious, important and substantive differences remained. Alatas made it clear that he first wanted agreement on the shape of a final settlement: the discussion could then focus on the details of that solution. He was prepared to discuss a wide range of issues, provided that the two sides agreed in advance that the final settlement of the problem would be based on "autonomy."

The Portuguese position was that in the absence of sufficient common ground to address the core issue of the status of East Timor, Gama at this stage preferred to tackle short-term issues (mainly improvement of conditions inside East Timor) and to seek an "interim" solution (including one based on some form of self-administration), pending a definitive settlement of the problem at the appropriate time. Gama also forcefully reiterated that Portugal had no right to decide on the final status of East Timor: that right belonged to the East Timorese, and the decision should be theirs.

Prior to their arrival in New York, we presented both Foreign Ministers with a short Non-Paper, which outlined the manner in which the Secretary-General proposed to structure the negotiations. Commencing with the Secretary-General's view that "there is a clear desire on the part of the two governments to intensify their efforts aimed at finding a just, comprehensive, and internationally acceptable solution to the question of East Timor," the Non-Paper went on to suggest that the Secretary-General and / or his Personal Representative would meet as often as necessary, and that day-to-day negotiations would be conducted by designated teams from the three sides.

The negotiators were to be given full authority to negotiate, ad referendum, and to engage in brainstorming. Frequency of the meetings was stressed, as was the necessity for confidentiality. In the event, these broad guidelines were accepted by the Ministers, and the pattern of negotiations proceeded in roughly the same fashion.

On the morning of June 19, 1997, the Secretary-General held separate tête-à-tête meetings with Foreign Ministers Jaime Gama and Ali Alatas. I was not privy to the discussions that took place then, except for Kofi's typically modest and laconic whispered comment to me as we went into the formal session, "It seems okay."

But, as I said earlier, the body language of each of the Ministers, both before and after the tête-à-tête, spoke volumes. To say that they each went in with a scowl and emerged with a smile might be an exaggeration, but only a slight one. During the early part of the first formal session, each of the Ministers made a skillful presentation of their respective cases, which placed on the record their concerns and reservations, but at the same time thanked the Secretary-General for his efforts and expressed a willingness to work for a solution.

The negotiating styles formed an interesting contrast: Alatas was almost flamboyantly eloquent yet sharply incisive, while Gama was equally incisive but much more restrained in expression. There were some sharp exchanges, but these never developed into acrimony, thanks essentially to Kofi's able chairmanship, which steered the discussions onto a pragmatic course once both sides had blown off steam. This took us to the afternoon session, which I chaired and which was intended to establish the basic framework of future negotiations.

I commenced the session by informing both Foreign Ministers, in unequivocal terms, that the formal positions of both sides were so diametrically opposed that any solution would necessitate a degree of compromise. Therefore, if we were to enter into realistic negotiations, then flexibility and a spirit of compromise would be absolutely essential. I further suggested that the very presence of both Ministers, and their previous conversations with the Secretary-General, implied that they were prepared to be flexible and that a compromise was possible.

I asked both Ministers to confirm, on a personal basis, my understanding in this regard, and to convey to me their personal assurance to this effect. Both Ministers quietly agreed, and in what I thought was a much more important gesture, Alatas and Gama each looked me in the eye as they softly assented. I knew then that I was dealing with two gentlemen who were not only able politicians, but were also statesmen of the highest order. And I silently thanked my stars. In turn, I assured them of the sanctity of this understanding, which would remain highly confidential, and that nothing would be said by me in public which could in any way detract from their governments' official position on the East Timor question.

Our two days of discussions concluded with an agreement on the format and framework of future negotiations. The Foreign Ministers would meet with the Secretary-General for a periodic review of the situation, while the substantive talks would be carried out at the level of senior officials, under the chairmanship of the Personal Representative of the Secretary-General (PRSG).

There would be absolute confidentiality of discussions and any statements to the media would be made only by the PRSG after clearing it with the two sides. The negotiators were mandated to explore possible political arrangements for East Timor without, at this point, determining whether any agreement would lead to an "interim" or a "final" settlement of the issue.

In the context of these arrangements, the elements for discussion would include, inter alia, military issues; the migration of non-East Timorese into East Timor, cultural, linguistic and religious issues; human rights and political freedoms; greater Timorization of all aspects of government in East Timor; economic and social issues; bilateral relations between Indonesia and Portugal; and the international verification of agreements already arrived at, as well as mechanisms for ascertaining the views of the East Timorese people.

In addition, there was agreement to restart the All Inclusive East Timorese Dialogue (AIETD). Finally, both governments agreed to show restraint in their public statements in order to "maintain the positive atmosphere of the talks": a very commendable sentiment, which was, alas, frequently honored in the breach. All this was substantive stuff, and as I was anxious to get moving on it as soon as possible, I was able to persuade both governments to accept July 28, 1997 as the first date for the Senior Officials Meeting (SOM), by which time we hoped to supply both capitals with provisional working papers, and receive from them, in turn, a list of the participating delegations.

As things turned out, there was a delay—the first of many slippages which were to dog the course of our subsequent negotiations—so that the Senior Officials meeting was eventually held from August 4-7, 1997. I used the intervening period to prepare the working papers in New York, and for a quick visit to Washington, DC for consultations at the State Department and on Capitol Hill. Since during this period I also managed to acquire, and cope with, a minor cardiac condition, the delay in convening the SOM meeting proved to be something of a providential respite.

The importance of the United States' role in the East Timor crisis, as in most other international crises for that matter, can never be underestimated, and I was determined to establish a pragmatic working relationship with Washington. On this first visit I met with Under Secretary Tom Pickering, a true and old friend and colleague, whom I regard as one of the most brilliant and versatile diplomats of our era, with Ambassador Aurelia de Brazael, and other officials of the State Department, as well as John Shattuck, the indefatigable Assistant Secretary for Human Rights. I did not on this occasion meet the Assistant Secretary for South East Asia, Stanley Roth, a formidable personality whose unstinted help and guidance and decisive approach would later prove to be of paramount importance in the search for a solution in East Timor.

Not unexpectedly, the United States position on the East Timor issue, at that point in time, possessed an element of ambivalence. While the Administration, and particularly the Department of State, was clearly mindful of its wider geo-strategic responsibilities as far as the unity and security of Indonesia was concerned, it was also conscious of its commitment to support human rights and to promote democracy. Thus, it remained measured in its responses to events in East Timor.

There had been an extremely effective and productive relationship between Washington and Jakarta throughout the Cold War and its immediate aftermath. Political and military links had been very close, and economic relations were extensive: the 1995 figures for two-way trade and new investments in Indonesia had amounted to approximately $7 billion on each account. On the other hand, in Congress there was a strong and vocal group which had agitated against Jakarta's human rights record in Indonesia generally, and in East Timor in particular.

My meetings with Senator Feingold and Representative Patrick Kennedy, two of the most outspoken legislators on the issue of East Timor, convinced me of the groundswell of support which they had managed to obtain on Capitol Hill. The United States Government therefore warmly welcomed the Secretary-General's initiative in revitalizing the East Timor negotiations, and promised to be as helpful to the UN effort as they could, a promise which, as time was to prove over the ensuing months, was neither pro forma nor empty.

Welcoming my appointment, Tom Pickering assured me that the US would be fully supportive of the UN effort, and would respond positively to any call for action or assistance. Tom's concluding remarks to me were typical dry vintage Pickering: he said that he was prepared to issue a statement either supporting or opposing the Secretary-General's initiative on East Timor, whichever I thought would be the more helpful.

Back in New York, I was confronted with two significant events which occurred just prior to the Senior Officials Meeting scheduled for August 4. The first was an increase in military activity, and consequently in tension, in East Timor. This was to become a pattern, caused partly by the spontaneous combustion of fears and expectations prior to the meetings in distant New York, and partly by deliberate actions designed to dramatize the situation on the ground as the negotiators went about their work in the detached safety of their conference chamber in the UN building.

I got quite used to this phenomenon, despite its manifest irritation and inconvenience, and accepted it as part of the larger problem on which we were working. On this occasion, the matter was both more serious and more high profile because we received reports of the death of David Alexander, a deputy to Xanana Gusmao and a very prominent resistance leader who was actually conducting guerrilla operations in East Timor.

There were ugly rumors that Alexander had not been killed in battle, but had been captured, tortured, and executed by the Indonesian forces. Despite the inquiries that we immediately instituted, we still do not know the truth of the matter: but there is no doubt that the incident added substantial darkening to the clouds that had foregathered prior to our meeting.

The second event was the fallout from the July visit of President Nelson Mandela of South Africa to Indonesia. The basic purpose of President Mandela's visit to Jakarta was to thank President Suharto and the government and people of Indonesia for the support that they had rendered to Mandela and the African National Congress (ANC) during its struggle against apartheid. But the emotional issue of East Timor became a major intrusion, and when Mandela made a public statement calling for the release of Xanana Gusmao, the side-show overtook the main event, as so often happens in such cases.

I shall deal with this matter in some detail at a later stage, but suffice it to say that in July of 1997 the observations and statements that emanated from all sides after the Mandela visit to Jakarta possessed for us in New York a Delphic quality, and left the Portuguese and Indonesian delegations, each for their own separate reasons, in a state of some confusion and barely concealed irritation.

Typical of the situation was a later bizarre incident in which a secret document on Indonesia / East Timor inadvertently found its way from the South African Department of External Affairs to the desk of the Portuguese Ambassador in Pretoria, from whence its contents were made public. In the resulting furore, the South African Government declared the Portuguese Ambassador persona non grata, and there was much recrimination on all sides. Fortunately, we did not permit the incident to intrude overly on the work of our negotiations, and with good sense prevailing all around, the general feelings of outrage and high dudgeon dissipated more rapidly than I thought they might.

We commenced the first round of the Senior Officials Meeting in New York under my chairmanship on August 4, 1997. The delegations consisted of six or seven members each, most of whom remained the same throughout the talks that extended over the next two years, and therefore developed a personal relationship and a camaraderie that became very agreeable when things went well and provided a safety net of sorts when things went badly, as they often did. I decided to put no limits on the quantum of participants, leaving it to the good sense of the delegations to fix their own numbers.

The rules of business were also kept as flexible as possible, but for the sake of good order I normally only took statements from and spoke directly to the two leaders of the respective delegations. The leader of the Indonesian delegation was Ambassador Nugroho Wisnumurti, Director General for Political Affairs in the Department of Foreign Affairs, Jakarta, and the leader of the Portuguese delegation was Ambassador Fernando Neves, the Director General for Special Political Questions in the Ministry of Foreign Affairs, Lisbon.

Nugroho Wisnumurti, who had until recently served as the Indonesian Permanent Representative at the United Nations in New York, was an old friend and colleague, and a proven expert in multilateral diplomacy. Fernando Neves had also served in the Portuguese Mission in New York, and had honed his considerable skills at Brussels, where he had served as Portuguese Ambassador to the European Union and had also worked in the Secretariat.

Both Wisnumurti and Neves possessed an impressive command of the English language, which was a tremendous advantage for the process of the negotiations. My two interlocutors were therefore not only thorough professionals, but were also experts in the specialized field of multilateral diplomacy. This made working with them agreeable for the most part, sometimes a trifle difficult, but always a fascinating exercise. Although they possessed different negotiating styles—Neves forceful and focused, Wisnumurti reticent but implacable—they had quite a lot in common.

Both possessed fine legal minds, were masters of detail, and above all each was a tough and formidable negotiator. I constantly kept in mind that, despite the flexibility ostensibly provided to the delegations under the original understandings, both Neves and Wisnumurti were operating under considerable political constraints. Apart from accountability to the highest political level of their respective governments was the caution imposed by the menacing nature of a watchful and suspicious domestic public opinion in both capitals.

The atmosphere of our talks was constructive and businesslike, and the format was a combination of bilaterals and trilaterals. We (the UN team) met each delegation separately in the mornings and had joint meetings with both delegations in the afternoons. This allowed for frank expressions of sensitive issues in the bilaterals, and the opportunity to concentrate on the specifics of less difficult issues in the joint sessions.

It also enabled me to assess the strength and sensitivity of a particular issue to each delegation, so that it could be introduced into the trilaterals in an appropriate manner. Apart from this, the importance of confidentiality was repeatedly stressed and the commitment not to disclose the substance of the discussions to the press was reaffirmed.

We agreed on the composition and agenda for the next AIETD meeting, and then went on to discuss possible political arrangements for East Timor. I gave the delegations two papers, the first one outlining the major features of various successful and unsuccessful arrangements that could have relevance to the East Timor situation. The study featured nine cases: Bhutan and India, Hong Kong and China, Macao and China, Catalonia and Spain, Eritrea and Ethiopia, the Aaland Islands and Finland, Puerto Rico and the US, the Federation of St. Kitts and Nevis, and the Autonomous region in Muslim Mindanao (Philippines).

The second paper summarized the main elements drawn from these cases, and in submitting it I emphasized that these were merely "food for thought," and were not meant to be "proposals" in any sense. Both sides stressed that their discussion did not prejudice their positions on the issue. The Portuguese, in particular, underlined that their willingness to look at these autonomous and other forms of arrangements did not mean that they were prepared to accept a permanent settlement of the problem without the people of East Timor exercising their right to self determination in a democratic way.

These ideas could at best help devise an "interim" solution pending final settlement. Predictably, the Portuguese felt that there should be the widest possible autonomy as a first step toward a long-term solution. On the other hand, the Indonesians, equally predictably, stressed that they were only prepared to consider measures to expand the existing autonomy in East Timor in terms of what would be possible within the context of the Indonesian constitution and law on autonomy.

I next took up with the delegations the important issue of prevention of escalation of tension on the ground. Both sides felt that this was an important issue, but came at it from different angles. The Indonesians said that as long as the threat to stability and security continued in East Timor, the security forces would continue to take appropriate measures, and that the onus therefore lay on Portugal and the resistance movement to ease tensions. The Portuguese argued that it was up to Indonesia to improve human rights and living conditions in East Timor, and indicated that in the next round of talks they intended to raise the topics of "demilitarization" and "human rights and political freedoms."

In reporting the results of this first SOM meeting to the Secretary-General, I believed that within the parameters of the political competence and authority of the participants the meeting was a success. It had kept the ball in play, and may have generated some ideas for the elements of an eventual agreement. But that was still a long way off, and while the working level meetings could perform a useful task in identifying the modalities of a final settlement, the latter would require weapons of much heavier caliber than those hitherto employed, and our next task should be the mobilization of the requisite political will at the appropriate decision making level.

I derived a measure of cautious satisfaction from the conclusion of the first SOM. We had started a process, and done so without spilling any blood on the carpet of Assistant Secretary-General Alvaro de Soto's conference room. But clearly there was much to be done, and we still had a long way to go. The old Chinese saying, of a journey of a thousand leagues commencing with one step, appeared to me, at that time, to stress the ominous rather than the optimistic aspect of the proverb.

6

The Consultations Widen

GENEVA, PRETORIA, VIENNA AND LONDON: AUGUST THROUGH NOVEMBER 1997

Tell me, Muse, of that man, so ready at need, who wandered far and wide, after he had sacked the sacred citadel of Troy, and many were the men whose towns he saw and whose minds he learnt, yea, and many were the woes he suffered in his heart upon the deep, striving to win his own life and the return of his company.

—*Homer*, The Odyssey: Book I
(Translation by Butcher and Lang)

Having got the negotiations off to a start in New York, I was eager to maintain the momentum, and accordingly visited, over the next few weeks, Geneva, Pretoria, Vienna, and London, before returning to New York to chair the next SOM meeting. Apart from looking through some papers on East Timor in the UN offices in Geneva, I had a short but most pleasant and productive meeting with Mrs. Mary Robinson, who had just assumed office as High Commissioner for Human Rights.

I suggested to her that although the issue of human rights constituted an essential component of my work, my basic objectives were political and diplomatic. I judged, therefore, that it would be unproductive for my political negotiations if I were to imprudently concentrate efforts on investigations into human rights violations, of which I knew there would be plenty. The latter, I felt, should come strictly under the purview of the Human Rights Commission, and would doubtless be handled with the due diligence and firmness characteristic of the Commission.

Mary Robinson was in total accord with this procedure and rela-
tionships moved smoothly: neither wires nor swords were crossed between
the Department of Political Affairs and the Human Rights Commission
during the course of the East Timor negotiations. Even at the very end,
during the period of the rampage carried out by the militias in East Timor,
Mrs. Robinson curbed her highly justified outrage, and adjusted her activities and her presence in East Timor in accordance with the overall emergency priorities set by the Secretary-General.

A meeting at the headquarters of the International Committee of
the Red Cross (ICRC) concluded my visit to Geneva. I was given a full
and comprehensive briefing on the situation and conditions in East Timor.
The ICRC is, of course, a unique organization, impressive in its expertise and commitment, with an ubiquitous presence in the trouble spots of
the world. It had an effective presence in East Timor also, and its representatives had an extensive but balanced perception of the situation on
the ground. I came to rely a great deal on the reports and the counsel of
the ICRC representatives in Jakarta and East Timor.

From Geneva we went to South Africa, where we stayed from August
22 to the 27 on a visit that included an encounter which was probably
one of the most impressive and memorable of my career—a meeting with
President Nelson Mandela. This was, of course, my first visit to South
Africa, in common with so many others who had either excluded themselves or been excluded by the odious conditionalities of the previous
apartheid regime.

The palpable sense of newfound freedom seemed to have enhanced
the natural beauty and majesty of this vast country, and although signs
of poverty and deprivation were everywhere evident in distressingly large
measure, there was an air of bustling, if sometimes chaotic, optimism
which lifted the spirits of every friendly visitor. Johannesburg, with its
combination of skyscrapers and urban insecurity, seemed no different from
any other megalopolis, but elsewhere there was a spirit of newfound hope,
combined with an understanding of the tremendous problems that faced
the new South Africa, and an evident determination to work toward their
solution.

I recalled a discussion in New York, not too many years earlier, when
a number of us viewed the future of South Africa with the utmost trep-
idation, and despairingly wondered what measures the United Nations
could possibly take to cope with a massive blood bath that seemed at that
time to be almost inevitable. This did not occur, of course, and the only
reason why it did not was Nelson Mandela.

Superlatives become superfluous when it comes to describing this extraordinary man, and when so much has already been said and written about him, it would be an impertinence to add anything further. Suffice it to say that his spirit pervaded the entire land, manifesting itself in the robust freedom and rambunctious peace that prevailed, and South Africans of all races and persuasions rightly respected and revered one of the greatest personalities of the century.

Tamrat Samuel accompanied me to our meetings at the Department of Foreign Affairs in Pretoria for the preliminary discussions, which were led on the South African side by Abdul Minty, the Director General in charge of Multilateral Affairs in the Department. Minty had spent years in exile during the apartheid period and had been an energetic activist mobilizing international opinion against the government. He was particularly effective in tracing attempts at UN sanctions busting by the apartheid regime.

During my tenure on the Security Council, I had served as the Council's chairman on the South Africa Sanctions Committee, and Minty's reports to us proved invaluable in enabling the Committee to take corrective measures over actual or intended breaches of sanctions. I once observed to the members of the Committee that but for the vigilance and initiatives of Mr. Minty, we could all find ourselves putting in for unemployment benefits.

Our talks with Minty provided a most useful background to the South African position on the East Timor issue. Despite the fact that Suharto had rendered such substantial support to Mandela and the African National Congress during the period of apartheid, there remained a very significant opposition to Indonesia among the South African political parties, on the subject of East Timor. There were many groups actively working for East Timorese independence and in an unpleasant rebuke to Jakarta all members of the South African legislature had boycotted the National Day reception given by the Indonesian Ambassador.

Part of these feelings could be attributed to the natural desire of a newly liberated people to support liberation movements everywhere. But in the case of South Africa, I thought that the neighboring Mozambique connection entered the equation in significant measure. The linguistic link between Mozambique, Portugal, and East Timor, combined with the commonality of the freedom struggle, had found fertile soil in South Africa. To this could also be added the fact that the issue had evoked the interest of the formidable Mme. Gracia Machel.

When President Nelson Mandela visited Indonesia in July 1997, the main purpose of his visit, as already indicated, was essentially a goodwill gesture of thanks to Suharto and the Indonesian Government for the substantial support that the latter had rendered to the ANC during its long struggle against apartheid. But obviously Mandela's concern over the East Timor issue was not going to be suppressed. Apart from discussing the subject in some detail with Suharto, Mandela not only called for the release of Xanana Gusmao, but also insisted on meeting with the latter—and got his way.

There is a report that Suharto at first refused Mandela's request to meet Xanana with the question, "Why do you want to meet him? He is only a common criminal." When Mandela responded by saying "that is exactly what they said about me for twenty-five years," Suharto promptly and magnanimously responded by arranging for Xanana to be brought from prison to the State Guest House for an intimate dinner with Mandela.

I cannot vouch for the veracity of this story, but it has an air of authenticity and, if true, has a legendary touch which says much for the caliber of both Presidents. However it may have been brought about, the fact remains that Xanana did have a most useful discussion with Mandela in Jakarta, and that they emerged from the dinner meeting with considerable mutual respect.

President Mandela received us in his office in Pretoria on August 26, 1997, first in a tête-à-tête with me, followed by a fuller meeting when we were joined by Foreign Minister Alfred Nzo, Abdul Minty, and Tamrat Samuel. This, in turn, was followed by a joint press conference. Later, Tamrat Samuel said to me that meeting Nelson Mandela in person was probably the most moving and emotional moment in his life. As for me, I can only say that I was not too far behind Tamrat in his sentiments, and that on meeting Mandela one immediately realizes that everything that has been said about him is true. Courteous, soft-spoken, gentle, and with a quiet sense of humor, he radiated dignity in his person and his bearing. His eyes are deep set, kind, and thoughtful and expressed in a deep glow the humane sensitivity that seems to emanate from his personality.

After the usual courtesies, Mandela assured me that his efforts were entirely in support of the Secretary-General's initiatives, and that "I am working completely under the instructions of my boss, Kofi Annan." Giving an account of his visit to Indonesia, Mandela said that he had urged Suharto, both in private and in public, to release Xanana Gusmao. Mandela was extremely impressed by Xanana's "intelligence and decisiveness" and felt that our joint efforts should be to secure his release, since his participation in the process of negotiations was crucial.

During their meeting in Jakarta, Mandela had expressed his doubts to Xanana about the efficacy of the armed struggle, as it only provided an

An early Strategy Session. The Secretary-General, with top aides, clockwise from left, Francesc Vendrell, J.M., Tamrat Samuel, Under Secretary-General, Sir Kieran Pendergast, Kofi Annan, and Assistant Secretary-General Alvarode Soto.

opportunity "for Indonesia to slaughter people," and had tried to impress upon Xanana the need for a compromise solution. The latter had made no commitment, but promised to consider the matter seriously. As regards President Suharto, Mandela said that "he told me that he was eager to solve the problem," but when Mandela asked whether he was prepared to give autonomy to East Timor, Suharto's response was that he was considering giving autonomy to *all* the provinces.

Suharto was due to visit South Africa in November, and Mandela asked me to convey to the Secretary-General the assurance of the continuation of South African efforts at that time. We discussed the possibility of Xanana's release and exile to South Africa, and while Mandela expressed his complete willingness to provide political asylum, we agreed that obviously this would be subject to acceptance by both Suharto and Xanana, the likelihood of which appeared very doubtful under the prevailing circumstances.

President Mandela then raised with me the idea of organizing a conference in the near future of "East Timorese leaders" in South Africa, with a suggested UN participation. This wild idea, I knew, was being urged on the President by some of his enthusiastic staff and political advisers. Knowing its explosive implications, I urged the strongest caution and restraint, particularly in the light of Suharto's forthcoming visit to South Africa, and the President immediately took the point.

We proceeded to a crowded press conference, where the President expressed his total support for the Secretary-General's initiative to find a peaceful solution to the problem of East Timor. In turn, I expressed the Secretary-General's thanks and appreciation for this support and stressed the importance of President Mandela's role in the peace process. We took a few questions on East Timor from the journalists, after which a South African correspondent raised a domestic issue with Mandela.

The breaking news that day was F.W. de Klerk's resignation from the leadership of his party, and the press corps was obviously keen to have Mandela's reaction to the announcement. The President said that in the first place this was a matter between the party and its leader. "But having said that," Mandela added, he personally felt that de Klerk had made a mistake, "as we all do from time to time."

"Be that as it may," he continued with quiet emphasis, "let none of us ever forget the vital contribution that Mr. de Klerk has made toward the creation of the new South Africa." This generous, thoughtful tribute, spontaneously conveyed in Mandela's customary dignity, put an end to further questions, and concluded the press conference on a very satisfactory note.

At the conclusion of my visit to South Africa, my recommendation to the Secretary-General was that we maintain close contact with President Mandela, keep him informed of what we were doing, and conserve the immense prestige of his authority for the moment when it could be most effectively deployed during the future course of negotiations.

In early October 1997, I convened the next session of the Senior Officials Meeting in New York. As usual, events on the ground ensured that we got off to an uneasy start. The Indonesians complained about Portugal's refusal to grant a visa to an Indonesian delegate to a meeting of the International Forum for Child Welfare, which was being held in Portugal. A more serious issue was an incident in Jakarta, when five East Timorese jumped over the wall of the Austrian Embassy and sought political asylum.

This type of occurrence was by no means uncommon, despite the increasingly stringent security measures taken by foreign embassies in Jakarta, and the usual pattern was for the Indonesian authorities to permit, after a short period of time, the asylum seekers to leave for Lisbon. In this case, however, two of the fugitives were not only prominent East Timor political activists, but were also criminally charged with the illegal possession of explosives.

The Indonesian authorities refused them safe passage, as a consequence of which they remained holed up in the Austrian embassy for several months. From time to time I did attempt a goodwill intercession, but these efforts were necessarily tentative, since the matter was essentially a bilateral issue between the Governments of Indonesia and Austria. Although it did not quite become an albatross around my neck, the issue obviously did nothing to improve the climate surrounding the start of the negotiations.

The SOM meeting dealt with three main issues. The first was a continuation of the discussions on the "models" and "elements" that might apply to autonomy in East Timor, and I undertook to provide, at the next meeting, a comprehensive working paper which would take into account our current discussions. The second issue was the AIETD, and here we reached agreement on the guidelines that were to be provided to the delegates at the conference. The third issue was that of Confidence Building Measures (CBMs).

I proposed that the resistance movement should be persuaded (by methods to be worked out) to cease all military activity for a period of three months. If this was done, and peace prevailed generally, then the Indonesian Government should respond by withdrawing a substantial number of troops from East Timor at the end of the three-month period of cease-fire. The process could then be repeated for another three months, and so on.

The preliminary response, from both sides, was predictably tentative and cautious, but did not evoke outright rejection. The Portuguese claimed that they had "no control" over the actions of the resistance (which was not quite true), and the Indonesians thought that any conditionality on troop deployment was an infringement of sovereignty, (which would only be true if the territory in question was not in dispute).

In my report to the Secretary-General I stated that the SOM negotiations were conducted in a reasonably friendly, and certainly professional, manner. The atmosphere was somewhat vitiated by the reports of the East Timorese asylum seekers in the Austrian Embassy, and by the Portuguese refusal to grant a visa to an Indonesian wishing to attend an international conference in Lisbon. I added, "Although these are elements which are either extraneous or peripheral to our main negotiations, we must continue to expect their ghostly presence, however unwelcome, to hover over our banquets."

Following the SOM meeting in New York, we flew to Vienna for the third session of the AIETD. The Austrian Government had very generously agreed to host this conference, and provided excellent facilities for this purpose at Schloss Krumbach, situated in the vicinity of Vienna in a region of almost breathtaking alpine beauty. The essential object of AIETD was to provide a forum for the East Timorese representatives, of all shades of political opinion to meet in an informal gathering and to freely exchange views and ideas.

Under the formal rules of procedure, the delegates were prohibited from discussing political issues, such as the future status of East Timor, but were encouraged to propose social and cultural projects that might be of benefit to the East Timorese. In reality, the prohibition on discussion of political issues was impossible to implement, except during the formal sessions, and the fact that the delegates lived together for three days and nights, in salubrious surroundings, provided an excellent opportunity for brainstorming and for getting to know each other better.

There were thirty-five participants at the conference, nineteen from Indonesia and East Timor, and sixteen from the diaspora, and the impressive list included Bishop Belo, Ambassador Lopez da Cruz, Jose Ramos Horta, Joao Carascalao, Mari Alkateri, and Abilio Soares.

The SOM had identified two specific issues for confirmation and elaboration by the AIETD. These were the establishment of an East Timorese cultural center in Dili, and the utilization of a Portuguese Government offer for human resources development on the island. The AIETD were unable to come up with anything substantive on the latter issue, but did produce some useful suggestions on the organization, funding, and management of the cultural center in Dili. Unfortunately, lack of agreement in subsequent meetings of SOM, coupled with bureaucratic impediments persistently applied by the Indonesian authorities, ensured that Dili never got its cultural center.

The delegates also struggled hard to obtain a final declaration, and almost succeeded, during the last late night moments of the conference, to obtain a reasonable text. But they could not get a consensus and the meeting broke with the usual recriminations and accusations of sabotage. A statement by Bishop Belo, issued more in sorrow than in anger, nevertheless incensed the Indonesians, who unofficially conveyed to me their sense of anguish: "Will no one rid me of this meddlesome priest?"

Nevertheless, I was satisfied with the outcome of the AIETD. It had served its primary purpose in getting the East Timorese together, which in turn had enabled us at the UN to get a first-hand impression of the participants and their political inclinations. Secondly, it had demonstrated to the East Timorese that they had not been totally excluded from the UN negotiating process.

In my opening remarks to the delegates, I tried to assure them of the nature of their participation in this process, and said:

> You are all aware that the terms of reference of the AIETD, adopted by the fifth round of Ministerial talks held in January

1995, remain valid. In particular, I should like to remind you that the dialogue should not address the political status of East Timor and does not constitute a parallel negotiating track or a substitute for the tripartite talks under the auspices of the Secretary-General. It is a complementary process that provides a unique forum for the East Timorese to make practical contributions to the search of a solution.

After Schloss Krumbach I spent a day in Vienna, thanking Staatsekretarin Benita Waldemar Ferraro for the splendid arrangements provided by the Austrian Government for the AIETD, and keeping her and her colleagues in the Ministry up to date with the process of negotiations. For a multitude of reasons, Vienna is one of my favorite cities. I spent a happy afternoon wandering through its streets, revisiting its baroque splendors, and ended the evening with an attractive performance of Weber's *Der Freischütz* at the Wiener Staatsoper. The fringe benefits of diplomacy can often be quite delectable.

From Vienna I went to London for two days of meetings at the Foreign Office with Foreign Secretary Robin Cook and Minister of State Derek Fatchett. The United Kingdom Government had displayed a lively and positive interest in the East Timor issue, and my contacts with the British Ambassadors in New York, Jakarta, and Lisbon had been continuous, intensive and very productive.

My meetings at the Foreign and Commonwealth Office were essentially a continuation of this process of consultation, and I was reassured by the positive attitude of the British Government, and its promises of cooperation and support. It was with great sadness that I later learned of the sudden demise of Derek Fatchett, a gentle and effective diplomat, whose influence and wise counsels were greatly missed by all.

7

Coming to Grips: The Negotiations Intensify

INDONESIA AND EAST TIMOR: DECEMBER 1997
PORTUGAL: JANUARY 1998
LONDON: APRIL 1998

Rebus sic santibus.

(Things have changed)

On November 14, 1997, I had a meeting with Secretary-General Kofi Annan in New York for a review of the current stage of negotiations and to plan a strategy for the future course of action. The current position, as I saw it, rested on the following five postulates:

> 1. At the June meeting there was a clear understanding that Indonesia and Portugal would work for a solution that would be less than their basic position.
>
> 2. Portugal, while insisting on the issue of self-determination, is prepared to be flexible on its modalities, and does not insist on a referendum as long as the East Timorese are satisfied with a solution.
>
> 3. Indonesia says it is prepared to make major concessions, including a wider devolution of power to the East Timorese and the release of Xanana Gusmao, as long as Portugal is ready to accept integration as the basis of the solution.
>
> 4. The senior officials' meetings have achieved only limited progress. Discussions have focused on three main issues: "models" for a possible political arrangement, confidence building measures (CBMs), and the AIETD.

5. My proposal for a three-month suspension of military activity by the resistance, followed by a reduction of Indonesian troops,
has not been accepted by Jakarta.

We thought that the forthcoming visit of Suharto to South Africa
presented a valuable window of opportunity, and the Secretary-General
accordingly contacted President Mandela and outlined for the latter our
views. In particular, the Secretary-General stressed the importance of
involving Xanana Gusmao in the negotiating process. It was suggested
to Mandela that he should propose to Suharto that the Indonesian Government should conduct direct talks with Xanana in absolute secrecy, and
that these talks should take place without disrupting the ongoing talks
between Indonesia and Portugal under the auspices of the Secretary-General.

It was emphasized that Xanana was the one leader who commanded
universal respect among the opponents of integration, and that he was a
pragmatic, if proud, leader who understood political realities and the need
for compromise.

President Mandela, in due course, conveyed to the Secretary-General an account of his discussions with Suharto. Mandela stressed to
Suharto that the release of Xanana was not just a political issue but "as a
matter of common concern to all of us." It would be very unfortunate if
the East Timor issue was once again permitted to raise its divisive head
during the forthcoming Non Aligned Conference.

Mandela felt that whereas Suharto did not explicitly accept the suggestion, the latter's "general demeanor" during the discussion appeared to
be "favorably disposed." However, events were to prove that these hopes
were in vain, and Suharto's decision on the continued incarceration of
Xanana remained as firm as ever, and the former thus continued to maintain a major obstacle to the progress of negotiations.

The next phase in the process of consultations began with a visit by
Tamrat Samuel and myself to Indonesia and East Timor just before
Christmas 1997. We adopted the standard procedure of meetings in
Jakarta with the Indonesian authorities, political leaders, and diplomats,
followed by a stopover in Bali for talks with the Udayama command, and
then on to Dili for meetings with the administration, the bishops, and
other East Timor personalities.

On our return to Jakarta we had a review meeting with Foreign Minister Alatas, and a wrap-up press conference before departure. It became
immediately clear to me, upon arrival in Jakarta, that the confident euphoria that had pervaded the capital during my earlier visit had by now considerably dissipated, to be replaced by a sense of disquiet and feelings of

apprehension at the ominous approach of the dark clouds of nemesis. The country had been ravaged by some of the worst forest fires in memory, and large parts of Sumatra, Java, and neighboring Malaysia and Singapore were shrouded for weeks in a dense pall of smoke and cinders.

The first fissures had begun to appear in the immense monolithic financial pyramid of Indonesia, and with the International Monetary Fund acting in an increasingly interventionist fashion, feelings of disquiet and concern had replaced the confidence that had hitherto characterized the attitude of the national, as well as multinational, corporations in Indonesia. The bulls were clearly being shoved aside by the bears. Finally, there was the matter of the President's health.

Suharto had been compelled, on medical grounds, to cancel his official visits abroad, and to restrict his activities and public appearances at home. For Indonesia, which had been accustomed for over thirty years to Suhartro's firm presence and grip on its body politic, these first signs of frailty and fallibility could not have come at a more crucial or inappropriate moment.

My arrival had been preceded by a series of difficult, complicated, and highly charged negotiations between the I.M.F. and the Indonesian Government, as a result of which the latter had been compelled to accept some major structural adjustments to its economy, measures which were bound to have widespread negative social and political consequences, and which in due course were to make a major contribution to the downfall of Suharto. A widely published photograph of Suharto signing the I.M.F. agreement document, while its Managing Director Michel Camdessus stands beside him with folded arms, had a humiliating effect on the proud Indonesian people and was, for the regime, a bit of a PR disaster.

In my talks with Alatas, I followed up on the initiatives of the Secretary-General and President Mandela regarding Xanana Gusmao and underlined the need to open quiet talks with the latter in whatever manner or format the regime thought appropriate. A decision on this was clearly beyond Alatas' powers, but even so there was a distinct reluctance on his part to address the matter. Then, somewhat to my astonishment and concern, Alatas went on to express in the strongest terms his opposition to an element in the formula agreed upon between the Secretary-General and the two Foreign Ministers in June 1997, specifically that the talks should avoid, for the time being, the difficult issue of whether to look for an "interim" or a "permanent" settlement.

He insisted that the talks should clearly aim at finding a permanent settlement, and that settlement should be based upon Portugal's acceptance of "the reality of East Timor's integration with Indonesia." If Portugal were to commit itself to such an undertaking, he said he would work to convince President Suharto and others to accept autonomy. Alatas continued his list of complaints by what he saw as Portugal's lack of seriousness in the negotiations. He said that by indefinitely postponing a decision on crucial matters, Portugal was using the talks as a means of pressuring Indonesia.

He deplored the extensive information that third countries seemed to have about the substance and stages of the negotiations. He said that Portugal was in for a surprise if it thought that in the post-Suharto era Indonesia would give up East Timor. He said some of the younger officers rising in the Indonesian military did not even have a full understanding of the history of East Timor, and saw it simply as an integral part of Indonesia which had to be defended at all costs.

He said that he himself might not continue as Foreign Minister after March, in which case he thought that my job would become much more difficult. Alatas said that now was the time to resolve this problem if the Portuguese were wise. When I raised the point with President Sampaio in Lisbon later on, the President said he saw some merit in this argument, but noted that while Suharto might have the power, he had not acted to resolve the problem in all these years.

We next discussed the issue of autonomy, on which Alatas said, "the whole world was pressing us." He said that an "autonomous region" was out of the question at present, but that some "autonomous steps/measures" were possible. He quickly added, however, that if the Portuguese were ready to accept autonomy as a final dispensation, Indonesia would negotiate in a reasonable way and he would do his best to obtain his Government's agreement. He said that the "sugar coating" for Portugal could be the release of Xanana and others, and Ramos Horta could return to take part in the politics of East Timor.

The trend and tenor of Alatas' presentation and argument fortified my conviction of the difficult role that he had been compelled to play, and that he was not only negotiating with the United Nations and Portugal, but was also having to cope with an extremely complicated, and possibly hostile, situation on the domestic front.

Alatas raised the issue of establishing interest sections in Jakarta and Lisbon. This was a matter on which the Secretary-General was very keen, and we thought that if it could be achieved then our negotiations would get a great boost, both in perception as well as in fact. The Indonesians were almost as keen as we were on the interest section issue, but Portugal maintained a rigid refusal. They felt that it was one of the few bargaining chips that they held, and were not going to give it up without securing substantial concessions elsewhere.

Jaime Gama told me that while he recognized that interest sections would be mutually advantageous, he indicated that it would not be easy for Portugal to justify such a step to its public without some progress in the situation in East Timor, and in the talks. My next meeting in Jakarta was with Major General Prabowo Subianto, the powerful son-in-law of President Suharto, and commander of the dreaded, elite Special Forces (KOPASSUS).

Our encounter took place under the previous conditions of secrecy and security, and Prabowo was as suave, self assured, and courteous as ever. I gave him a frank assessment of my observations in East Timor and said that while a case could be made for the argument that political realities compel the acceptance of integration, there were equally compelling political realities that the people of East Timor should be persuaded to accept this view.

Currently, this was far from the case, and although Jakarta had taken impressive measures to improve economic conditions in East Timor, and although there was a welcome increase in the restraint exercised by the army, the Government was a long way from winning the hearts and the minds of the people of East Timor. I stressed the necessity for a meaningful political dialogue on as broad a basis as possible, and one that should certainly include Xanana Gusmao (whether in or out of prison) and the two bishops.

Prabowo agreed with me and said that he had been working in this direction since our last meeting in March. He stressed that what he was about to tell me was in his "personal capacity only," but long experience has taught me to take such caveats with much reserve. Prabowo said that he had managed to persuade the "entire Army Command and the General Staff" that if integration is accepted by the Portuguese then Jakarta would grant the territory "special autonomous status," withdraw all military forces, release all political prisoners, and allow the East Timorese to run the province in genuinely autonomous fashion.

The problem remained the President, and "you must help us to convince him." Prabowo suggested that a special appeal, conveyed in confidence by the Secretary-General, and backed by world leaders such as Kohl, Chirac, Mandela, and Lee Kwan Yew, might provide the requisite persuasion. I told Prabowo that I would sound out the Portuguese in Lisbon, before reporting to the Secretary-General, and suggested that we meet again, either in Paris or New York, to try and develop the idea further.

However, the projected meeting did not take place, and this was the last that I saw of Major General Prabowo Subianto. Events in his country had already begun to move at a pace and in a direction that would lead to a rapid diminution of his power and influence, and eventually to his exile.

I visited Xanana Gusmao in Cipinang prison shortly after my meeting with Prabowo. The meeting commenced by a request from Xanana for a private conversation. I strongly endorsed this request, and after some anxious hesitation on their part, the prison authorities and the Foreign Ministry escorting officer left us on our own. Xanana started by saying that he had reconsidered his previous position as stated to Mandela, and that he was now prepared to accept exile in South Africa, so that he could organize his political campaign. However, the proposal for this should emanate from the United Nations and he would accept it.

Xanana also reiterated his assurance that he wanted to follow a peaceful, political campaign, and that he had no intention of causing "the Indonesian military to lose face." He urged me to convey this to the relevant quarters in Jakarta. I welcomed this flexibility and farsighted approach, and said that I would do my best to convince the Indonesian authorities of his sincerity. I pointed out to Xanana that the Indonesian position remained firmly predicated upon the acceptance of integration. I added that there was reason to believe that East Timor could secure the broadest measure of autonomy, coupled with troop withdrawals and release of political prisoners, once the reality of integration was accepted.

One option available to Xanana was to commence negotiations on this understanding under the aegis of the UN, which would guarantee its implementation, provide special economic assistance to East Timor, and ensure through a UN mission that the East Timorese were not abandoned once an agreement was signed. The other option available to Xanana was to continue the struggle by military means, implicit with further bloodshed and hardship for his people. Xanana acknowledged this, adding that he had been "told the same thing by Mandela."

He queried whether "an interim arrangement" was possible, and I told him that the Indonesians had categorically opposed the idea. Personally, I thought that at some stage we might be able to find our way out of the dilemma, but it would clearly have been inappropriate for me to indicate even an inkling of this to Xanana at that time. After some deep reflection, Xanana reiterated that he had "abandoned the military approach" and pointed out, quite logically, that he would need both time and facilities "to convince the people," and work for an understanding.

In the ensuing general discussion I expressed admiration for his leadership and asked him to take further bold initiatives for peace and for his people. I said that I had been urging the Indonesian authorities to commence a secret dialogue with him, and had been told that something might commence in the near future. I believed, from my latest talks with the Indonesian leadership, and particularly with Prabowo, that the Indonesian authorities were beginning to realize the value of opening a direct dialogue with Xanana, and that something would soon happen. In this belief I was, of course, quite wrong, and I was equally mistaken in my belief that Prabowo and I would be able to continue our critical discussions on this subject in Paris the next week.

In Dili I had the usual round of meetings with the civil and military authorities in the administration, and discerned that the earlier attitudes of self-assurance and confidence had been replaced by a sense of uncertainty and restiveness. In my meetings with the East Timorese leaders, I was able to encounter a number of former adherents of integration, led by Manuel Carascalao, who had just formed a new movement calling for "reconciliation" and "self-determination."

A meeting scheduled for thirty minutes went on for over two hours. The group bitterly complained about the manner in which integration had been carried out, and that even when they had supported Indonesia they had expected integration to come with dignity for the East Timorese. After years of misrule, they said, "The path of integration has been closed by injustice." Nevertheless, they said they favored dialogue and compromise rather than confrontation, and their main demand was for the inclusion of East Timorese leaders in the process of negotiations.

They also expressed fears for their safety because of the open way in which they had spoken, and asked for "UN protection." I knew that their fears were well-founded, and knew also how frail were my promises to ensure their security. Haunted by these thoughts, I did not sleep much in what was left of the night after our meeting ended. The next morning I spoke in the strongest terms to the military and civil authorities in Dili, and warned them against taking any measures against those whom I had met the previous evening. Subsequently I was to learn that my admonition had not prevented retribution, but had only made it less severe.

As always, at all the talks with East Timorese in Dili, the importance of Xanana and the need for his direct involvement in the process of dialogue was emphasized. Equally recognized was the importance of Bishop Belo, whose rocky relationship with the military and the government had continued unchanged. He drew a gloomy picture of the human rights situation and linked General Prabowo's Special Forces to many of the atrocities. The Bishop was also concerned about the alienation of the younger generation of East Timorese, who were not only increasingly resorting to violence, but were doing so with the use of more sophisticated weaponry.

Back in Jakarta, I had a series of meetings with my kind friends the
Ambassadors of the United States, the United Kingdom, Australia, Canada,
Japan, the Netherlands, Austria, South Africa, and the Philippines, and
also with the able representatives of the ICRC. Much of our talk was about
the current political and economic situation in Indonesia itself, and of an
impending crisis that would soon become a reality. There was much speculation as to how it might effect Jakarta's policies toward East Timor, and
no one was quite sure as to how things might turn out. There was a distinct possibility, in my view, that the Indonesian position would harden.

Herodotus had observed that "it is evil to acquire an empire, but it
is dangerous to give it up." A similar sentiment could well prevail amongst
Jakarta's ruling elite at this time. Notwithstanding these concerns, I was
determined to maintain the pace of the negotiations, as I was convinced
that we should remain pro-active and not await events in hopeful anticipation. I accordingly flew to Lisbon in early January 1998, and informed
my high-level trio of interlocutors, the President, Prime Minister, and Foreign Minister, of my discussions in Jakarta and Dili, and of my ideas for
pushing the negotiations further, and made the following points:

> A) During my visit to Indonesia in mid-December, I noted a
> degree of flexibility in the position of both sides, the government
> and the resistance, but considerable distrust still remains.
>
> B) The dismal economic situation, coupled with the uncertain
> political climate, creates a situation of considerable unpre-
> dictability.
>
> C) The economic crisis, though very severe, was, in my view,
> of an extended temporary phase and would eventually be overcome,
> given Indonesia's vast natural and human resources.
>
> D) Long-term political predictions were much more difficult,
> but I was certain that a solution to the East Timor problem could
> best be achieved during the Suharto regime. His successor, who-
> ever he may be, was unlikely to possess the authority to push
> through its implementation. Time was not on our side, and it
> would be a grave error for us to think otherwise.
>
> E) I inquired as to what would be Portugal's bottom line on this
> issue. Could they accept integration if the East Timorese were to
> be given maximum autonomy, all Indonesian troops withdrawn,
> political prisoners released, etc.?
>
> F) Would Portugal be prepared to exchange interest sections in
> Jakarta and Lisbon, as a confidence-building measure?

Subsequent events, and history itself, have revealed that whereas I
was correct in most of the above assessment, I could not have been more
wrong on the vital issues indicated in (D) above. In exculpation, I can
only say that the name of B.J. Habibie had not entered into anyone's cal-
culations at that time, other than as subservient to the powerful Suharto,

nor could anyone have anticipated the far-sighted and dramatic decision on East Timor that this unpredictable but remarkable man would take, and implement, precisely one year later.

The Portuguese response to me, on the fundamental question regarding the acceptance of integration, was predictably firm. It was argued quite logically by Foreign Minister Gama that negotiations were pointless if one party was required to commence by accepting the maximalist position of the other. All three Portuguese leaders were quite firm that there should be no change to the understanding reached in June. They were equally firm that they could not accept a solution that was not based on the freely expressed choice of the East Timorese people.

They stressed that Portugal had neither a territorial claim nor a preference for one form of solution over others—full integration, autonomy, or independence. What matters, they insisted, was that the solution was based on the freely expressed wish of the people. While a referendum remained Portugal's basic demand, it continued to stress that it was open to any suggestion that could satisfy the free choice test. However, pending a final resolution of the problem, which Portugal thought might take some time, they proposed some interim measures.

This was a three-phased approach which envisaged, in first phase, an improvement of conditions in East Timor, in the second "interim democratic arrangements" with international monitoring (which could extend up to ten years), and finally an act of self-determination to settle the problem. Here it was emphasized by President, Prime Minister, and Foreign Minister alike that they would not insist upon a referendum, provided the will of the East Timorese people could be ascertained in some impartial and internationally acceptable form.

In my response, I indicated that the interim method of dealing with the issue was anathema to the Indonesians, that it had already been rejected by them, and that I saw no possibility of convincing them otherwise. While agreeing with Jaime Gama that it would not be possible to revise the understandings reached the previous June, I suggested that Portugal give assurance to Indonesia that it was ready to work for a permanent settlement, without at the same time abandoning its position of principle on the question of self-determination. On the question of interest sections, the Portuguese attitude continued to be negative and they continued to rate reasons of public opinion. I thought this to be somewhat specious, but decided to continue our efforts.

During my meeting with Prime Minister Guiterrez, we had the usual brainstorming session, when we considered various alternatives and possibilities of advancing the negotiations. We discussed the forthcoming meeting in London of the Heads of Government of ASEAN and the European Union, and Antonio Guterres said that he was prepared to meet Suharto on this occasion, in any format that the UN might devise. I thought this to be a truly bold decision on his part, and he confirmed my sentiments when he remarked, with a wry smile, that there were not too many democratic political leaders who would seek a photo opportunity with Suharto these days.

On my return to New York I conveyed this to the Secretary-General, who duly contacted both President Suharto and Prime Minister Guterres, proposing a meeting under his aegis, and also contacted the British Government who were the hosts for the ASEAN-EU meeting in this regard. For my part, just after my meeting with Guterres in Lisbon, I informed the able British Ambassador, Roger Westbrook, of this development and sought the cooperation of his government.

In view of the sensitive nature of the proposal, we took measures to preserve its confidentiality, and I left Lisbon for New York to report to the Secretary-General and commence work on a project that could have crucial implications for our efforts. My meeting with Prime Minister Guterres was, as always, lively and meaningful. This remarkable man was under great personal stress at that time, because of the grave illness of his beloved wife. In fact, immediately after our meeting he flew to London, where she was undergoing treatment, and where she passed away shortly thereafter.

These visits to Indonesia, East Timor, and Portugal convinced me that we now had in place a working mechanism for a solution of the East Timor problem, that the parties to the conflict had exhibited a demonstrable desire for UN mediation, and that the UN should retain the initiative. It was now up to us to move the negotiations into the next stage, which should be more intensive, more focused, and dare I say it, more creative.

One way to do this was to intensify our contacts with the New York representatives of the core group of nations, which had evinced interest in the East Timor problem, and I accordingly met, individually and collectively, and on a frequent and regular basis, Ambassador Penny Wensley of Australia, Ambassador Stuart Eldon of the United Kingdom, Ambassador Nancy Soderburg of the United States, Ambassador Michael Powles of New Zealand, and Ambassador Yuldo Takasu of Japan.

In addition, I set up a regime of regular telephone contacts with the indomitable Stanley Roth, the Assistant Secretary at the State Department in Washington. Our meetings, discussions, and consultations with this elite coterie, high-powered in knowledge and diplomatic skill, and representative of states that could bring to bear meaningful influence on both Indonesia and Portugal, was a most invaluable adjunct to our negotiation process. Their contribution to the solution of the East Timor problem was absolutely crucial, and really needs to be recognized and placed on record. The United Nations owes much to their dedicated efforts and substantive contributions, enthusiastically rendered throughout the process of negotiations.

We next began working on the project for a meeting in London between President Suharto and Prime Minister Guterres, under the aegis of the Secretary-General. The British Government was most cooperative, designated Admiralty House as the venue, and made the requisite administrative and security arrangements for the purpose. The Portuguese readily accepted the Secretary-General's invitation to the meeting, but confirmation from Jakarta was not forthcoming, even though Suharto had earlier told the Secretary-General on the telephone that he would attend the tripartite meeting if his doctors permitted him to travel to London.

Following a flurry of telephone calls, we were informed that, for medical reasons, President Suharto would not be attending the ASEAN-EU Conference, and that the Indonesian delegation would be led by Vice President B.J. Habibie. We were also informed, in the clearest terms, that Indonesia was opposed to the trilateral format of the meeting proposed by us, and that a high-level meeting between Guterres and Habibie, in any form, was out of the question.

The Indonesians advanced the somewhat unconvincing argument that Vice President Habibie was unfamiliar with the East Timor problem, and rejected our suggestion that perhaps he could leave the discussions to Foreign Minister Alatas. However, the Indonesians were prepared to meet with the Secretary-General for a bilateral discussion of the East Timor issue. What I had hoped would be a First Division match had thus been relegated to a Second Division fixture, but we decided to make the best of it anyway.

Notwithstanding the setbacks which form a constant element in his occupational hazard, discouragement is a sentiment which is totally alien to Kofi Annan's temperament, and indeed finds no place in his vocabulary, either. He unhesitatingly decided to meet the Portuguese and Indonesian leaders individually while in London, and accordingly took a brisk walk from the Dorchester to Habibie's suite at a nearby hotel on the morning of April 3, 1998. The word brisk is a bit of an understatement, for Kofi is a fast walker and some of us arrived at the destination a little short of breath.

We were ushered into Habibie's presence for what was to be, for most of us, our first encounter with this extraordinary man. After greeting the Secretary-General warmly, Habibie immediately launched into an exposition of the political and economic strength of Indonesia, reading out a series of statistical figures from a paper presented to him by a nervous aide. He then went on to say that Indonesia would shortly be signing an agreement with the IMF. Turning to the issue of East Timor, Habibie went into a tirade about the Portuguese, and said that he distrusted them so much that there was absolutely no point in his meeting with their Prime Minister.

He thanked the Secretary-General for the efforts made by the UN to find a solution to the problem, and pointed out that Indonesia had already shown its goodwill by being willing to establish interest sections in Jakarta and Lisbon, a gesture which the Portuguese continued to reject. As far as East Timor was concerned, Jakarta had made considerable efforts to improve the living conditions of its inhabitants, who had suffered from years of colonial domination, and that the majority of the people in the island were aware of this.

The Secretary-General pointed out, gently but firmly, that this massive economic investment had still not changed the political climate, that Jakarta had not succeeded in winning the hearts and minds of the people of East Timor, and that a major political problem continued to exist. The United Nations would therefore continue to seek a just solution, as it was required to do by the relevant General Assembly and Security Council resolutions.

This did not go down terribly well with Habibie, but he accepted it with good grace, especially after Alatas chipped in to say that Indonesia had always cooperated with the United Nations on this issue. It was difficult to immediately assess the significance of the meeting, punctuated as it was by Habibie's effervescent, alternating tirades and enthusiasms. But it was quite clear that Habibie was still very much under Suharto's control, and that as far as East Timor was concerned his brief was very rigorously circumscribed.

That afternoon we went to Admiralty House to meet Prime Minister Guterres, who was assisted by Foreign Minister Jaime Gama and Ambassador Fernando Neves. The Secretary-General told Guterres that during our morning meeting Habibie had indicated that Indonesia was about to sign a new agreement with the IMF. The Prime Minister saw this as a positive development; though Portugal wanted self-determination for East Timor, it had no desire to see the people of Indonesia suffer. Gama added that Portugal had made no attempt to complicate Indonesia's dealings with the IMF, implying that it could have done so if it wished.

On the question of interest sections, Guterres said that Portugal was not attaching conditions to the idea, but felt that there should be a series of CBMs to be considered together. When a comprehensive settlement is not possible, it should be possible to have "small" or "big" packages of ideas while a long-term settlement is awaited.

The small package could include: freedom of East Timorese prisoners and improvement of human rights conditions in East Timor, in return for which Portugal could end its pressure on Indonesia and its current efforts toward the adoption of a resolution on East Timor in the Human Rights Commission.

The larger package could be autonomy for East Timor, in return for which Portugal would lift all the restraints it had put on Indonesia. Then, in perhaps five to seven years, the problems could be resolved by themselves.

Our meetings in London, it seemed to me, produced only one positive result: Both sides were prepared and willing to continue the dialogue and negotiations, and that while intransigence remained as strong as ever, there was a marked decrease in bitterness. But to be realistic, we had made no progress on the fundamentals, where the positions of both sides were as far apart as ever.

Our minutes on the meetings conclude with the phrase: "He (the Secretary-General) emphasized that the UN will continue to work hard and persevere, adding that Mr. Marker would try some innovative ideas." I flew out of London with this sobering injunction weighing heavily on my mind. Fortunately, this kind of load is not subject to excess baggage charges on airlines.

8

Negotiations Continue in the Shadow of Indonesia's Summer of Discontent

NEW YORK AND WASHINGTON: APRIL AND MAY 1998

... Experience teaches us that, generally speaking, the most serious moment for a bad government is one when it seeks to mend its ways. Only consummate statecraft can enable a King to save his throne when after a long period of oppressive rule he sets to improve the lot of his subjects. Patiently endured so long as it seemed beyond redress, a grievance comes to appear intolerable once the possibility of removing it crosses men's minds.

—*Alexis de Tocqueville*, The Ancient Regime and the French Revolution

In early April of 1998, I held a brainstorming session in New York with my colleagues in the Department of Political Affairs to decide on our next move. We also had consultations with the Ambassadors in our core group, and I made a quick trip to Washington for a meeting with Stanley Roth, from whom I received, as usual, a most accurate and up-to-date reading on the turbulent events in Indonesia.

The news from Jakarta was cause for increasing concern. The whole of ASEAN had begun to reel under the disastrous economic crisis that had struck the region, turning the aspect of its financial structures, almost overnight, from institutions of opulent dynamism into ones of near desperation. The worst hit, of course, was Indonesia, where the hitherto stable rupiah suddenly shot through the roof, as the dramatic signal of a widespread economic and financial crisis of immense magnitude.

The IMF was again compelled to step in and check the hemorrhage. The conditionalities, including long overdue measures of fiscal discipline, imposed by the Fund triggered the now familiar pattern of aggravating social unrest, which in turn added to the prevalent volatile political situation within the country. The ailing but still autocratic Suharto's physical health was a matter of obvious concern, but it seemed to me that his political health was even more precarious, with a prognosis that was far from reassuring.

Countrywide agitations were leading to a situation that was becoming dangerously unpredictable, with Suharto making concessions that were always too little and too late. I recall contemplating the situation in April 1998, and observed that in the case of East Timor we were dealing with half an island in an archipelago of sixteen thousand islands, and with a population of under one million in an overall population of over two hundred million. God forbid, but if Indonesia were to implode, then there was not much that we could do about East Timor.

Mentioning these flights of fancy, at that time, to the Secretary-General, I said that working on East Timor under these circumstances was a bit like polishing the dinner silver on the Titanic. Kofi's response was a soft chuckle and a quiet, "Well, let's go on doing it." Of course, doomsday scenarios occasionally cross the minds of all negotiators, and I knew that we had no option except to go on doing what we had commenced. In this instance, however, I was quite convinced that notwithstanding all the odds, and despite all the civil and social unrest that prevailed at the time, Indonesia would overcome its difficulties.

This was largely because of the intrinsic nature and civilization of its people, a characteristic which I had just begun to know, and one which I admired tremendously. What confirmed and added immensely to my admiration was the fact that the same people, within a few short months, would defy all doubters and a general international pessimism, would overcome all obstacles imposed by a prolonged dictatorship and a wrecked economy, and would go on to hold free, fair, and generally peaceful elections, and commence the process of creating democratic institutions.

It may be necessary to continue this brief diversion reviewing the chronology of events in Indonesia, in order to place this narrative in perspective. Contrary to his undertakings given to the IMF for its "rescue package" in October 1997, Suharto introduced a budget in January 1998, which, inter alia, increased government spending and subsidies, and left monopolies unregulated. Following mounting domestic and international pressures, Suharto renegotiated the agreement with the IMF in February 1998.

But by that time increasing unemployment and rising food prices had provoked countrywide agitation against Suharto's rule, and had made a major issue of his family's corruption. There was widespread rioting in April, in which the students took a leading part, culminating in the death of six students at Jakarta's Trisakti University on May 14. This sounded the death knell for the Suharto regime, as it triggered riots and massive demonstrations all over the country, and ended with students occupying the National Assembly building in Jakarta.

On May 21, 1998, with Indonesia in almost total paralysis, Suharto resigned and handed over power to his Vice President, B. J. Habibie. Thus ended thirty-two years of rule: clearly the ruler had failed, in his last days, to display the consummate statecraft that de Tocqueville had considered necessary on such occasions. The consequences of Suharto's departure became immediately apparent in Indonesia, and their political impact was and continues to remain both uncertain and far-reaching. Certainly it changed the dynamic of the East Timor problem in a manner which will be traced in subsequent chapters.

As for Suharto, and his long rule in Indonesia, it is still too early to make any definitive judgment and this is a task that should be left to qualified historians. One would have to await the outcome of the process of de-Stalinization, which is currently under way, and is inevitable under the present circumstances. Only then can there be an objective historical catharsis. One is reminded of Chou En Lai's famous observation that it is as yet too early to make a definitive analysis of the French Revolution. In the case of Suharto, one may not have to wait quite as long.

Notwithstanding the concern caused to us by the volatile situation in Indonesia, we decided to press on with our efforts. I felt that they should be focused on four main issues. The first and most important was to continue the negotiations in the SOM format, and to simultaneously push along the AIETD. The other three items were basically CBMs, which would require constant prodding and the discreet application of pressure. These were (a) the release of Xanana Gusmao and his participation in the negotiations process, (b) the withdrawal of a substantial quantity of troops from East Timor in a manner which could be verified, and (c) the establishment of interest sections in Lisbon and Jakarta.

I felt that all three of the latter objectives were attainable if one persisted and went about it the right way. Success in achieving them would not only be a great spur to our efforts, but would also carry useful practical as well as publicity impact and value. I accordingly mounted a sustained campaign of persuasion on the three issues in both Jakarta and Lisbon, and invoked the formidable support of our core group of states. Stanley Roth was particularly active and helpful in this regard, flourishing carrots and sticks from his plentiful stock in appropriate manner and at appropriate moments.

I convened the next Senior Officials Meeting in New York from May 6 to 8, 1988. The agenda consisted of two items, (a) a discussion on "ideas for a possible political arrangement," and (b) the organization of the next AIETD. We submitted in advance to both sides a Non-Paper, with a "strictly confidential" security grading, which outlined certain thoughts on the first item.

In so doing, I wrote to both Neves and Wisnumurti:

> The following ideas are being submitted with a view to continuing and enriching the previous discussions of the Senior Officials Meeting concerning possible political arrangements for East Timor. They are intended to serve as a basis for discussion, and do not, as such, constitute a formal proposal. The ideas are being submitted in the letter and spirit of the Secretary-General's meeting with the two Foreign Ministers (June 19 and 20, 1997).
>
> They are an element in the attempt to find a just, comprehensive and internationally acceptable solution. Thus, they do not in any way prejudge the outcome of the negotiating process, and are without prejudice to the basic position of either side. They provide the general principles delineating spheres of authority in a possible future power sharing arrangement for East Timor, with details to be expounded at a later stage.

The outlines of the arrangement were for the Indonesian Government to have competence over foreign relations, defense, currency, and finance. The East Timor regional authority would exercise legislative, executive, and judicial powers in all areas except those designated as the responsibility of the Indonesian Government. East Timor would also have complete cultural autonomy, including in education, language, and the promotion of culture.

The paper went on to detail the suggested respective areas of competence in respect to foreign relations, defense, economy, currency, and finance, the applicability of Indonesian laws, and the competence of the East Timor authority in terms of legislative, executive, and judicial power, and of public order.

In consonance with our malign tradition, the Senior Officials Meeting in May commenced on a sour and unpleasant note, and at the end of the first day the distrust and bitterness increased to an extent that could have jeopardized the entire process of negotiations. Fortunately, wiser counsels prevailed and we were able to bring the meeting to a reasonably successful conclusion. Most importantly, both the Indonesian and Portuguese delegations were scrupulous in maintaining the confidentiality of the discussions, so that most people were unaware of our close call.

The Human Rights Commission had just ended its session in Geneva by expressing, in a presidential statement, its deep concern on violations in East Timor, and had secured a pledge from the Indonesian Government to allow the UN to investigate, within one year, the arbitrary detentions in the territory. Following intensive negotiations between Indonesia and the European Union, the latter had withdrawn its strongly worded draft resolution in exchange for a consensus statement.

This was a satisfactory outcome, from my point of view, and could have established a reasonable climate for our SOM meeting. Unfortunately, it was more than offset by another event, also in Europe, which had also occurred in late April. The Portuguese Government, largely, I felt, at the initiative of President Sampaio, had organized a meeting of the various disparate East Timor resistance groups on April 26 at Peniche, near Lisbon, the outcome of which was the establishment of an umbrella organization called the National Council for Timorese Resistance.

The two hundred delegates unanimously adopted a draft charter unifying all the resistance groups, setting out the statutes of the CNRT, and electing Xanana Gusmao as the "Lider Maximo" (supreme leader) and President of CNRT, with Ramos Horta as Vice President. During our earlier meetings, President Sampaio had urged me to send a UN observer to this conference, but for obvious reasons I had firmly declined the invitation. The Indonesian reaction to Peniche was predictably sharp, but it exceeded my expectations by going beyond a strong verbal condemnation.

Indonesia maintained that the Peniche convention was an attempt by Portugal and Ramos Horta to intensify pressure on Jakarta, and was against the spirit of the AIETD. Consequently, it maintained that the AIETD should be discontinued, and Wisnumurti said that he was under instructions not to discuss the implementation of its previous agreements, nor was he to discuss arrangements for the next AIETD.

The Portuguese reaction was equally strong. They insisted that there was no linkage between the activities of the resistance and the AIETD. In their view, the only thing that had changed as a result of the Convention was that the resistance now had a united organization. They accused Indonesia of using the issue as an excuse to end the AIETD. Portugal acknowledged that it had supported the Peniche Convention, as was its right as the Administering Power.

If Indonesia was going to stick to its position, the Portuguese warned that it might have to reconsider the whole tripartite process, because it had been agreed at the June 1997 meeting between the Secretary-General and the two Foreign Ministers that the AIETD would be part of the SOM agenda. Consequently, Neves declined to discuss the fixing of dates for the next round of talks, before reporting to Foreign Minister Gama and receiving instructions.

This put me in a rather delicate position, and I knew that I was faced with something much more than a tantrum of prima donnas. I felt it necessary to initiate some intensive dialogues on a bilateral basis with the Indonesians and the Portuguese. In my talk with Neves I regretted that the resistance convention had become an issue in our negotiations, and added that the suspension or discontinuance of the AIETD would be a major setback for our negotiations, and an embarrassment to the UN.

I intended to try and resolve this issue in my discussions with the Indonesians, and also intended to continue our discussion on the "model" during the current session. In this connection, would Portugal accept discussing autonomy as a final settlement, subject to eventual acceptance by the East Timorese?

To Wisnumurti, I expressed regret that the resistance convention had become a complicating factor, but I emphasized that jeopardizing the AIETD would be counterproductive: inevitably Indonesia would be blamed by others, irrespective of Indonesia's views on the matter. It would also be a setback for the tripartite efforts at a time when we were entering into serious negotiations. I recalled that the UN had declined an invitation from the sponsors to send an observer to the convention, and that I would speak to the representatives of the resistance and ensure that the AIETD would not be adversely affected by the Convention.

After some more shuttling between the Indonesian and Portuguese delegations, and using every form of persuasion that I was capable of— short of threatening to jump off the 38th floor of the UN building or throw myself into the East River—we managed to secure an understanding to set aside the issue of the AIETD for the time being, and to resume our discussions on the autonomous arrangements.

I commenced our trilateral meeting by suggesting that the guiding spirit of our discussions should be to devise solutions through free-thinking and not hard-nosed bargaining—the time for the latter would come in due course. I also urged the negotiators not to argue over the past, but instead to discuss the future and see where there could be some reconciliation of views. Both Neves and Wisnumurti took these suggestions in good spirit, and conducted negotiations in a businesslike and constructive manner, so that by the end of the session we had some useful input to our working paper on autonomy.

I met with Ali Alatas in New York on May16. He was obviously deeply concerned and preoccupied with events back home in Indonesia, but we did discuss East Timor in some depth. I stressed to him the need to reconsider his decision on the AIETD, pointing out that this was the only organized channel for consultations between the UN and the East Timorese. If this was to disappear, we would be obliged to intensify our direct contacts with East Timorese leaders such as Ramos Horta.

Alatas promised to reconsider the matter, but in view of the prevailing uncertainty of the situation in Indonesia, we agreed to await developments before embarking on the next phase of negotiations. It was clear to me, at that time, that the future course of our talks was going to be largely determined by the evolution of events in Indonesia.

While keeping a troubled eye on the Titanic from distant New York, I continued to work on the East Timor negotiation process, and decided to invigorate our autonomy proposal. The paper that we had prepared and discussed until now had contained the broad outlines of our objectives, and I felt that we ought to present to both sides a much more substantive and sophisticated document, which would contain both ideas of principles as well as details, and would merit serious, in depth discussion.

I felt, with all due respect, that our resources within the Department of Political Affairs were insufficient for the purpose which I had envisaged, largely because the document I wanted would need not only legal expertise and professionalism, but also a full-time effort, which the overworked officers of the Department could obviously not provide. Vendrell had the bright idea of entrusting the task to Professor Hurst Hanum of the Fletcher School of Law and Diplomacy at Tufts University in Boston, and we were most grateful that he accepted the challenging offer.

Hurst Hanum proved to be an ideal choice, for he was not only a recognized expert on international law, but also had considerable experience in human rights issues. At our first meeting I explained our basic requirements to Hurst, and within a very short time he produced an excellent document, extremely well structured and substantive in content. I immediately sent copies to Lisbon and Jakarta, and the document became the basic working paper for our subsequent discussions, with Hurst joining in as a participant, providing explanations and drafting amendments. The paper that we eventually negotiated was so complete, in my view, that its elements could well form the basic framework of a constitution for an independent East Timor.

We also pursued our other objective, the release of Xanana Gusmao.

Shortly after assuming office, President Habibie had released a number of political prisoners in Indonesia. In his message of congratulations to the new President, the Secretary-General had expressed appreciation for this gesture, and suggested that it may also be extended to Xanana. By the end of May we were all very conscious of the vast changes that were taking place in Indonesia, but despite the uncertainties that they evoked, and unsettling as they might appear at first sight, I was sure that the new situation would provide a window of opportunity. The trick was to recognize it when it occurred, and to seize it.

9

The Second Innings: Indonesia in Transit and Tumult

New York, Lisbon, Jakarta, and East Timor: June and July 1998

> In all negociations of difficulty, a man may not look to sow and reap at once: but must prepare business, and so ripen it by degree.
> — *Francis Bacon,* Essays: "Of Negociating"

We did not have to wait too long. Early in June, Alatas called me from Jakarta to say that he would shortly arrive in New York to deliver to the Secretary-General "an important proposal" on East Timor, an essential element of which would be a "special autonomous status" for the region. Alex told me in confidence that he was "seizing a window of opportunity to obtain a consensus among the present Indonesian leadership."

Given the uncertainty of the prevalent Indonesian political situation, with its economic hardship and the divergence of opinion generally, his task could not have been an easy one. I hoped that the proposal would provide scope for positive negotiations, be worthy of serious consideration, and be one which we could convey with credibility to the Portuguese. An important factor in examining the proposal would obviously be the involvement of the East Timorese people.

Their position of the resistance had by now been greatly strengthened, both internally and internationally. What form of consultation did

Jakarta envisage, and were they prepared to release and negotiate with Xanana? Stanley Roth had told me that he had met Xanana in prison two weeks previously, and that the latter continued to display an impressive objective and statesmanlike attitude.

In a typically friendly meeting with the Secretary-General, Alatas delivered Habibie's proposals in the form of a verbal demarche, but later handed over to us a paper which contained his "Talking Points" and stated:

> 1. The Indonesian Government is prepared to grant a special status to East Timor, with wide-ranging autonomy, in the context and as part of a comprehensive, just and mutually acceptable end-solution to the question of East Timor. Toward this end, Indonesia is ready to negotiate the substantive elements of such a special, autonomous region of East Timor within the ongoing tripartite talks under the auspices of the U.N. Secretary-General.
>
> 2. Indonesia is of the view that considering the historical, political, socio-cultural, and geographic factors and conditions pertaining to the East Timor question, the creation of a special, autonomous province within the unitary Republic of Indonesia represents the most realistic, viable, and peaceful solution to the problem. On the other hand, the proposal to conduct a referendum would, in view of the long history of bitter strife and bloodshed in the province, only re-open old wounds, re-ignite violent disputes, and conflict and may even lead to renewed civil war.
>
> 3. Indonesia believes that this proposal reflects, once again, the sincerity and determination with which it has always approached the peaceful solution of this long standing issue and now expects the same degree of political will and sincerity to imbue and motivate the Portuguese side.
>
> 4. A new opportunity is now being provided in order to arrive at a comprehensive settlement of the question and all sides should grasp that opportunity and not allow it to be lost because of an erroneous or speculative assessment of the prevailing situation.

Although the proposal had formally come from President Habibie, the skill and mastery of Alatas' draughtsmanship, both in ideas and presentation, was quite unmistakable. As far as I was concerned, this was a great relief: Alex would continue to play a key role in the new dispensation. We felt that the Habibie proposal was clearly a step in the right direction, and should be pursued even though we did not think it went far enough. Our analysis of the situation was as follows:

> 1. East Timor was at the crossroads. Although, as Alatas had said, "President Suharto's departure has opened a window of opportunity," there was still a wide chasm between the growing demand in the Territory for self-determination and what the Habibie Government was prepared to give.
>
> 2. Habibie's offer of a "special status" had provoked widespread opposition in East Timor. In the latest of these actions, reminis-

cent of the Jakarta student protests in the days preceding Suharto's resignation, hundreds of East Timorese youth had occupied the local parliament building in Dili. In the new atmosphere of freedom, the demand for a referendum was now being expressed even by some former pro-integrationists.

3. In Indonesia itself, for the first time, opposition politicians, NGOs, and human rights activists were calling for a political solution on the basis of a free choice of the East Timorese, although opinion was divided on the question of independence.

4. On the other hand, the military seemed reluctant to withdraw troops, even though it had acted with unprecedented restraint in the face of the recent protests.

5. Thus far, Jakarta had ruled out referendum as an option, and had shown no intention of opening a dialogue with the East Timorese leaders. But with the growing demand for a referendum, we felt that the government should urgently start talks with figures like Xanana Gusmao and Bishop Belo.

6. We ought to revitalize the AIETD, and in order for it to achieve its full potential its format should be amended to include participation by Xanana, together with a lifting of the ban on discussion of the political status of East Timor.

7. An overall solution would have to include a mechanism that would allow the East Timorese population to express its views: the Senior Officials' Meeting had already been directed to seek "possible mechanisms for ascertaining the views of the East Timorese people."

8. There was an urgent need to mobilize international support for the Secretary-General's efforts at this critical juncture, in order to encourage Indonesia to take bold steps to resolve the East Timor issue.

In his meeting with the Secretary-General on June 18, Alatas made his usual persuasive presentation. He warned that it was not easy, in the prevailing volatile political climate in Indonesia, to obtain agreement to the proposals, which he had just presented. Such a significant shift in position was unimaginable under the previous regime, and every effort should be made to consider the proposal in a serious and realistic manner. The Secretary-General's response was contained in a letter that he sent to Habibie, immediately after the meeting with Alatas.

The Secretary-General described the proposals as "important, and ... receiving the most careful study by us here in New York. Your ideas will shortly be conveyed to the Portuguese Government by my Personal Representative, and you will be informed of their reaction." The Secretary-General expressed his appreciation of the President's initiative, and requested that this exchange of views remain confidential.

Accordingly, I flew to Lisbon in the last week of June for consultations with the Portuguese Government. We discussed the UN working paper on autonomy, which Lisbon found to be a useful document. President Sampaio, in particular, was impressed by the paper and had obviously gone through it with a very fine-tooth comb. It was discussed in some detail, and added to the stimulus and pleasure of a delicious working dinner, which the President graciously provided at his residence.

The other, more important, issue was the Indonesian proposal for wide-ranging autonomy, which Alatas had just presented to the Secretary-General. I was happy to notice that on this visit there had been a substantial change in Lisbon's attitude toward Jakarta. The Portuguese generally welcomed the Indonesian proposal as a positive development that gave the clearest signal of the changing attitude in Jakarta. However, they remained skeptical about the real value of the proposal, as it did not represent any fundamental change in the basic Indonesian position, i.e., that self-determination for East Timor was not an option, and that any concession on autonomy was conditional on Portugal's and the UN's recognition of its sovereignty in East Timor.

Foreign Minister Gama said that the recent developments vis-à-vis East Timor were "very, very positive," but he stressed that the reform in Indonesia had not yet crystallized and no one knew where it was heading. He said that autonomy meant different things under a dictatorship and a democracy, and it was not clear which was being offered to East Timor. Gama expressed the hope that Indonesia would provide more details about its proposal in order to see whether they fit into a democratic frame, and whether they could be reconciled with the principle of self-determination.

For example, would the Indonesians permit the formation of East Timorese political parties? I replied that my understanding from Alatas was that the proposal involved a genuine autonomy that would only exclude foreign affairs, external defense, and currency from the areas of East Timorese authority, and that freedom of association in East Timor would be permitted, with details being discussed at a later stage.

Gama warned that what should be avoided was the consolidation of Indonesian control under the guise of a more benign policy that would effectively allow Indonesia to get what it had not been able to achieve by force. I assured the Minister, somewhat peremptorily, that the United Nations could never be a part of any such scheme. I then urged Gama to consider the opening of interest sections in Jakarta and Lisbon, in the light of the change of attitudes in Indonesia and the new developments, including the release of some East Timorese political prisoners.

I also reiterated Alatas' assurance that Portuguese diplomats would be allowed free access to East Timor. We discussed the importance of holding the next AIETD in an amended format, and more importantly, the dates for the next meeting between the Secretary-General and the Foreign Ministers, which we tentatively set for early August.

My session with Prime Minister Guterres was as productive and pleasant as always. He regarded the Indonesian proposal as a positive sign, and reiterated Portugal's readiness to consider it provided that Indonesia did not ask Portugal to recognize Indonesian sovereignty over East Timor as a precondition. He also stressed the importance of obtaining East Timorese agreement to any settlement.

Guterres added that Portugal had already eased its diplomatic pressure on Indonesia, and was prepared to withdraw its reservations about opening interest sections in Jakarta and Lisbon, and even consider full normalization of relations, if Indonesia were to take more concrete positive steps, such as the improvement of human rights conditions in East Timor, and the release of Xanana Gusmao.

On the latter point, the Prime Minister and I were in complete accord, and I assured him that I would do my best during my forthcoming visit to Indonesia. My main objective, at this point in time, was to move the political process forward before it was overtaken by forces on the ground.

President Sampaio thought that the latest Indonesian proposal was "a very clever one," and implied that it was an attempt by Alatas to sell an old idea in a new package. While agreeing with my view that the present opportunity must be seized, he stressed that everyone must be clear as to what was being sought. Although he was prepared to give Indonesia the benefit of the doubt, he said that presenting autonomy as the conclusion and then embarking on negotiations would not work. He thought that "we need to engineer" some kind of modalities for a gradual approach, such as a period of transition when the issue of status would remain suspended.

I had a series of meetings with the leaders of the newly formed umbrella organization of East Timorese, the CNRT, which revealed, to no great surprise, a very reserved reaction to the Indonesian proposal. There was profound distrust, and an insistence on concrete evidence of good faith by the Indonesians, such as the release of Xanana Gusmao. I reassured the CNRT that no solution on East Timor could be reached without the involvement and agreement of the East Timorese people, but in order to avail of the present changed circumstances it was essential that the resistance carry out a peaceful political campaign and not resort to violence.

The visit to Lisbon had gone as well as could be expected. I had anticipated that the Portuguese would maintain their position of principle on the autonomy issue, but I had also hoped that their attitude would display some flexibility and a realization of the changed and changing circumstances in Indonesia. I was right on both counts, and was particularly encouraged by the obvious desire in Lisbon for an intensification of negotiations and for participation in constructive fashion.

It was a reassuring thought to keep at the back of one's mind when talking to the Indonesians in Jakarta. Immediately upon my return to New York I was confronted with a glitch, unexpected and unwelcome as glitches always are. Tamrat Samuel told me that he had called Bishop Belo in Dili to verify the reports of a document being circulated in East Timor as "Ambassador Marker's proposal for resolving the question of East Timor." The document was the untitled "model," which we had sent to Jakarta and Lisbon prior to the May meeting of the Senior Officials in New York.

Not only was this a most serious breach of the confidentiality under which our negotiations were proceeding, but worse still, it was a selective leak which omitted the fundamental caveat that the contents did not in any way represent a proposal but were only for the purpose "of enriching the previous discussions." Even more disturbing was Bishop Belo's report that he had received a visit from Governor Abilio Osorio Soares and some military officers who handed him "a six-page document bearing Ambassador Marker's signature" and informed him that it was the United Nations' proposal for a final settlement of the problem of East Timor and that "there was no other alternative for people in East Timor but to accept it."

The Bishop was asked to present this to the people as an accomplished fact and to persuade them not to oppose it. Moreover, according to Belo, Indonesian officials and pro integration figures close to the Governor were widely distributing the document and telling the people not to expect anything beyond what was contained in the paper.

Clearly, no actions could be more outrageous or mala fide. I immediately made an indignant telephone call to Foreign Minister Alatas in Jakarta and reported the incident. He expressed what I thought were genuine surprise and shock, and said that he would institute an immediate inquiry into the matter. His anguished immediate response was that "somebody is trying to sabotage our efforts."

I said that we would be issuing an appropriate official statement, and Alatas told me that he, too, would issue a statement that "no proposals have been made either by the United Nations, or by Indonesia or by Portugal." This flurry of statements served to contain, to a certain extent, the immediate damage. But the incident left me with an uncomfortable sense of foreboding: the fluid and volatile political situation in Indonesia was beginning to provide a fertile climate for disruption and mischief by dissident reactionary elements.

My next visit to Indonesia and East Timor was from July 16 to the 22, 1998, and confirmed my expectation that the trip would be an eventful one. Political ferment was palpable in both Indonesia and East Timor, with a plethora of political parties enthusiastically exercising their newfound freedom and a hesitant establishment reacting to events in a series of uncertain fits and starts. At the end of June, a Troika of European Union Ambassadors, led by the British Ambassador, who was its current President, had visited East Timor on a fact-finding mission.

The Indonesian Government had provided the Troika with all the necessary facilities and the members were able to meet East Timorese of both the pro-independence and pro-integration groups. But in the tense, charged political atmosphere that prevailed in the island, the presence of the high profile Troika of ambassadors created an emotional focal impact that the local administration was unable to handle.

Things went reasonably smoothly during the early part of the visit in Dili, but tensions began to build up, and during the later stages, when the Troika were visiting Bishop Nasciemento in Baucau, there was a demonstration followed by a serious clash between the pro-independence and pro integration groups, resulting in some casualties. In a rapidly deteriorating security situation, the Troika had to be evacuated from the island by a military aircraft.

There were dramatic reports of the incident in the Indonesian press, so that by the time that I arrived in Jakarta, there was already a perceptible feeling of jitters about any further visits to East Timor by VIPs. With Francis Bacon's ever-wise counsels as deep background in my thoughts, I felt that I "must prepare business, and so ripen it by degree."

Apart from the obvious and valuable need to advance the dynamics of the overall negotiating process with the new Habibie administration, I set the following objectives for the current session in Jakarta:

> A. Deepen contacts with the leaders of the main newly active and assertive political parties.
>
> B. Press vigorously for the release of Xanana Gusmao, or at least for his transfer from Cipinang prison to a residence, under some form of "house arrest." At the same time, involve him in active political negotiations with the Indonesian authorities, and possibly others.
>
> C. Arrange for a verifiable withdrawal of troops from East Timor.
>
> D. The establishment of interest sections in Jakarta and Lisbon.

As for the first issue, the prevailing political conditions were obviously propitious for broadening my earlier contacts with the leaders of different political parties and giving them an authoritative account of what the United Nations was trying to do about East Timor. I was convinced that any relationship that we would be able to build at this stage with the leading, highly competent Indonesian politicians would not only be most helpful in terms of advice and guidance during the negotiations, but would be vital for the implementation process of the agreement, whenever it came, and whatever shape it might eventually assume.

Accordingly, I had a series of meetings with the leaders of the main Indonesian political parties, notably Abdurrahman Wahid, "Gus Dur," Megawati Sukarnoputri, and Marzuki Darusman, and had the good fortune to develop a relationship with each of them that rapidly became both valuable and productive.

I started my visit to Jakarta, as usual, with a meeting with Foreign Minister Alatas. And, as always, it was as frank, friendly, and productive as one could wish, or as the circumstances of political realities could permit. I conveyed the Portuguese response to Indonesia's autonomy proposal, stating that they had welcomed it as a positive development and were ready to continue the negotiations, but that Portugal could not, in advance, be expected to agree to autonomy as a final settlement of the problem without the East Timorese expressing their views on it.

Alatas was somewhat dismayed that the Portuguese could not be more forthcoming, and hoped that eventually Portugal would see that autonomy was the only viable solution, and would work toward that end, even if it could not say so in public. I stressed to Alatas that there was an urgent need to involve the East Timorese more closely, and that Xanana Gusmao had a key role in this, as he was the only leader who had the strength and following in East Timor to bring the people around and pacify the territory.

Unfortunately, Alatas' view of Xanana did not correspond with mine, so we did not get very far on that one. Nevertheless, I continued my strong pleas to move Xanana from prison to "house arrest," so that he could have more access and be more directly involved in the negotiating process. In this, I was adding my voice to an international diplomatic chorus, which I was furiously orchestrating in the demand for Xanana's release.

We discussed the possibility of an expanded role and function for the AIETD, and I pointed out that since the political future of East Timor was now being openly debated in the streets of Jakarta and Dili, it would be quite invidious to exclude it from the agenda of the AIETD. Alatas did not agree, as he thought that it would constitute a "second track" to the UN sponsored tripartite negotiations. He suggested, instead, that the UN intensify its direct contacts with the East Timorese of all political persuasions. This "back channel" consultation could be conducted by the UN as a way of assessing the views of the East Timorese people.

We were received by President B.J. Habibie in the opulent splendor of his office, with its regalia of guards, liveried staff, and important looking officials scurrying in and out of the vast corridors. The contrast between this meeting and my first one with his predecessor in the quiet, shady Suharto residence could not have been more stark. And yet, I thought to myself, it was the soft-spoken recluse who had the mind set of the dictator, while the voluble extrovert Habibie possessed the more liberal temperament and had demonstrated this by a number of measures that he had already taken, such as removing restraints on the trade unions and the press.

He recounted these and other similar achievements to me with a zestful absence of modesty. As often happens in political life, there appears a leader who has greatness thrust upon him by fate and by circumstances which are frequently adverse. Habibie was a prime example of this eventuality, taking office at a time of the most severe national adversity, with Indonesia in the throes of the worst political, economic, and financial crisis that it had known in thirty years.

An intrinsically religious man, Habibie had assumed his responsibilities with a profound faith in Allah, and a deep devotion to his country. He exercised his duties with obvious relish which, combined with his impetuous and often idiosyncratic behavior, gave many the impression that the ship of state was under somewhat erratic pilotage. But I always thought that behind the impulsiveness and theatrical gestures that formed such a prominent feature of his personality, there was a keen, far-seeing mind, a basically generous and liberal spirit, and a deep and genuine patriotism.

These are the attributes that motivated his profound decision, six months later, to allow the East Timorese to choose their destiny. And the decision itself was pronounced in typical Habibie style, dramatic and impulsive according to his detractors. Dramatic it certainly was, but impulsive? Could he have done so if he had gone into long, convoluted consultations with his multifarious advisers with their diverse opinions?

Or was it more appropriate, once he had instinctively (and correctly) decided that it would be better for both Indonesia and East Timor for the latter to freely choose its future, to announce his decision with the full, unencumbered force of his newly acquired presidential authority?

These are intriguing, speculative questions, to which perhaps only B.J. Habibie can have the right answer. What is beyond question, however, is that the decision was both bold and historic.

With President B.J. Habibie, in his usual ebullient form. Left to right, unidentified Indonensian official security officer, J.M., Ian Martin, Mark Quarterman and President Habibie, whose crucial decision in January 1999 expedited the solution of the East Timor issue. Photograph: Ministry of Foreign Affairs, Indonesia.

But we are getting a little ahead in the narrative. At our meeting in Jakarta in July 1998, President Habibie maintained the position that his offer of special autonomy for East Timor was as far as he was prepared to go. He ruled out the possibility of a referendum, now or in the future, arguing that it would lead to the disintegration of Indonesia. He leapt out of his magnificent leather armchair, which appeared to be three sizes too large for his diminutive build, and rushed to an enormous map of Indonesia that adorned one of the walls.

Waving both arms vigorously as he made a rapid cartographic traverse of his nation, and pausing to firmly demarcate his own home region in Sulawesi, Habibie stressed the enormous diversity of Indonesia and the danger of centrifugal disintegration that could ensue if East Timor were allowed to break away. He was also categoric in his assertion that he would neither release Xanana Gusmao, nor engage in direct talks with him, even though he would permit "indirect contact" with the latter. Our meeting concluded with Habibie thanking me for all that I had done for Indonesia, and assuring me of his fullest cooperation in future. I reckoned that it was a stand off, but by no means a disagreeable one.

We met individually with three of the top ranking officers of ABRI, the Indonesian Armed Forces. The first was Major General Zacky Anwar, the Head of Military Intelligence. A thorough professional officer, belonging to the elite Special Forces, he was reputed to be a hard-liner and a "Prabowo man." But none of this came through in his conversation, which was always low-key, pleasant, and geared toward accommodation and not confrontation.

He readily agreed with my assessment that the Army, despite its recent restraint, had not succeeded in winning the confidence of the East Timorese. We went through the numbers game of the troops stationed in East Timor, and he told me that there had been a decision to withdraw some troops in the near future. I welcomed this, and made two suggestions.

The first was that the next phase of withdrawals should be given full publicity in the press and media, the second was that these troops should comprise of elements of the Kopassus, which were the most feared in East Timor. Zacky accepted the first suggestion with alacrity, but was noticeably less enthusiastic about the second, and gave a wry grin as I looked pointedly at the "Special Forces" tabs on his uniform. His equanimity on this, as on other occasions, elicited the fond respect that I had for General Zacky, despite the profound differences that I had with him on the conduct of operations, particularly at a later stage.

The next senior officer whom we met was Lieutenant General Susilo Bambang Yudono, Chief of Staff for Social and Political Affairs of the Armed Forces. A thoughtful and obviously intelligent officer, General Susilo Bambang engaged us in a most interesting discussion on the current state of affairs in Indonesia. His views were liberal, far-thinking, and entirely pragmatic. We emerged from our discussion considerably enriched and fortified by the thought of a possibility of a genuine change in the thinking of the Indonesian military.

In our meeting with General Wiranto, the Defense Minister and Commander of the Armed Forces of Indonesia, I commended the restraint now being exhibited by the army in East Timor, as well as the recent decision to make members of the armed forces accountable for human rights violations. We discussed force reductions in East Timor, as well as the disbandment of paramilitary organizations on the island. We also had a lengthy discussion on the future of East Timor and the implications of the special autonomy proposal.

At this point in time General Wiranto was a major political figure in Indonesia, and was being wooed by many political leaders, not excluding President Habibie himself. Wiranto's Sphynx-like attitude, not to mention his appearance, did much to enhance his personal prestige, while inducing a sense of uncertainty amongst the politicians and keeping them slightly off balance. At the end of our meeting, Wiranto said to me in confidence that he was confronted by so many multifarious problems in Indonesia itself that he would greatly welcome an early settlement of the East Timor issue.

My assessment was that there had been a major change in the attitude of the Indonesian military. Senior officers agreed that past policies had not won the hearts and minds of the East Timorese. The autonomy plan appeared to enjoy the general support of the military, but because it was seen as a big concession, it seemed to have raised the unrealistic and somewhat dangerous expectation that it would lead to an early settlement of the issue.

General Wiranto and other senior officers had assured me that there would be a reduction of troops, and President Habibie had indicated that Wiranto would work with Bishop Belo on a plan for troop reduction. I felt at that time that one of my objectives was about to be achieved, especially when we saw pictures in the newspapers of Indonesian troops embarking at the port in Dili. Alas, this was largely illusory: as subsequent events were to prove, this was a kind of a box and cox affair, and troops withdrawn in a blaze of publicity were subsequently re-inducted in a less public, indeed surreptitious, fashion.

My meeting with Xanana Gusmao was as interesting as ever, and perhaps more productive than before. Xanana's views on a solution involved what he termed a "phased approach." In the first phase, a "Security Phase" of six to eighteen months, there would be a de-escalation of tensions and reduction of Indonesian troops, whose new role would be one of "peace keeping," and a UN presence.

In the second, a "Reconstruction Phase" which would last five years alongside infrastructural development efforts, there would be political preparations for resolving the political status of East Timor and related problems in which the Indonesian military would not be sidelined. He was prepared to accommodate the military in the transition, as he said his desire was to end all animosity with Indonesia. He was also determined to give an assurance that once there was a political settlement, no vengeance or investigation into the past would be sought by the East Timorese.

At the end of the five-year period, a referendum would be held to determine whether the East Timorese wanted independence or integration with Indonesia. He remained convinced that independence was the best option, but expressed his readiness to work with other East Timorese leaders, through the AIETD, to build a consensus and to compromise toward an acceptable solution and a mechanism for settlement.

I told Xanana that I thought his ideas, so meticulously worked out behind prison bars, and yet so eminently reasonable and far-sighted, could find our support, but that was obviously not enough. I said that I would convey the gist to the Indonesian authorities in general terms, and urge them to enter into direct talks with him in any manner that they considered appropriate. But I warned Xanana that Jakarta now appeared to be hurtling along the Habibie track of "special autonomy" and were unlikely to be diverted from it. We would have to seek common ground, if any, between the two proposals, but the task would not be easy.

I then discussed the issue of interest sections with Xanana. He confessed his unfamiliarity with diplomatic procedures and terminology, but once I explained the details and implications to him, he firmly supported the idea and asked me to convey his views to both governments. On the spur of the moment, I decided to go one better, and asked him if he was prepared to announce this to the press which had, as always, gathered in large numbers outside the prison gate each time I visited Xanana.

When he expressed his willingness to do so, I contacted the Indonesian Foreign Service officer who had escorted me to Cipinang prison and told him to get clearance from his Ministry for Xanana to announce to the press that he supported the idea of establishing interest sections in Lisbon and Jakarta. I undertook to guarantee that Xanana would not hold a press conference, or take any questions, and would confine himself to the one statement on interest sections.

After a short but proverbially agonizing delay, the clearance came through. We escorted Xanana to the gates of the prison, where he was given a tremendous ovation, and I announced that he would make a statement. Xanana was true to his word, made his statement with the cheerful dignity that only he can display, and we retreated back into the prison, with sighs of relief from the Indonesian officials, including the Prison Governor.

Thanks to Xanana, we had made a breakthrough on the important issue of interest sections, and all that remained now was for the two governments to complete the formalities, which was done at the Ministerial meeting in New York two weeks later, and to work out the modalities.

The next hurdle that we faced on this visit was the trip to East Timor. As I said earlier, the signals were less than propitious. The existing tensions were already at a high level, and had been further exacerbated by the very recent visit of the European Union Troika ambassadors. The Foreign Ministry officials were genuinely concerned about my personal safety, and did their best to dissuade me from going to East Timor.

Both the pro-independence and the pro-integration groups had declared their intention to hold demonstrations during my forthcoming visit to Dili. During our talk in Jakarta, Xanana Gusmao had also expressed his apprehension about my going to Dili. Bishop Belo called me from there to advise against my visit, and then made his views doubly clear by making a public announcement to that effect.

The press, notably the foreign correspondents, had already sharpened their pencils and polished their camera lenses and flown off to Dili. I told Alatas that I was very conscious of his concerns, and did not wish to be the cause of any disturbance that might damage valuable lives or property, but I nevertheless did have a duty to perform, and did have to meet with representatives of the East Timorese people on their territory.

Alex tried to be as helpful as he could, and suggested that I go to Bali, where he would arrange to ferry any or all of the East Timorese personalities that I wished to meet. From the point of view of personal comfort and safety, there could not have been a better suggestion, but I had to remind Alex that I was, after all, the Personal Representative of the United Nations Secretary-General for East Timor, and that it was therefore necessary, as a matter of principle, for me to carry out my functions of consultations on the soil of the territory.

After further discussions with Alex and with Bishop Belo on the telephone, I suggested that I should go to Baucau, where tensions were less than in Dili and where I was not expected. In consultation with the Bishop, we selected the names of the East Timorese that I would meet, and they duly proceeded to Baucau. Our delegation was provided with a military aircraft, thanks to Alex's strenuous efforts, which flew us to Baucau, where I spent the entire day in meetings and talks with the East

Timorese leaders, who came in their individual capacities, and were compelled, for logistical reasons, to leave their respective mobs behind in Dili. The press, too, duly arrived in Baucau, in time to receive a rather dull briefing by me, instead of the more newsworthy incendiary reports that they might have filed from Dili.

Back in Jakarta, I had the accustomed round of stimulating meetings with the core group of ambassadors with whom I regularly met. Lavish in their hospitality, and generous in the dispensation of their knowledge and counsel, they invariably provided the greatest of food for mind and body, returning a fully nourished itinerant back to his place of duty in New York. In summing up the results of my July visit to Indonesia, I felt that we were beginning to get somewhere.

The negotiating process was in an operating mode, and was holding its own despite the uncertainties of the political conditions in Indonesia. We had managed to extend our close contacts and ongoing relationship with the Indonesian administration to the wider range of political parties and their leaders. There had been a public display of troop withdrawals from East Timor. Notwithstanding the sleight of hand used in this exercise, the fact remained that Jakarta had done something in public which it had consistently refused to do before.

The situation of Xanana, though still in incarceration, had considerably improved, both in terms of his accessibility to outside visitors and in his ability to run affairs in East Timor. Finally, there was the imminent prospect of the establishment of interest sections in Jakarta and Lisbon, thus bringing to an end a diplomatic breach that had lasted for over twenty years.

I felt that the August meeting of the Secretary-General with the two Foreign Ministers would provide a fresh impetus to the negotiating process, would probably add further problems to the ones that we already had, but at the same time take us on to the next sector of our work. I looked forward to the continuation of the challenge and its excitement.

10

The Doctor's Dilemma: The Negotiations Intensify, but So Does the Conflict

NEW YORK, VIENNA, AND LISBON: OCTOBER AND NOVEMBER 1998

> Men commit the error of not knowing when to limit their hopes.
>
> *—Machiavelli*

A Senior Officials' Meeting was held in New York from October 6 to the 8, 1998. The agenda focused on three issues: (a) the autonomy plan for East Timor, (b) modalities for the opening of interest sections in Jakarta and Lisbon, and (c) the next All Inclusive East Timorese Dialogue (AIETD).

As usual, Ambassadors Fernando Neves and Nugroho Wisnumurti led the respective sides, and the atmosphere during the session was both constructive and friendly. We submitted a proposal for a wide-ranging autonomy for East Timor, while leaving aside the question of final status. The basic draft of the plan came, of course, from Hurst Hannum of the Fletcher School of Law and Diplomacy, who sat in with us on the consultations, as usual.

The plan envisaged complete autonomy, except in the areas of foreign policy, external defense, and monetary and customs issues, and was strong on political freedoms and human rights issues, which were in keeping with Hannum's expertise. The Portuguese were generally supportive of the proposal, despite their continued unease in discussing autonomy without the direct participation of the East Timorese.

The Indonesian reaction, while showing readiness to accept many of the important elements, was also concerned that the proposed autonomy was "too wide," and that in some respects would place East Timor on a par with Indonesia. The constant problem in these negotiations was the issue of the fundamental difference over whether the autonomy was for a province of Indonesia or for a Non-Self-Governing Territory still awaiting decolonization.

We discussed the technical and legal modalities for the establishment of interest sections and presented a document, which would serve as a basis for agreement. This was accepted by both sides, and they agreed to establish offices by January 1999, following negotiations with their respective protecting powers, Thailand and the Netherlands. There was also agreement on the composition of delegates and the modalities for the next AIETD meeting, scheduled for later in the month.

The meeting took place against a backdrop of rising tensions in East Timor itself, although curiously, this was not reflected in the genuine spirit of accommodation that prevailed in the discussions. Persistent reports of an increase in troop levels in East Timor were followed by a series of operations launched by the army against the guerrillas, leading to a number of casualties, primarily on the Indonesian side.

We were receiving mixed tidings from East Timor. On the positive side was news of a two-day dialogue at Dare, near Dili, convened by Bishops Belo and Nasciemento, and attended by most parties and groups in East Timor. The purpose was to discuss the political situation, and in particular the proposals for autonomy. The meeting, for which Xanana Gusmao voiced public support, took place in a very good atmosphere, and appeared to have had a calming effect on the island.

But shortly after it was over, Governor Abilio Osorio Suares, who was never less than his abrasive self, made an announcement that all East Timorese Government employees would be required to support East Timor's integration into Indonesia, and that those who failed to do so would either have to retire or face dismissal. The reaction was predictable, but its extent and violence must have penetrated even the Governor's thick political skin.

A public strike brought Dili to a standstill, and a large demonstration of about thirty thousand people demanded the resignation or removal of the Governor. We received reports that the agitation had spread from the capital to other towns in East Timor. This, in turn, prompted an unhelpful pronouncement from Udayana Headquarters that "there is a limit to the new era of openness, a limit to our tolerance."

The events that unfolded in Alas shortly thereafter were a grim reminder that the warning was not pro forma. Under these circumstances, I thought that it would be a good idea for Tamrat Samuel to make a brief visit to the region, and get an assessment of the situation on the ground before our next SOM session later in the month.

The Fourth Meeting of the AIETD took place, as before, at Schloss Krumbach, near Vienna, at the end of October 1988. As usual, the Austrian Government provided the excellent facilities requisite for the conference, and the East Timorese participation was both increased and more wide-ranging than before. Although none of us could have guessed it at that time, this was to be the last session of the AIETD. In my opening address to the participants, I stressed the necessity for the active participation of the East Timorese representatives in the negotiating process:

> Your meeting takes place at a critical stage in the efforts to find a peaceful solution to the problem of your homeland. These efforts have reached the crossroads. The convergence of important developments has ushered in a new phase in the long effort to find a just and honorable solution. However, as much as this period offers promises and opportunities, it also carries its own risks and dangers.
>
> At the landmark meeting of the Secretary-General with Foreign Ministers Alatas and Gama on August 5, 1998 in New York, agreement was reached to begin in-depth discussions on a special status for East Timor based on a wide ranging autonomy, without prejudice to the position of principle of the two sides. In other words, Indonesia and Portugal agreed to proceed with elaborating the details of the shape of a possible autonomous status for the Territory while putting aside, for the time being, the question of the final status of East Timor.
>
> The Secretary-General's intensification of his consultations with East Timorese leaders is closely tied to this new phase in the negotiations. The outlines of the proposal have been conveyed to several East Timorese leaders and representatives, and we expect to receive their input as we continue our consultations with them. The commitment to closely involve the East Timorese in the discussions derives from the UN's firm conviction that any viable solution has to be acceptable to the people of East Timor, and therefore their leaders should be engaged in active consultations during the process.
>
> These consultations, which we have been conducting both inside and outside East Timor, will also continue on the sidelines of this meeting, the United Nations hopes that the East Timorese leaders will rise to the occasion and seize the new opportunities that have arisen and provide well considered ideas and proposals on the specific elements and aspects of autonomy which we have asked many of you to focus on.
>
> Your input to the discussions of the tripartite process is of cru-

cial importance. We believe that the East Timorese have the primary responsibility for developing and producing ideas and for
building a consensus amongst themselves. It should not be
expected that ideas and initiatives will come from the United
Nations or the tripartite process alone.

Notwithstanding this exhortation, and despite the fact that during
the meeting the atmosphere was reasonably civil, it came as no surprise
that the AIETD could not come up with an agreed final declaration. The
main sticking points were on the issue of a referendum for East Timor,
and whether to call, in the joint declaration, for the release of Xanana
Gusmao. The media correctly reported the failure of the AIETD to reach
an agreement, but this did not dismay me. An important ancillary objective had been achieved: we had enabled the East Timorese to get together
and jointly review, as well as react to, the ongoing tripartite negotiations.

On my way back to New York from Vienna, I stopped in Lisbon for
meetings with the President, Prime Minister, and Foreign Minister, as
well as with Members of Parliament. A positive assessment of progress
in the tripartite negotiations was tempered by a mutual concern over the
situation in East Timor, from where there were reports of increasing violence.

In the meanwhile, as had already been arranged, Tamrat Samuel went
on a mission to Indonesia and East Timor for an assessment of the situation on the ground before our next Senior Officials' Meeting, scheduled
for November19th. His report was as perceptive as ever, and his findings
were a matter of considerable concern.

"There is," he noted, "a new political climate in East Timor, marked
by an unprecedented degree of open defiance of Indonesian authority.
The ranks of the pro-independence activists is swelling. Many East Timorese, emboldened by the political transformation sweeping Indonesia and
the weakening of the military's position, have seized the opportunity to
seize and consolidate new political space in East Timor.

"The general docility of the Indonesian military is interpreted in two
ways: Either it is genuinely paralyzed and fearful of the international
backlash that any violent crackdown would provoke or, as many people
in East Timor believe, it is deliberately allowing the situation to deteri-
orate in order to prove its point that there is still a serious security problem in East Timor requiring its continued large scale presence. It is evident
that powerful forces within the military are resisting the international
pressure for a substantial withdrawal from East Timor."

I thought that the latter of Tamrat's assumptions was probably the
correct explanation, and therefore feared the possibility of a strong mili-

tary backlash. Accordingly, I called for calm, both in my public statements and in personal appeals to Xanana and Bishop Belo on the one side, and the Indonesian administration and military on the other. I said that all sides had a responsibility to ease tensions and avoid steps that might jeopardize the negotiations.

The volatile political atmosphere that prevailed in Indonesia had by now blown into East Timor with a vengeance, and by linking itself with the tensions already existing on the island, had created the tinder that awaited the tiniest spark to set off a combustion.

Expectations of both the pro-independence and pro-integration groups had never been higher, and the spirit of compromise was a commodity that was dwindling rapidly and inexorably. Xanana's call for calm, issued from his prison cell, did not evoke the same immediate response as before, and my own, increasingly desperate calls to the Indonesian administration to release Xanana met with an ominous silence.

In this charged atmosphere, Tamrat worked on the second objective of his mission, which was to explain to the East Timorese people the UN proposal on autonomy. Since the document itself was still under discussion in the SOM, as well as under scrutiny of the Indonesian and Portuguese Governments, Tamrat was left with the delicate task of framing his explanations in broad terms, enumerating the main areas that the proposal tried to address.

He found an enormous mistrust, because many regarded autonomy as an Indonesian proposal, synonymous with integration. The fact that the Indonesians had, indeed, made some attempts to foster the idea that the UN had itself proposed autonomy did not make Tamrat's job any easier. He was obliged to forcefully reject the allegation that the UN proposal amounted to "an attempt to legalize an illegal situation."

But by patient and persuasive reasoning, and by skillful diplomacy, Tamrat was able to convey the correct position to the East Timorese, and thereby bring them into a receptive frame of mind. He did this largely through a tactic that was as simple as it was honest and intelligent.

"I started every meeting," he reported, "with an explanation that the August agreement had not compromised any principles, that it represented an important agreement to define the shape of a suitable autonomy for East Timor, in close cooperation with East Timorese leaders, and without prejudice to the respective positions of principle of Indonesia and Portugal, i.e., that the two sides had merely set aside, for the time being, the question of the final status of East Timor, and at some point, that issue would have to be addressed. There was greater interest and involvement once such assurance was given."

The next Senior Officials' Meeting took place in New York from November 19 to 21 with an agenda that included a review of the last AIETD. More importantly, there was a continuation of the discussions on the autonomy proposals, following the consultations that the delegations had held in their capitals. The talks got off to a good, businesslike start, but we were soon overwhelmed by events in East Timor.

Political tension had erupted into violence, as I feared it might, and soon horror stories were being flashed from the island to the rest of the world. Indonesian security forces had reacted to provocations with ferocity, particularly in a small town called Alas, from where there were reports of harsh and serious human rights violations. The authorities had expelled reporters and members of NGOs from the area, and sealed off the town.

The resulting international outcry naturally had its impact on our negotiations, and I fully expected our afternoon session to commence with strong statements of indignation by the Portuguese delegation. Somewhat to my surprise and discomfiture, it went well beyond that.

Ambassador Neves called me shortly before the meeting was due to commence, and said that he was under instructions to stop negotiations immediately. He said that public opinion in Portugal was so incensed over what he described as "the new atrocities in East Timor," that his government felt that it could not be seen to be treating with the Indonesian Government in the prevailing circumstances.

I could understand that it would be awkward for Portugal to be seen negotiating autonomy proposals in New York with the Indonesians, while the latter were breaking East Timorese heads in Alas, yet I nevertheless felt that Lisbon's decision was both unfortunate and abrupt. My immediate response was to tell Fernando that in my book, a crisis is precisely when negotiations should be intensified, and not abandoned, but since he was acting under instructions I could understand that there was nothing he could do.

I next informed Wisnumurti about the Portuguese decision, together with its reasons, not to attend the afternoon session of SOM. Wisnumurti's response was that he was quite ready to pack his suitcase and take the evening flight to Jakarta. I persuaded him to put his travel plans on hold until I had spoken to Lisbon, and accordingly telephoned Jaime Garna.

I was informed that the Foreign Ministry had already announced Portugal's decision not to participate in the ongoing New York talks, and had done so in response to the public indignation that prevailed in the country over the incidents in East Timor. We then went back and forth over the telephone for a while, and I pointed out that since the UN deplored the violence in East Timor just as much as anyone else, I would, as a matter of course, carry out my own thorough inquiry into the incident, and would designate an official for the purpose.

This assurance, coupled with a strong recommendation on the importance of the continuation of the tripartite talks, appeared to have struck a responsive chord in Gama's eminently sensible and pragmatic attitude, and he agreed to send his delegation back to the table.

I then called Alatas in Jakarta and gave him a run-down of the whole episode, pointing out that the scale and nature of the violence in East Timor had made it incumbent upon me to look into the matter, regardless of what the Portuguese felt or said. Alex was not at all happy either about the developments, or about my decision, but again displayed an understanding of the situation, and its wider implications, and accordingly instructed his delegation to continue the negotiations.

But we were not yet out of the woods. The Portuguese made a public announcement to the effect that their decision to suspend the talks had been justified because it had compelled the UN to send a mission to investigate the incident in Alas. Of course, this was stretching things a bit, and I would not have minded it too much as far as I was concerned. But the effect on the Indonesians was predictably provocative.

Alatas responded in an indignant statement to the effect that Jakarta would never permit a formal UN investigation in Alas. We had thus now reached the stage of public posturing, with expressions of high dudgeon emanating from both sides. This was inevitable and I left it to blow over, while we quietly ushered the two delegations back to serious negotiations in our airless little room in New York.

At the same time, we issued a press statement which would hopefully lay the matter to rest. By now, the draft document was beginning to look purposeful and in reasonable shape. Our attempt was, on the one hand, to persuade the Indonesians to yield the concessions that would make autonomy as wide ranging as possible, so that it could be sold to the East Timorese. On the other hand, we tried to persuade the Portuguese to temper their demands to the extent that one could reasonably expect Jakarta to bear.

We concluded the Senior Officials Meeting with both delegations taking to their capitals the completed drafts of the autonomy proposals for final scrutiny and provisional concurrence at the next SOM. We would then need to take up the all-important and most vexatious question, the final status of East Timor. At this point in time, Machiavelli's observation was very much in my thoughts. Would there be any limitations on hopes?

11

Sailing into the Squall
INDONESIA AND EAST TIMOR: DECEMBER 1998

> Aux armes, citoyens!
> Formez vos bataillons!
> — *La Marseillaise*

Tamrat Samuel visited Indonesia and East Timor in the first week of December 1998, and presented his usual excellent report, wide ranging in content and admirable in its perception. It confirmed my impression that our next visit to the region (Francesc Vendrell was to accompany me this time) was unlikely to lack interest.

Although he was not allowed to visit the town itself, Tamrat put together a very succinct account of events in Alas. This was the incident, it may be recalled, which had caused a suspension in our tripartite negotiations in New York earlier in November. It was the usual story of an escalation of violence, as so often occurs in areas of high tension.

A militant student demonstration got out of hand and provoked a typically disproportionate military reaction, resulting in about fifteen deaths and the destruction of houses and property. Alas remained off-limits while the army conducted a search for weapons stolen from the local armory, and the National Human Rights Commission said that it would carry out an investigation as soon as access to Alas was permitted.

Apart from indicating that tension in East Timor remained very high, Tamrat also said that skepticism about the autonomy proposal appeared to have increased considerably. "The Security situation is further deteriorating," he reported, and added, "The Peace and Justice Commission reports that there has been an overall increase of 22 per cent in reported human rights violations in nine categories in 1998. There has been an increase in the number of attacks on the military and on East Timorese with ties to Indonesia. The radicalization of the youth continues.

"Our concern that moderates like Xanana might soon lose their grip is beginning to happen, according to Bishop Nasciemento. He said that the youth were increasingly defying instructions from Xanana and the guerrillas. A lawless situation is emerging as people take their own action to settle scores with those that had worked with the military and the intelligence....

"Most East Timorese seem to have decided that this is their chance to free themselves from Indonesian rule. While outsiders and Minister Alatas talk about a window of opportunity, many in East Timor see in the present situation a door that has cracked ajar and needs to be pushed open for a rapid exit before it closes again."

With Tamrat's realistic assessment usefully stacked in our briefing dossier, we set off for Jakarta and Dili in mid-December. At our transit stopover in Singapore, Arnaz had a medical emergency that necessitated hospitalization, so I left her in the care of the excellent clinical facilities for which Singapore is justly renowned and the affectionate ministrations of our dear friends Tommy and Siew Aing Koh and of Arnaz's twin sister Aban, who flew in from Karachi.

Arnaz's indisposition in Singapore was somewhat inauspicious, and also inconvenient, but it would have complicated matters a great deal more if the emergency had struck two days later in Dili, where treatment, if at all available, would have been much less reassuring. She recovered in time to travel just as I finished my Indonesian trip, and we left Singapore together to spend Christmas in Karachi.

The reports that we received upon arrival in Jakarta spoke of increasing lawlessness and militancy in both Indonesia and East Timor, of the distribution of arms and the discoveries of arms caches, of inflammatory statements from leaders of various factions, peppered with sporadic outbreaks of violence.

East Timor seemed to be particularly unsettled, with all sides acquiring arms in anticipation of a conflict that they appeared to deem inevitable. I noted, too, that there was an ominous increase in the sophistication of ordnance, with machetes and muzzle-loaders being superseded by grenades and automatic weapons. The prospect of a peaceful transition, in East Timor at any rate, did not appear to be too bright.

My first meeting in Jakarta was with Major General Zacky Anwar

Makarim, Head of ABRI Intelligence, followed later in the day by a meeting with Lieutenant General Susilo Bambang Yudhoyono, the Chief of Staff of the Territorial Armed Forces. Both general officers were amongst the most competent of the senior Indonesian military hierarchy with whom I had dealt, and while each matched the other in intelligence, politeness, and sophisticated negotiating skills, there were subtle differences in their political attitudes and inclinations.

Zacky Anwar was a crypto hard-liner, which was not surprising in view of his Kopassus background. Susilo Bambang, on the other hand, appeared to be the contemplative liberal, wrestling with the problem of maintaining political and civil order, yet making concessions without giving too much away.

Both general officers expressed to me their concerns about the rapidly deteriorating situation in East Timor, and Zaky Anwar told me quite frankly that he had been obliged to provide arms to some of the pro-integration East Timorese, whom he described as "loyal, law abiding citizens," in order to "defend themselves" against elements of the FALANTIL.

I thought this decision was particularly ominous, and said so to Zacky, pointing out that the best way to improve matters was to employ political methods, such as the release of Xanana Gusmao and his active involvement in the process of consultations. Of course, I did not get very far in convincing Zacky Anwar with that argument, but hoped that at least the vehemence of my demand might be conveyed to his superiors.

I did the same with Susilo Bambang, with whom I thought I struck a slightly more respondent chord, especially when I pointed out the positive impact of a "half-way solution," such as shifting Xanana from prison to house arrest. Apart from providing Xanana with the opportunity for more active political participation, such a measure would evoke a significantly positive international reaction.

The General's response was to imply that such a decision was clearly above his pay grade, but he maintained a discreet, thoughtful silence on the merit of the proposition. I came away from my meetings with the two Indonesian generals with the feeling that there might be some give on the issue of the release of Xanana. On the other hand, I was somewhat perturbed by the probability of supply of arms to the pro-Indonesian East Timorese irregulars in East Timor: this was bringing the flame dangerously close to the tinder.

I next met Mario Caralascalao, an able East Timorese and former Governor of East Timor, whose moderating influence had always been a bridge between the East Timorese and the Administration. His assessment of the situation in his home island was somber, realistic, and disturbing. Previous distrust on both sides had by now hardened into antagonism, and the pro-independence groups, encouraged by the air of rambunctious freedom that was now sweeping the rest of Indonesia, were getting increasingly militant.

There was a plethora of arms and an increasing inclination to use them, particularly by the East Timorese youth who were "getting out of control." The other meetings on that first day in Jakarta were lunch and dinner sessions with Ambassador Stapleton Roy of the United States and Ambassador John McCarthy of Australia, respectively. Apart from the splendid meals, we received from these two good friends the customary succinct and valuable assessments so necessary for our work.

Reports of the unease and tension in East Timor were supplemented by perceptive analyses of the current political climate in Indonesia itself. In turn, I informed them of the present status of the negotiation process, as well as indicating some ideas on my future strategy. The most immediate of these was to work on the release of Xanana, for which objective I called upon both Ambassadors to deploy the maximum pressure on the Indonesian Government, both personally and through their governments.

The next day I met Toni Pfanner, the Head of the ICRC Delegation in Indonesia, together with two of his colleagues who had just returned from East Timor. Their first-hand accounts of events in the island were disquieting, particularly in view of their obvious authenticity and objectivity, and confirmed the existence of the air of uncertainty and militancy that had now seized most of East Timor.

Our next appointment was with Xanana Gusmao, with whom we had a long session in Cipinang Prison. The authorities had by now considerably eased constraints, so that Vendrell and I were able to converse with Xanana in private. I was delighted to see him again, and even more delighted to find him in such good form. Polite and pleasant, self assured and dignified as ever, Xanana continued to exude his quiet dynamism.

He emphasized the critical stage of the historic process in which we all found ourselves at this moment, and expressed disappointment at the slow progress of the tripartite negotiations, as well as the failure of the AIETD. I brought Xanana up to date on the status of the negotiations, and in the ensuing discussions we were told by him that he was prepared to accept a five-year period for provincial autonomy in East Timor.

Xanana also told us of the feelers that he had extended to General Zaki Anwar, and Ambassadors Wisnumurti and Lopez da Cruz, in an attempt to establish a direct political dialogue, but despite some initial positive signals, no meeting had as yet taken place. Talking of the situation in East Timor, Xanana said that tension had greatly increased, and

A visit to Xanana Gusmao at his house of detention in Jakarta. Left to right: J.M., Xanana and Arnaz Marker. Photograph: Tamrat Samuel, author's collection.

that considerable hostility existed on all sides. He had issued appeals for calm, and supported the efforts of Bishops Belo and Nasciemento to organize a dialogue between the different East Timorese groups.

Nevertheless, the situation remained tense and volatile. In this connection, Xanana told me that he had received reliable reports of a plan to take me hostage during my visit to Dili. He had issued the strongest instructions to his followers to ensure my personal security, but he nevertheless remained apprehensive. He urged me to remain in my hotel as much as possible, and not to go out on the evening walks by the seaside, which I had always enjoyed so much.

That afternoon we took a long drive through the suburbs of Jakarta to the residence of Abdurrahman Wahid, commonly known by his popular and affectionate honorific, "Gus Dur." This extraordinary man, who was reported to have a personal and absolute following of over eighty million devoted adherents to his organization, lived in a simple Jakarta suburban house, situated in the compound of a neat and modest little mosque.

Half-blind and partially paralyzed, he shuffled into the sparsely furnished living room on the arm of an aide, and warmly welcomed us, speaking in perfect English. As soon as we began our discussion, I was struck by an awareness of the vast chasm that separated mental agility from physical infirmity in this remarkable person. He possessed a razor sharp mind, and like many people with weak eyesight, had compensated for one failing faculty by sharpening and developing the other senses, particularly that of memory.

Possessing vast knowledge on a number of issues, including politics, history, theology, and the arts, Gus Dur was a fascinating interlocutor, punctuating his discourse with anecdotes replete with a puckish sense of humor. A bust of Beethoven was almost the only decorative object in the room, poised in silent testimony to the eclectic good taste and sophistication of its owner, and in seeming disregard of religious cant, for statuary is not normally discernible in such close proximity to a mosque.

In response to my request for an assessment of the current political situation in Indonesia, Gus Dur made a succinct presentation, analyzing the causes and reasons for the prevailing uncertainties, and forecasting the future with a prescience and foresight which subsequent events would prove to be largely and astonishingly accurate. All this was related with quiet assurance, a total absence of pomp and rhetoric, and with flashes of dry humor.

I described the course of our negotiations on East Timor, and Gus Dur encouraged me to "continue your efforts." He was pragmatic in his assertion about drawing Xanana into the negotiating process, and said that he would do whatever he could to bring this about. On the broader issue of East Timor itself, he felt that it would be in the interest of all parties if the East Timorese could have broad ranging autonomy within the Republic of Indonesia.

This was not an unexpected viewpoint, but his next remark took me somewhat off guard and sent Vendrell's pencil scurrying over his note pad. "But if they truly want independence, then why not? Why should we stop them?"

This was as stimulating a note as any on which to end our fascinating discussion, and we set off on our long road, to return in the dusk, from the wood-smoke-filled outer suburbs of Jakarta to the neon and monoxide of the city center. And as we drove back to the hotel, it seemed to me that this ecological contrast found reflection, in some ways, in the myriad thoughts that coursed through my mind after the meeting with Gus Dur. In Indonesia, contrast is a normal component of coexistence.

We left Jakarta for East Timor on December 18 making the obligatory overnight stop in Denpasar for a meeting with Major General Adam Dhamiri, the Udayana Military Commander. It was not a very satisfactory encounter: always the hard-liner, Dhamiri seemed more belligerent than ever. He thought that the situation in East Timor had deteriorated to the extent that it could only be controlled by "firm action."

For increased emphasis, he informed me that for security reasons we would be lodged in the senior officers' military quarters instead of the Makhota Hotel in Dili. I did not think that we would greatly miss the hostelry's rudimentary creature comforts, but I accepted the enforced military hospitality on the strict condition that it would not impede my accessibility to any and all of the East Timorese that I wished to meet.

The next day we took a commercial flight from Denpasar to Kupang in West Timor, from where we flew to Dili in a military helicopter. Colonel Tono Suratnam, the able Military Commander in East Timor, received us and immediately transported us to his headquarters, where he provided me with a long, detailed, and very useful situation brief, which ended with the report that earlier in the day he had "spoken to both sides," and secured their agreement to "remain peaceful."

The rest of the day was spent in meeting a large number of East Timorese representatives from both the pro-independence and pro-integration factions, including Manuel Carascalao, Leandro Isaac, Herminio da Silva da Costa (an ex-partisan of the 1975-76 civil war), and Mauhono and Mauhodo, who were Xanana's deputies, still carrying on the armed struggle, and who came down from the hills to meet me. The Indonesian authorities had been true to their word, and facilitated my meetings with everyone on my list, despite the fact that many of these were clearly high on ABRI's anathema list.

The meetings were held in seriatim, and went on almost until dawn. These were highly charged encounters, full of emotion and expectation, with feelings of anguish and expectation thrown in for good measure. As the evening went on, the hot, sticky room became increasingly permeated by cigarette smoke, creating environmental discomfort of suffocating proportions. But this paled in comparison to the discomfort generated by the tone and tenor of the political discussions.

The pro-integrationists, who were loud and firm in their support for the status quo, were also menacing in their determination to maintain it. The pro-independence groups, on the other hand, described their sufferings over the past years in vivid and most painful terms, and expressed their determination to seize the present opportunity, provided by the prevailing period of national uncertainty, to obtain total freedom. The spirit of compromise was as evasive as the presence of fresh air in the musty, smoke-filled room, but I nevertheless thought it important to allow each delegation to let off steam and have its full say, even if it sometimes meant listening to each member of the delegation repeating almost exactly the same thing that was said by each of his colleagues.

I would then respond by stating that the UN objective was to obtain a peaceful and just solution to the problem, that the two requirements of peace and justice were inextricably linked, and that the United Nations would never be party to any solution that did not have the consent of the East Timorese people. After that, we would try and examine the main elements of the autonomy proposal, but the plethora of conflicting responses made it a somewhat difficult exercise. I also laid great emphasis on the need for maintaining peace and avoiding violence, and this was perhaps the only issue on which I obtained a positive response from all sides, even though it was often conditional.

It was easy enough to identify the political color and inclination of each delegation as it entered the room, for the contrast in the appearance and physical bearing of the opposing groups could not have been more stark. The pro-independence people were either simply or more often shabbily dressed, looked undernourished, nervous and fidgety, with looks that carried all the emotional and physical years of conflict, deprivation, and repression.

They had a palpable sense of urgency in their desire to make a grab for freedom, regardless of consequences, and to that extent I judged them to be less likely to exercise restraint. The pro-integration groups, on the other hand, were sleek, well-dressed, and well-fed. They spoke with much assurance, and took up a lot of my time trying to convince me that all was well, and that a considerable majority of East Timorese felt the same way as they did.

In my later visits to East Timor, I found that this attitude of smug self-assurance had faded considerably, and had been replaced by an apprehensive mood of uncertainty over an unpredictable and uncertain future. In fact, following many private conversations with some of these gentlemen, I detected that a process had begun to set in, one which I somewhat irreverently described to my friends as "self-dequislingisation," or abandoning ship.

On the morning of Sunday, December 20, following a brief rest, shower, and change after our nocturnal session, I was about to set off for a meeting with Bishops Belo and Nasciernento, but as the diocese was surrounded by a large crowd of demonstrators, the Bishops very kindly came to the army quarters for our meeting. Our conversation strengthened my admiration for these two clergymen, whose daily lives were spent not just in tending to the spiritual well-being of their parishioners, but also in the hard temporal task of combating repression and injustice, and controlling the violent protests that were inevitably provoked by these evils.

The Bishops told me that the excessive presence of the military was a major source of resentment and conflict, but while they strongly urged a significant withdrawal of forces, particularly the Kopassus units, they nevertheless realistically realized the necessity for a modicum of military deployment for security purposes. They recounted many instances of harsh treatment and of egregious human rights abuses by the authorities, which had resulted in widespread fear amongst the East Timorese and an increasing hatred of the Indonesian authorities. Finally, they reiterated the observation of others about the increased radicalization that had occurred in the island, one example of which was the demonstration that was taking place in Dili even as we spoke.

On the conclusion of this, the last of our meetings, I set off for the airport, accompanied by Francesc Vendrell and Dino Patti Djalal, the intelligent and lively Indonesian Foreign Service official who had been our escorting officer. We set off in a convoy under heavy military escort, and had not gone very far when we were diverted from the main road onto a dirt track, because we were told that the normal entrances to the airport had been blocked by hostile crowds.

Our jeeps bumped their way through the bush and eventually emerged at the end of the airport runway. But a convoy of six vehicles, most of which were loaded with fully armed military, is not easy to disguise, and we were soon spotted and trailed by a number of young men, riding on motorcycles, waving flags and excitedly chattering into their cell phones. After streaking across the runway, we made it to the terminal building, outside which a large crowd of demonstrators had already gathered.

A number of civilians, including some priests and nuns, were urging restraint on the demonstrators, who at this time were quite peaceful and merely shouted slogans. However, within half an hour the crowd had vastly increased and its mood had become much less benign. Colonel Tono Suratman, the Dili military commander, had earlier arrived at the airport and brought with him a substantial military contingent, which now took up position around the terminal building.

I was a bit disturbed by this, and immediately gave firm orders to Colonel Suratman that his troops were not to open fire on any account, no matter what the provocation. I was fairly certain that Suratman's inclinations were the same as mine, for he was a cool and professional officer, with obvious ability and experience in crowd control, and I was therefore quite certain that he would neither panic nor overreact. Just then our tension was somewhat eased by the arrival of the Merpati plane, which was scheduled to disembark its Dili bound passengers and board us for our return to Denpasar.

But the appearance of the aircraft seemed to have further ignited the feelings of the crowd, who correctly sensed the imminence of the flight of their quarry, and attempted to prevent this by making a forceful assault on the fragile airport barriers, breaking into the terminal building and spilling onto the apron. Meanwhile, the captain of the Merpati aircraft, who had taxied toward the terminal building, obviously decided that coping with a hostile reception committee was not an item that was included in his manual on standard operating procedures.

He prudently guided his aircraft past the terminal, proceeded to the end of the runway, and took off in a defiant roar. Francesc, Dino, and I, who had a short while earlier said to each other, "our plane has arrived," now made the equally obvious and fatuous observation, "our plane has left."

I contacted Colonel Suratnam and suggested that perhaps we might try to get an army helicopter, but this resourceful officer had already made the necessary arrangements, and shortly thereafter the craft arrived, taking up station as close to the terminal building as was prudent. Meanwhile the demonstrators were milling all over the terminal building and apron, but had not yet got to the VIP room where we were holed up.

Suratman was as cool and collected as ever, and he and his men, together with a number of civilians, priests, and nuns, were doing a splendid job, holding back the demonstrators through peaceful persuasion and a little gentle shoving. The rest was Keystone Cops. A jeep was brought to the entrance of the VIP room, we were bundled in, the driver tore his zig zag way through and past the crowd, and deposited us fifty yards from the helicopter, whose rotor blades were already turning.

We leapt out of the jeep and made an undignified sprint to the helicopter, beating our nearest pursuers by a few uncomfortable yards. As the helicopter lifted off I gave a cheerful wave to our self-invited send-off committee, and they, in turn, returned it in equally cheerful fashion. For better or for worse, elements of the international press and TV were present at Dili airport to record our precipitate departure.

The military helicopter took us to Kupang from where, after a brief layover, we took a commercial flight to Jakarta. Sensing the possibility of some dramatic, if not lurid, reports of our exit from Dili, I put through two reassuring calls, one to the Secretary-General in New York and the other to Arnaz in Singapore. To my companion Francesc Vendrell, I suggested that he and I now had material for collaboration on a new Broadway musical: "Miss East Timor."

Back in Jakarta, I went through a series of meetings with President Habibie, Foreign Minister Alatas, Law Minister Muladi, and General

"Miss East Timor." A hurried photograph from the helicopter as we made our precipitate departure from Dili. **Photograph: author's collection.**

Wiranto, the Armed Forces Chief. We reviewed the UN negotiation process, taking into account the changed and still evolving political situation within Indonesia, as well as the impressions that I had formed during my current visit. It was encouraging to note that all four leaders, each in his own fashion, continued to be supportive of the UN process.

Habibie was the most enthusiastic, not only because that is his natural bent, but also because he genuinely felt that the wide ranging autonomy that he had proposed to the East Timorese was in consonance with the genuine policy of liberalization which he had proudly proclaimed, which he was now in the process of implementing within Indonesia, and with which he hoped his name would for ever be associated.

Wiranto was a little more reserved. He said that he was beset by so many major problems throughout Indonesia that he would warmly welcome getting East Timor off his list if a reasonable solution could be found, and that he was prepared to do all he could to help the process. However, when I suggested that substantial troop withdrawals from the island and the cessation of arms distribution to the militia would be a most valuable first step, he grew reticent.

As was to be expected, Alatas was the most professional, substantive, and measured in his responses. He looked forward to the January meeting in New York, when we could finalize the autonomy proposals and begin to tackle the vital issue of whether the solution was to be temporary or final. On the substance of the autonomy proposal itself, I was pleased to note further flexibility on the part of Alatas, particularly on the key issue of the establishment in East Timor of political parties supporting independence.

This item had hitherto threatened an impasse in our negotiations. In a subsequent private conversation Alex recounted, in his own fascinating and inimitable manner, his long and intimate association with the East Timor problem, and of his earnest desire for a solution before he left office, the time for which he thought was now not far off.

I thought that my old friend could not have been more sincere or convincing in his remarks. I responded by welcoming his desire for a solution of East Timor, but was truly sad and apprehensive about any prospect of his departure from office. Indonesia, and indeed all of us in the international community, would have need of his statesmanship, his brilliance, his talents, and his diplomatic skills for many years to come.

Apart from pushing the ongoing tripartite negotiations, I had, during this particular visit to the region, set out to obtain two objectives. The first and most important of these was the release of Xanana Gusmao, and the second was the establishment of a United Nations office in East Timor. I raised both these issues very vigorously in my talks with Habibie, Alatas, Wiranto, and Law Minister Muladi, but in doing so I reversed the order of my priorities, emphasizing as a matter of tactics the issue of the UN office.

I argued that since Indonesia had already accepted and cooperated in such exemplary fashion with the Personal Representative of the Secretary-General for East Timor, there should be no objection to the PRSG establishing his own liaison office in Dili. The Indonesians, of course, resisted this fiercely, since it held for them obvious implications of sovereignty in respect of East Timor. Whether this intractability influenced their view to be more accommodating on my second request, the release of Xanana Gusmao, remains a matter of conjecture.

For on the issue of Xanana's release I continued my vigorous campaign, arguing with Habibie, Alatas, Wiranto, and Muladi that if he could not be set free by a presidential decree of amnesty then he should, at least, be removed from Cipinang prison, lodged under custody in a private residence, and permitted public access so that he could carry out his political work. I did not accept the contention that under Indonesian law there was no provision for the concept of "house arrest," and thought that an exception could well be made as a goodwill gesture in response to the special request of the Secretary-General of the United Nations.

I pointed out to Alatas that the house arrest concept was an old and tried political device in circumstances of this nature. The British had used it in the 1940s when they arrested Mahatma Gandhi and lodged him in the Poona residence of the Aga Khan, having previously satisfied the legal technicalities by declaring the residence as a prison, as defined in the official Jail Manual.

The upshot of all this was that I left Jakarta with the hopeful feeling that the Indonesians would be likely to respond positively to one of my two requests, and that the one most probable would be the release of Xanana. As for the UN office in Dili, I regarded it as a bit of a red herring. Thanks to the prevailing cooperative attitude of the Indonesian government, we already had as much access to East Timor as we wished, so that the absence of a UN office was, at most, a mild inconvenience. But the release, or the relaxation of constraints, on Xanana Gusmao was, in my view, a matter of substance and importance, particularly at this point in time.

With uncertainty, lawlessness, and violence so much on the increase in East Timor, it was imperative that Xanana be provided with the possibility to exert his moderating influence over events in the island. I called Stanley Roth in Washington, conveyed to him the impressions of my latest visit to Indonesia, and requested him to lend weight to the pressure for the release of Xanana Gusmao.

Needless to say, Stanley's prompt response, in his usual splendid, energetic fashion, added immeasurably to our effort. It was beginning to look as though our moves might at last meet with success, and I was determined to keep at it. "Hard pounding this, gentlemen," observed the Duke of Wellington famously, at the height of battle at Waterloo, "let's see who will pound longest."

12

A Dramatic Decision, and an Opportunity Seized
NEW YORK: JANUARY AND FEBRUARY 1999

Dans les crises politiques, le plus difficile pour un honnête homme n'est pas de faire son devoir, mais de le connaitre. (In political crises, the greatest difficulty for an honest man is not to do his duty, but to know what it is.)

—*La Rochefoucauld*

January 1999 was an important month in the calendar of the East Timor negotiations. On January 5 the Australian government, which up till now had been unique in its acknowledgment of Indonesian sovereignty over East Timor, suddenly reversed its position with a proclamation that East Timor had the right to self-determination. The weighty and substantive nature of the relations that exist, and must always exist, between Indonesia and Australia made this announcement the precursor of major consequences, both immediately and in the later part of the year.

This was followed, on January 27, by a dramatic and largely unexpected statement by the Indonesian government. Emerging from a Cabinet meeting, Yunus Yosfiah, the Indonesian Information Minister, with Foreign Minister Ali Alatas standing by his side, said that in accordance with a Cabinet decision, "a Regional Autonomy Plus will be awarded to East Timor. If this is not accepted by the mass in East Timor we will suggest to the new membership of the Peoples Consultative Assembly (MPR), formed as a result of the next elections, to release East Timor

121

from Indonesia." The MPR was the highest legislative body in Indonesia: it was due to be formed after the Indonesian general elections in June, and was scheduled to hold its first session in August.

At the same time, and on the same occasion, Alatas also announced the Government's decision to move Xanana Gusmao from Cipinang prison to a residence of private detention. This was being done in response to an appeal from the Secretary-General of the United Nations, in order to enable Xanana to play an active role in the East Timor negotiations.

I first got this astonishing news through the media, and although I had anticipated some positive movement on the matter of Xanana's release, the announcement of the offer to "release East Timor from Indonesia" took me by complete surprise. I had been in regular telephonic communication with Alex on a number of topics, and I got the feeling that there was some major rethinking going on in Jakarta, but I did not imagine that it would be anything quite so radical. Our attention had hitherto been entirely focused on the autonomy proposals, which had by now reached final shape and were awaiting Ministerial approval.

Naturally, I rang up Alex as soon as I saw the wire reports of his January 27 announcement, and sought both confirmation and elaboration. I received both, as well as a request for an early meeting with the Secretary-General and the Portuguese Foreign Minister. This was set up for Sunday and Monday, 7 and 8 of February, and was to be preceded by a Senior Officials Meeting at which we were to finalize the autonomy proposals for submission to the Secretary-General and the Foreign Ministers.

The SOM text was a reasonably compact document, many elements of which could be applicable in either an autonomous or independence constitution, whichever was adopted. The proposal envisaged the allocation of external defense, foreign affairs, and currency and finance, to the Indonesian government. Responsibility for legislation in all other areas was to rest with the East Timorese, who would set up a Regional Council, elect the Governor, and nominate members of the Advisory Board of the Government of the Special Autonomous Region of East Timor (SARET).

The Governor would be elected by the Regional Council from a list of persons already approved by the President of Indonesia and subject to his confirmation after the election. The police and judiciary were to be under the control of SARET, but East Timorese courts were to be subject to the Supreme Court of Indonesia as court of final appeal. The Indonesian Army (TNI) would be deployed in East Timor for purposes of external security only, but could be used for internal security "in exceptional cases" if requested by SARET. The Indonesian flag would continue to fly over the territory, with SARET having its own coat of arms.

Natural resources were to be under the control of the regional government, except those already designated under Indonesian law as being of strategic importance. While having competence over local taxation, the region would be subject to national taxation, and would be incorporated into national monetary and fiscal policies. A senior Indonesian central government representative would establish an office in Dili for purposes of coordination between the central and regional authorities. Finally, the UN Secretary-General would have the responsibility and authority to monitor and verify the implementation of the Agreement, and would establish offices in East Timor for that purpose.

On February 5, I announced the results of the Senior Officials Meeting to the press, stating, inter alia, that "in general, there is a basic agreement on a broad autonomy regime for East Timor, but on certain points the parties have agreed to disagree. At this stage we still cannot make the document public. It is still to be discussed by the Ministers and the Secretary-General, and then with key East Timorese leaders."

I then went on to add, "Obviously, you are wondering how all this is going to be reconciled with the important announcement made in Jakarta in the past one week. These are all issues to be discussed by the Secretary-General with the Ministers. We expect Minister Alatas would provide further clarification on the policy announced last week." Needless to say, and notwithstanding my soothing and soporific words, it was quite clear that the Indonesian government's announcement of January 27 had overtaken, if not entirely displaced, the relevance of the autonomy proposals. At our initial private meeting in New York in early February, Alex gave me a background briefing on Habibie's decision, the details of which he elaborated at the formal meeting the next day.

The Tripartite meeting took place on Sunday, February 7, at the residence of the Secretary-General, and lasted all day, at the end of which the Secretary-General left New York for Amman, in order to attend the funeral of the King of Jordan. Alatas commenced the proceedings with a succinct summary of the Indonesian position:

> A. A wide-ranging autonomy as an end solution is Indonesia's first option.
> B. If that is not acceptable to the East Timorese, the government would recommend allowing East Timor to become independent.
> C. Indonesia insists that any autonomy agreement must acknowledge Indonesian sovereignty, and that autonomy followed by a referendum was not acceptable.
> D. The Indonesian Cabinet has decided that, should the autonomy proposal not be acceptable to the East Timorese, it would rec-

ommend to the new parliament (the MPR), to be elected in June and likely to convene in August, to adopt a law rescinding the integration of East Timor.

E.) If the parliament accepts this recommendation, Alatas said that Indonesia recognizes that it has a moral, legal, and political obligation to ensure an orderly transition through the involvement of the UN.

F.) Finally, Alatas reiterated Indonesia's readiness to "exhaust the exercise" to find a final solution based on a wide ranging autonomy through the UN process.

Alatas next informed the Secretary-General and Jaime Gama about the Indonesian decision on Xanana Gusmao. He said that the action was taken in response to the Secretary-General's request, and that Xanana would be given "a special status." He would shortly be moved from Cipinang prison to a house, which will technically be designated as an extension of the prison. However, Xanana would have complete access to visitors, and would be able to carry out his political work.

The Secretary-General expressed his appreciation of this gesture of the Indonesian government, and said it would go a long way toward helping all of us in our search for a solution. Kofi then took up the main issue, which was the latest Indonesian proposal. There was a long, free, and wide-ranging discussion, deftly steered by the Secretary-General into a congenial atmosphere, which I could only describe as a heady brew of anticipation, excitement, goodwill, and a desire for expedition. Having thus firmly set, in his unique, quiet, and inimitable manner, the positive tone, tenor, and direction of the negotiations, Kofi took off for Amman and left us to get on with it.

Our discussions on the next day revolved around the two options that had constituted the basis of the latest Indonesian proposals, and the Foreign Ministers reached an understanding that they would meet again in early March, after the UN had prepared a working paper based upon the discussions that had just been held. While there was general agreement that the two options proposed by Indonesia would form the framework of the settlement, it was left to the UN to work out a proposal for the method of consultations.

For the Indonesians, the use of the word "referendum" was total anathema, while for the Portuguese anything that did not resemble a referendum was equally neuralgic. But they both agreed to leave it to us "to be creative." Responding to this challenge, I suggested that we designate the exercise as a "popular consultation," a suggestion that appeared to find provisional acceptance by both ministers. I further suggested that the simplest course for us to now follow would be to use the just completed auton-

Left to right: Foreign Minister Ali Alatas of Indonesia, J.M., and Foreign Minister Jaime Gama of Portugal at a press conference at UN headquarters. The media always had a lively interest in East Timor, and did a splendid job in promoting international attention through bold and scrupulous reporting. UN/DPI Photograph by Evan Schneider.

omy proposal as the document on which the East Timorese would be required to exercise their option. This suggestion was also accepted, ad referendum, by the ministers, who now prepared to return to their capitals for further consultations with their respective governments.

There was thus a large measure of accord at the end of the meeting, and Alatas said at his press conference that he hoped Indonesia and Portugal will agree "by April at the latest" on a package for broad ranging autonomy as a final solution for East Timor. This would be put to a vote by the East Timorese people, and that if the package was rejected, the Indonesian parliament would revoke the 1976 act of annexation and Indonesia and East Timor "would part ways."

Jaime Gama was in complete accord with this arrangement, and in his own press conference he paid tribute to Alatas' spirit of cooperation. In a somewhat uncharacteristic burst of effusiveness, Gama purred, "Alatas sounded almost like a Portuguese diplomat when he talked about East Timor. I felt like saying to him, 'Hello, Mr. Gama!' " However, the session was not a complete "bataille des fleurs," as the following extract from an Associated Press report would indicate:

> After Sunday's meeting with Alatas and UN envoy Jamsheed Marker, Gama declared that Indonesia had agreed to a UN sponsored ballot on autonomy and to return East Timor to its 1976 status as a non-governing territory of Portugal in the event of a "no" vote on autonomy.... Alatas disputed Gama's comments later Monday. He said his government wants to consult the residents of East Timor, but there would be no ballot because of the risk of vio-

lence. He said he had asked Marker and UN Secretary-General Kofi Annan to find a solution "short of a referendum" to consult the views of the East Timorese. "And voting is out," he insisted. Marker said the United Nations was looking at ways this could be done. "But one thing I'd like to assure you is that there are no short cuts to democracy, much less a question of short-circuiting the democratic process. That is out. That cannot be done," said Marker in what appeared to be a veiled reference to Indonesia. He did not elaborate.

It was clear that years of suspicion and distrust could not be dispelled overnight, and serious problems and difficulties had yet to be overcome. Some idea of the shadow boxing that took place, during what was really quite an unusually agreeable session, is reflected in the Associated Press report that has just been cited.

In the follow up departmental conferences that we had after the departure of the Indonesian and Portuguese delegations, the Secretary-General stressed not only the need to seize the opportunity that was now available, but also maintain and pursue the UN initiative. Apart from doing our homework on the next phase of our tripartite negotiations, we intensified our consultations with a number of delegations, establishing for the purpose a "Group of Friends of the Secretary-General on East Timor."

This group consisted of representatives of twenty two countries, plus the World Bank, and included the five Permanent Members of the Security Council, Australia, New Zealand, Japan, Brazil, Austria, Germany, South Africa, the Philippines, the Netherlands, and Norway. For practical reasons, we established from these delegations a smaller "Core Group," which consisted of the United States, the United Kingdom, Australia, New Zealand, Japan, Brazil, and Austria, and it was with this latter steering committee that we remained in almost daily contact.

This permitted us to establish a most useful, friendly, and productive relationship. Our meetings, which were informal and free-ranging, enabled us to collate information and plan strategy on a regular and continuing basis. My office was located on the thirty-third floor on the west side of the UN building, and was spacious enough to accommodate all the core group participants to the meetings, which was a great convenience.

Moreover, it provided a superb view of Manhattan and its skyscrapers, from the East River clear across to the Hudson. The panorama, whether at dawn, midday, twilight, or dusk, whether in sunshine, rain, or snow, was always enchanting, and never failed to delight. For the sake of these visual pleasures I was quite prepared to overlook the dismal furnishings, which could charitably be described as either rudimentary or utilitarian, depending on the level of generosity of one's prevalent mood.

Included in these fixtures was a standard metal hat stand, and on one of its hooks was perched a dark, grayish green felt hat. The hat was in situ on the day that I moved into the office, and I decided to leave it undisturbed, anticipating that its possessor would one day come back and claim it. But this never happened, so to this day his identity remains a mystery. But the hat, as time went on, began to acquire an identity of its own, as if to disparage its delinquent owner, and proceeded to establish its own occupancy rights.

It is a difficult article to describe, being a somewhat wide brimmed, pork pie number, whose origins my limited expertise in haberdashery would trace to East Central Europe. Needless to say, its obtrusive presence combined with its extensive tenure did not escape the attention of my Core Group colleagues, whose comments ranged from curiosity to ribaldry, and in the process made the hat something of a mascot.

In an unguarded moment I once mentioned that I would throw it out of the window once the East Timor problem was solved. This provoked a collective awareness in the fate of the hat, and the U.S. Ambassador, Nancy Soderburg, in particular, developed a special interest in the chapeau issue. After the May 5 Agreements were signed, she made a determined effort to bring about the destiny that I had decreed for it, but I thought the occasion was premature and fended her off until December 1999, by which time UNTAET had come into existence. Nancy then came over to my office, bearing a camera and a bottle of champagne, and took a picture as I sent the hat twirling its way down to the UN entrance driveway. With such lovely friends around, how can anyone ever lose?

To return to more serious matters, it is perhaps now necessary to interrupt the chronicle of this narrative for a brief review of the policy of Australia on the East Timor issue. This is important for three main reasons: a) because of the obvious geopolitical dimensions of the Australian-Indonesian relationship; b) because of the impact on both Indonesia and East Timor of the dramatic volt face of Australian policy implicit in the January 1999 proclamation; and c) because of the crucial role that Australia would be destined to play in East Timor later in the year.

The Australian Government, regardless of the party in power, had from the early days accorded a de facto recognition of Indonesian sovereignty over East Timor, and the 1985 agreement between Australia and Indonesia, over oil exploration rights in the Timor Sea, was a virtual de jure extension of this recognition, despite the slight international opprobrium that was occasioned. At the same time, public opinion in Australia was getting increasingly restive about the government's policy on East Timor.

This was due to a combination of factors, including indignant reactions to human rights violations in East Timor, the presence of a considerable and active East Timorese diaspora in Australia (Ramos Horta was a Professor of Law at New South Wales University in Sydney), and a lively media activity that always kept East Timor in the public view.

Accordingly, in August 1998, the Australian government carried out an informal review of East Timor opinion, in the diaspora as well as the territory itself, and ascertained that there was almost no support for the idea of integration as a precondition for autonomy. The conclusions of this report were informally conveyed to us at the UN, and also, I was given to understand, to the Indonesian government.

Then, in December 1998, Prime Minister John Howard went one step further, formally conveyed his findings to President Habibie in a letter, and recommended that the Indonesian Government enter into direct negotiations with the East Timorese on the issue of self-determination. Howard went on to suggest the New Caledonia model, wherein a review process was included in the autonomy package.

Habibie's reaction to the suggestion was an outright refusal. He was particularly incensed at the idea of deferring the final outcome, and told the Australian Ambassador, John McCarthy, that Indonesia was not going to act as "a rich uncle" to the East Timorese for a fifteen-year period. But on the main issue of self-determination Habibie was more responsive, and went about it in a skillful and pragmatic manner. He sent out a handwritten note to some of his key Ministers, enclosing Howard's letter and report, and suggesting to the ministers that they consider the option of recommending to the MPR an honorable parting of ways with East Timor.

Habibie argued that if, after twenty-five years, the East Timorese still refused to accept integration, the norms of democracy and justice would suggest that they should be permitted to peacefully exercise their right of self-determination. I understand that once his note had been circulated, it took Habibie a week to firm up his decision to offer the East Timorese the choice of integration or independence.

In the meanwhile we in New York could only get tantalizing glimpses of the drama that was being played out in the corridors of power in Jakarta. We had out all our antennae, the most powerful of which were obviously the Australian, U.S., and British, and sensed that something important was going on, but could not tell exactly what it was.

At this point it is perhaps appropriate to continue the interruption of the chronological narrative to speculate on the motivations and actions of President Bacharuddin Jusuf Habibie. His decision to terminate twenty-five years of Indonesian national, political, military, economic, and emotional involvement in East Timor could not have been easy, especially for a person who had not hitherto been in the opposition, but was very much a part of the establishment. But there is not the slightest doubt that Habibie's epic action was the turning point in our negotiations, and paved the way to eventual independence for East Timor.

There has, of course, been a great deal of speculation on the reasons that prompted Habibie's precipitate announcement of January 27, 1999, much of which has centered on Prime Minister Howard's letter to Habibie and their subsequent meeting. My own impression is that while the Howard contact was an important and significant factor, it was not the determining one. In his own mind, Habibie had already made the determination, and that he used the Howard letter, with his usual skill and dexterity, as the instrument with which to effect the implementation of his will.

Habibie's disposition, as I discovered over the several formal and informal meetings that I had with him, was capricious and idiosyncratic, replete with histrionics, imprecations, and dramatic gesticulations, and with an occasional egotistical outpouring that was almost infantile in its bombast. His outward manner displayed some symptoms of an immature extrovert, and yet behind the smoke screen and pyrotechnics there were the unmistakable signs of a thoughtful and pragmatic mind, a subtle capability for manipulation, and above all, of a kind and courageous man.

It has been said, with good reason, that Habibie had made a deliberate attempt to distance himself, as cautiously as he could, from the policies of Suharto, whose known standing, as both benefactor and predecessor, must have made the exercise somewhat awkward and difficult. The near revolutionary changes that occurred in the political life of Indonesia, following the downfall of Suharto, were generated by forces which were manifestations of popular will, and Habibie had nothing to do with them. Nor was he able to exercise much influence over their control and direction.

But in the case of East Timor, the initiative seems to have emanated almost entirely from Habibie, who made the project his own, and launched this particular raft on the rough tide of freedom that was surging through Indonesia at that time. The East Timor issue thus became an extremely personal matter for Habibie, and one to which he had firmly hitched his political star. Habibie's decision to free East Timor could certainly have been made with a view to garner political capital in the quest of his ambitions in the emerging new Indonesia.

It was also, I believe, motivated partly by genuine feelings of human-
itarianism, but mostly on the cool calculation that the rapidly increasing
cost of the shackles was far in excess of the value of the object that they
restrained. This made him an intelligent statesman. Habibie also knew
that his actions would provoke strong adverse reactions from the country's most powerful groups, the military and the politicians with vested
interests in East Timor.

But he went ahead with his decision anyway, because he knew that
morally and realistically it was the right thing to do. This made him a
brave statesman. Instinctively, he appears to have discerned the ethical
distinction, expressed in La Rochefoucauld's observation, between doing
one's duty and knowing what it is.

In retrospect, as I think of Habibie's actions and motives (as I still
sometimes do), I am tempted to recall the events of January 29, 1960, when
Charles de Gaulle, dressed in full military uniform as an impressive
reminder of his authority, went on French television and reaffirmed the
right of the Algerians to choose their own future. This was truly one of
the defining moments in history. Not only did it lead to Algerian independence, but it also prevented France from becoming, in de Gaulle's
words, "a broken plaything."

There are, I sometimes feel, some slight similarities to the East Timor
situation, including the curious coincidence that both announcements
were made in the month of January. In the first place, there is the specter
of an unsettled region in revolt threatening overall national stability. Next,
in both cases there was the danger of a backlash, emanating particularly
from a powerful and entrenched military establishment. A third coincidence is that, in seeking a solution, both the controlling powers, France
and Indonesia, resorted to similar diplomatic and constitutional devices
for framing the enabling measures for the transfer of power and sovereignty.

The French insisted that independence for Algeria should be granted
by France, and not wrested from her. Hence the Evian agreements did
not constitute a treaty, since Algeria was not yet sovereign, and transfer
of power was accordingly effected through a Declaration made by the
French Government. In the case of East Timor, constitutional procedures
were devised in order to meet similar Indonesian sensitivities, and the
MPR enacted a law, which rescinded the July 1976 parliamentary law
under which East Timor was incorporated as a province of the Republic.

However, notwithstanding the temptations of these intriguing speculations, prudence imposes an element of caution in seeking similarities
between the Algerian and East Timor situations. De Gaulle's task was

monumental, fraught with consequences and political risks of devastating proportions. It was executed with statecraft of the highest order, and with a firm decisiveness that brooked no opposition. Above all, it was magisterial, like everything that General de Gaulle ever did.

The dissimilarity between de Gaulle in Algeria and Habibie in East Timor is just about as stark as the contrast in the stature, both political and physical, of the two men. And yet, I sometimes wonder, was there not somehow, somewhere, a similar tiny spark that flashed in the souls of both men—the diminutive, unknown transient from North Sulawesi, and the heroic, historical colossus from Colombey-les-Deux-Églises?

It is an intriguing thought, but is perhaps best left at that. Speculative imagination and reality dwell on different planets.

13

Substantive Progress in Negotiations in New York; Ominous Signals from East Timor

New York, Jakarta, and East Timor: February to April 1999

> It was the best of times, it was the worst of times;
> It was the age of wisdom, it was the age of foolishness ...
> It was the spring of hope, it was the winter of despair.
> — *Charles Dickens*, A Tale of Two Cities

The Habibie proposal was a seed that had fallen on soil that was already rich and fertile. Thanks to Kofi Annan's foresight and initiative, the UN had in position an active, ongoing process of negotiations over East Timor. So that when Alatas brought the project to New York we were ready to run with the ball, so to speak, and did not have to scurry around in search of plans and players to move it forward.

The Secretary-General's initiative thus played a dual role, as an incentive for settlement as well as a framework for final agreement. The problems that now confronted us were likewise twofold, the first being to further the diplomatic process, and the second, much more serious, being to cope with the deteriorating security situation in the territory.

The former, diplomatic issue was dealt with on the basis of the Secretary-General's suggestion during the meeting of February 7. We drafted an agreement, which maintained the basic positions of both sides, but nevertheless agreed that the autonomy proposals be submitted to the East Timorese for acceptance or rejection. In the event of acceptance, the Indonesian government would take the necessary measures for the incorporation of East Timor into the Republic, and in the event of rejection Indonesia would take the requisite measures to restore East Timor to its former status of Non-Self-Governing Territory. The method of consultation was left to the United Nations. The relevant portions of the text of the Agreement stated as follows:

> Having studied the draft constitutional framework for a wide-ranging autonomy regime for East Timor attached hereto as an annex:
> Taking into account the position of the Government of Indonesia that the proposed wide-ranging autonomy regime can be implemented only as a permanent regime with full recognition of Indonesian sovereignty over East Timor;
> Taking into account the position of the Government of Portugal that the proposed wide-ranging autonomy regime should be a transitional regime, not requiring acknowledgment of Indonesian sovereignty over East Timor or the removal of East Timor from the United Nations list of Non Self Governing Territories, pending a final decision on the status of East Timor by the East Timorese people through an act of self-determination under United Nations auspices;

The parties hereby agree as follows:

> 1. That the draft constitutional framework providing for a permanent wide-ranging autonomy regime for East Timor within the unitary Republic of Indonesia should be presented by the Secretary-General to the East Timorese people for their consideration and approval or rejection through a popular consultation.
> 2. In devising the method and procedures for the popular consultation, the Secretary-General shall take into account the views of the Governments of Indonesia and Portugal, and the representatives of the East Timorese people.
> 3. The Secretary-General shall inform the Governments of Indonesia and the East Timorese people of the results of the consultation.
> 4. If the Secretary-General determines that the attached framework is acceptable to the East Timorese people, the Government of Portugal will initiate within the United Nations the procedures necessary for the recognition of East Timor as a special autonomous region within the Republic of Indonesia and the Government of Indonesia shall initiate within Indonesia the procedures necessary for the realization of that arrangement.

> 5. If the Secretary-General determines that the autonomy
> model is not acceptable to the East Timorese people, the Gov-
> ernment of Indonesia shall take the steps necessary to terminate
> its links with East Timor, thus restoring under Indonesian law the
> status it held prior to the 1976 incorporation of East Timor into
> Indonesia.

Thus, the autonomy proposals, which we had so assiduously crafted over the previous months, was now made the trigger mechanism for the implementation of the process of "popular consultations" in East Timor. Having gained acceptance to the agreement by the two Foreign Ministers, our next task was to devise the modalities and method of consultation.

Back in March 1999, we were, of course, aware of the imponderables. Could Habibie maintain course until August, in the likely event of an East Timorese vote for independence? What was the guarantee that the MPR would, in fact, accept Habibie's proposal "to part company" with East Timor?

Already, Megawati Sukarnoputri, whose populist support was at its height, had rejected Habibie's authority and denounced his proposal. She felt that East Timor should remain a part of Indonesia, and that Habibie, as an un-elected, interim President, had no competence to make such a far-reaching political offer. I decided that although these concerns were real, they were not of an immediate nature.

The important thing to do now was to secure and beef up an agreement, which would both accept the principle of a "popular consultation" and also leave the modalities to be worked out by the UN. Once that was done in New York, I could proceed to Indonesia and East Timor and try to persuade any recalcitrants to accept the fait accompli.

Accordingly, we set to work on the nature, manner, and procedures for consultation. One method, as originally suggested by Alatas, was for the UN to undertake "a democratic sampling of views," whereby a UN team would go round the Territory and obtain as broad a range of East Timorese views and opinions as possible. The second option was to elect a "Council of Representatives," which would initially decide upon the acceptance or rejection of the autonomy proposal, and then serve as an interim government until elections were held. The third option was, of course, a straightforward direct ballot.

We discarded the first option, because it was lengthy and cumbersome, lacking in credibility and subject to challenge. The second option, which found favor amongst some of my colleagues, and also Xanana and the Bishops, was given serious consideration. I had considerable reservations, and pressed for a direct ballot. This was the option that was finally adopted, at a meeting that the Secretary-General held with the two Foreign Ministers in New York in March. This decision met the Portuguese demand that the consultations should be democratic and universal, while by designating the ballot as a "popular consultation" we overcame the Indonesian objection to the use of the term referendum.

During my earlier talks with Bishops Belo and Nasciemento, we had discussed the idea of setting up a "Committee for Peace, Stability, and Reconciliation" in East Timor, composed, inter alia, of Xanana Gusmao, the two Bishops, and the local Indonesian civilian and military authorities. Following a decision in New York we did, in fact, set up such a committee. But as later events were to show, it was skillfully hijacked by Wiranto, whose effective manipulation turned a potentially very useful institution into an ineffective body.

To return to the subject of the modalities for the "popular consultation" process, it was obvious that the United Nations would be responsible for devising and implementing the procedures, which we would then present to both governments for their approval. But before we did so I deemed it necessary to obtain agreement on the form of the question that was to be put to the East Timorese.

The issue generated considerable discussion, which could have become quite heated, but for the level-headed directions of Ministers Alatas and Gama. In the end, it was decided that the East Timorese would be asked to choose between two carefully phrased options: "Do you accept the proposed special autonomy for East Timor within the Unitary State of Indonesia?" or "Do you reject the proposed special autonomy for East Timor, leading to East Timor's separation from Indonesia?" In other words, the ballot paper not only offered a choice to the East Timor voter, but also clearly indicated the consequence of that choice.

On this note of substantive progress, the two ministers left for their capitals, with an understanding to reconvene in New York in early April in order to finalize the agreement. In the meanwhile, we got busy in two directions. I was getting increasingly concerned about the situation on the ground in East Timor, and we accordingly sent a mission, led by Tamrat Samuel, to the region, in order to assess and evaluate our requirements for organizing the consultation process, and equally importantly to assess whether the security situation would enable us to do our job.

In New York, we got cracking on the political and administrative requirements for our new task: the Security Council was to be briefed, personnel were to be selected, and budget allocations made. Our consultations with the Core Group of the Friends of the Secretary-General for East Timor assumed new levels of intensity and, thanks to the unstinted and enthusiastic cooperation of its members, of productivity.

Tamrat's report, on return from Jakarta, was, as usual, clear and perceptive: it was also disturbing.

> The process that for years moved sluggishly is now in danger of being overtaken by events that are proving very difficult to keep pace with. Absent a defined course for the remainder of the diplomatic process, the heightened sense of uncertainty in East Timor, combined with the continued fluidity of the political situation in Indonesia, could easily translate into an unguided and quite possibly violent transition in East Timor.

Tamrat sensed that East Timorese political opinion was generally in favor of a transitional autonomy, which could ease the way into independence and reduce the possibility of violence.

But it was Tamrat's assessment of the security situation that caused me the gravest concern, and substantiated the daily reports of violence and killings that emanated from East Timor:

> The most pressing issue is the security situation in East Timor. Political killings and clashes are almost a daily affair. The pro-independence camp, increasingly confident that victory is at hand, but also responding to Xanana's instructions ... is showing considerable restraint. On the other hand, the pro-integrationists, whose leading figures are almost to a man government officials and civil servants, now feel greatly threatened and betrayed by Habibie, and some have taken up arms (with the thinly-veiled support of ABRI or elements within ABRI) vowing to resist by all means any move toward independence. Several new militia groups, some with modern automatic weapons, others using traditional and home made ones, have multiplied.

Tamrat's observation of the humanitarian situation was equally grim:

> The outflow of non-East Timorese settlers continues. They fear the consequences of a rejection of autonomy. It is also clear that there has been intimidation by young radicals. At the same time, ABRI is said to be encouraging the departure of the settlers and the non-East Timorese civil servants, doctors, and teachers. The distribution of food and other essentials is already affected ... there are no surgeons left in the whole of East Timor.

During this period, there was a bizarre contrast between the overseas messages and the internal working papers that crossed my desk. The latter reflected the full steam ahead approach to post agreement preparations, confident in the realistic anticipation that an accord would soon be forthcoming. Yet, on the other hand, the telegrams and news items from Jakarta and Dili carried constant and alarming reports about the deteriorating security situation in the region.

The increased belligerence of the pro-integration groups was attributed to the support and the arms which they were receiving from ABRI, and while the pro-independence groups were generally following Xanana's call for restraint, there was still a great deal of combat on the island. My frequent telephone calls to Alex in Jakarta generally covered two issues: the more agreeable aspect was discussions on matters that progressed our diplomatic negotiations; the less pleasant were the protests about the escalating violence.

I felt that it was imperative that law and order be rapidly restored in East Timor, as otherwise we could find ourselves in the ridiculous situation of possessing an agreement but lacking the ability to implement it on the ground. This was truly a case of the best of times and the worst of times.

The next meeting between the Secretary-General and the Foreign Ministers of Indonesia and Portugal was scheduled to be held in New York on March 10 at which time it was expected that the autonomy proposal text would be approved by both sides, and we could begin discussions on a final agreement. However, this was not to be.

Some disquieting reports from Jakarta had begun to trickle in. Habibie's proposal had already been quite a hornet's nest, and now the revelation of the text of the autonomy proposal, with its wide-ranging concessions, had added further sting to the apiarian infliction. There were dark, but unconfirmed, reports of a stormy cabinet meeting at which Alatas had been quite unfairly accused of giving away the store.

So when I got a phone call from the Indonesian mission in New York informing me that the Foreign Minister wished to meet me, before the start of the Tripartite Meeting, in order to discuss an important matter, I had an inkling of what it was likely to be. At a tête-à-tête breakfast at his hotel the next morning, Alex told me that at a meeting in Jakarta three days earlier the Cabinet had thoroughly discussed the autonomy proposals and had raised a number of serious "and quite valid" objections.

The text was accordingly being reworked in Jakarta and would be submitted to us in a couple of weeks. Alex went on to emphasize that there had been no change in his government's basic position regarding the popular consultation proposal, and that they were anxious to get the process going as soon as possible.

Clearly, a postponement at this late stage would not go down very well. The Portuguese were on tenterhooks and could react adversely to a perception that confirmed their darkest suspicions. The media, too, was poised for an announcement, and a postponement would provide them with a field-day for speculation. Nevertheless, I could appreciate the reasoning that compelled the Indonesian request.

It was not spelled out by Alex, but I knew that I could count on our years of friendship and understanding to speak frankly and spell it out to him. I expressed my appreciation of the fact that during the long and arduous negotiations over the autonomy proposals, which had taken place well before the Habibie offer, the Indonesian delegation had made concessions, frequently at my request, in order to make the autonomy as wide ranging as possible. This was done in order to make the package attractive, and therefore salable, to the East Timorese.

Now that the circumstances had changed and the Indonesian offer of "the second option" was on the table, Jakarta might well find itself in the unenviable position of losing East Timor and being left with a rejected but nevertheless liberal autonomy document on its hands. And regions like Aceh and Irian Jaya might be tempted to demand from Jakarta the same special offer that had been made to the East Timorese.

I could, therefore, well understand the concerns of the Indonesian Cabinet. Habibie and Alatas had made a bold and far-reaching proposal, and Alex's expression of their continued commitment to it was most reassuring. It would therefore be imprudent on the part of any of us to complicate Habibie's task any further by insisting on adherence to the negotiated wide-ranging autonomy document.

I immediately reported the gist of my talk with Alatas to the Secretary-General. After approving my action, he decided that we should inform the Portuguese, and that we should avail of the presence of both Foreign Ministers to explore the modalities and requirements of the consultation process. We took the position that since the autonomy document was now basically a trigger mechanism for activating the "popular consultation," there was no merit in tinkering with the details. Jaime Gama, calm and pragmatic as ever, said that as long as the UN could go ahead with administering the ballot, Portugal had no intention of holding up an agreement over the text of the autonomy proposal.

The Trilateral meetings between the Secretary-General and the Foreign Ministers of Indonesia and Portugal, together with their delegations, on March 10 and 11, 1999, did not produce any concrete results that the media could convey to the general public. And yet, judging by the exchanges that took place, the sessions were exemplary in terms of quiet, productive diplomacy.

Alatas presented a frank and lucid analysis of the political situation that prevailed in Indonesia: "We already have thirty-eight political parties, there may be more, and some are likely to form coalitions. But nobody can predict the outcome of the June elections." We discussed the ways, means, and possibilities of synchronizing our joint objective of organizing the ballot process in the climate and context of a rapidly changing and constantly evolving political situation within Indonesia. We had some useful preliminary discussions on the requirements and procedures for the education and familiarization of voters, on the Indonesian electoral system, and on the electoral infrastructure of East Timor.

Most important of all, we discussed the security issue, and expressed in the strongest terms our concerns over a matter which was obviously central to the whole exercise. The suggestion of a UN presence for security purposes was indignantly rejected by Alatas, who argued forcefully that this was a matter of national honor and sovereignty, since security was a function that was intrinsically Indonesia's responsibility.

A UN military presence in East Timor, before the balloting, would imply Jakarta's relinquishment of sovereignty over East Timor even before the votes were cast. These were powerful arguments, but as later events were to so tragically demonstrate, the powerful assertions of responsibility in the council chambers were not matched by an equally powerful execution of responsibility in the field.

The issue of security, which had loomed darkly in the background over the last several months, was brought to the fore in the March 1999 Tripartite meeting. Henceforth the problem would increasingly dominate our considerations, posing dilemmas of compulsion and resistance, and leading to an outcome that should never have been as tragic as it eventually became.

At the conclusion of the Tripartite Ministerial meeting in New York on March 11, 1999, the Secretary-General told a crowded press conference, after thanking the two Foreign Ministers for their presence and the co-operative spirit that they displayed, that:

> A. We have just completed a very positive and constructive round of talks, at which the main issues discussed were, 1) the autonomy proposal for East Timor and its finalisation, 2) the method of consulting the people of East Timor on the autonomy proposal, and 3) the situation in East Timor.
> B. Foreign Minister Alatas informed the meeting that he will convey to the tripartite forum Indonesia's revisions to the autonomy plan as soon as these are completed.
> C. On the means of consulting the East Timorese people, the meeting has reached agreement that a method of direct ballot will be used to ask the people of East Timor whether they accept or reject the autonomy proposal. The specific modalities of how the popular consultation will be carried out are being worked out.
> D. Members of my Personal Representative's team will soon be visiting Jakarta, East Timor, and Lisbon to continue the process of consulting the East Timorese leaders and personalities.
> E. While the situation in East Timor remains a matter of con-

cern to all parties, I welcome the recent positive steps to promote dialogue and reconciliation amongst the East Timorese. In particular, I am encouraged by efforts to set up a mechanism for fostering peace and stability in East Timor, to which I am prepared to lend my full support.

F. The Senior Officials Meeting will convene in New York on April 13 and 14, 1999 under the chairmanship of my Personal Representative, Jamsheed Marker. The two Ministers and I will meet in New York on April 22, 1999.

Shortly thereafter we sent an assessment mission to the region. It signified the intensification of our efforts, and served as a link between the Ministerial Tripartite Meetings of March and April 1999. The mission, which lasted from March 18 to April 6, 1999, visited Indonesia, East Timor, Australia, New Zealand, and Portugal. It was led by Francesc Vendrell, and included Tamrat Samuel, Horaceo Boneo, the able and energetic expert on electoral affairs, Mike Dora and Henry Thompson of the Field Administration and Logistical Division, who were experts on communications and logistics, and Terry Burke from the Security Division.

As its composition would indicate, the mission was a practical one, designed to survey and actively prepare for an early UN presence in East Timor. In addition, it would also pursue the political agenda with the Indonesians and East Timorese. On its return to New York, the mission reported that it "found a dangerous level of tension and political violence, which, if not quickly curbed, could easily spiral out of control."

> Indeed, unless ABRI adopts a neutral stand and disarms or otherwise neutralizes the militia, the situation risks becoming unmanageable in the period prior to and after the consultation, particularly if the result is in favor of East Timor's separation from Indonesia. An independent East Timor could become a failed state at its very birth. It is abundantly clear that a free and fair poll could not be held under the prevailing circumstances.
>
> At the same time, the Mission concluded that for a consultation to take place by the end of July, a minimum of three months would be required and this on the assumption that there was full cooperation from all the parties concerned, and from the Indonesian authorities in particular. Such an assumption cannot, of course, be made.

The valuable but sobering content of the report convinced me that we needed to expedite the overall process and secure an agreement as soon as possible. Our two main enemies, time and violence, had begun to rear their ugly heads, and would from now on play an increasingly disruptive role in our lives.

In the first instance, we set about increasing pressure on the Indonesians to improve the security situation in East Timor. We did this not only by direct demarches to Jakarta, but also through the Core Group nations, with whose representatives we shared the contents of the Mission's report. Madeleine Albright, the U.S. Secretary of State, visited Jakarta in early April, and in a forceful meeting with Habibie, demanded that he improve the law and order situation in East Timor, while Stanley Roth followed this up by a public statement calling for the disarmament of the militia.

While all this was going on, the Indonesian military and militia, who were never less than themselves, once again provided two instances of their extraordinary faculty for thumping the football into their own goal. Both events would appear to be incredible, in the light of the prevailing circumstances.

On April 6, the church in Liquica, where over two thousand people had taken shelter, was ruthlessly attacked by the militia, resulting in about fifty deaths and a large number of injuries. This wanton massacre, which was witnessed by Indonesian troops and police, who remained callously indifferent, had repercussions throughout the world. The Secretary-General issued a strong message of condemnation, as did President Clinton, who called upon President Habibie to take stem measures to control the militia.

When I visited the Liquica church a few weeks later, the effects of the attack were very much in evidence in the damaged building, but the refugees, while still in an obvious state of shock, had pulled themselves together and organized a defense system which, though rudimentary in effect, was impressive in terms of morale and symbolism.

Hard on the heels of the Liquica massacre, there followed a similar attack by the militia in Dili on April 17. A rally by pro-integration militia outside the Governor's office led to a rampage in which a number of people were killed, and many houses burned. The Foreign Minister of Ireland, Mr. David Andrews, was visiting Dili at the time, as a representative of the European Union. He not only witnessed the incident, but was also a victim of its effects, and observed the complicit inaction of the Indonesian security forces.

His subsequent report, conveyed in justifiable terms of indignation to Habibie and Alatas in Jakarta, added considerable weight to the international concern that was now being expressed. As a result, General Wiranto flew to Dili and arranged for representatives of the pro-independence and pro-integration groups to get together and sign a "peace accord," which Wiranto also signed as a witness.

The gesture was obviously designed to placate international opinion, and did not produce any appreciable effects on the situation on the

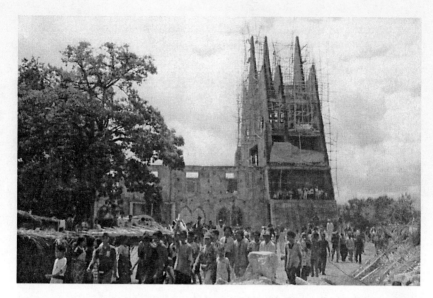

The church of Liquicia, and the refugees who took shelter there. Note the breast-work of stones and thatch which the occupants built in their successful defense against militia attacks. Photograph by Arnaz Marker.

ground. The Secretary-General brought the matter to the attention of the Security Council in a strong statement:

> You will be familiar from press reports with the appalling violence in Dili carried out over the weekend by thousands of pro-integration militiamen, in which many people have been killed and wounded and houses and other property looted and vandalized, including the offices of the main daily newspaper. The information available, including from foreign journalists who witnessed the events, indicates that the Indonesian military and police made no attempt to intervene or to protect the lives and property of the population.
>
> These events occurred while the Irish Foreign Minister was visiting Dili. They follow credible reports in the past few months of weapons being distributed to pro-integration groups, particularly since the announcement by President Habibie in January that Indonesia would be willing to allow East Timor to separate from Indonesia, should a majority of the East Timorese reject autonomy within Indonesia. I, as well as my Personal Representative, have repeatedly raised our concerns with the Indonesian authorities. Following the initial deterioration of the situation a fortnight ago, I have spoken and subsequently written to President Habibie urging that measures be taken by the authorities to take control of the situation and carry out their duty to maintain law and order.
>
> On Thursday, two days before Saturday's events, my Personal Representative brought to the attention of the Indonesian Per-

manent Representative information indicating that the militias were planning to carry out such an attack. In the last forty-eight hours, my Personal Representative has been in frequent contact with Foreign Minister Ali Alatas, who has assured him that the Indonesian authorities would take all necessary steps to control the situation.

It seems to me that the only way to avert a wider conflagration in East Timor is, first, for the Indonesian authorities to take the steps they have promised to restore security and, second, for the current diplomatic process to be brought to a swift and successful conclusion. In this connection, I hope that, at my meetings later this week with the Foreign Ministers of Indonesia and Portugal, agreement will be reached on the specifics of the direct ballot in East Timor to determine whether the autonomy proposal under consideration is acceptable to the East Timorese in a consultation that I have been asked to conduct as early as possible. As soon as an agreement is reached, I intend to dispatch a preliminary team to lay the groundwork for the popular consultation.

The Australian and Japanese governments, each in their own fashion, also weighed in, adding up to an impressive pressure group on Jakarta, and reports of these actions were received by us in New York with much appreciation. Nevertheless, I continued to remain disturbed, because I knew that we were dealing with a new Indonesia wherein the writ of Jakarta, so comprehensively and imperiously exercised in Suharto's day, no longer held the same sway.

The entrenched militants and their powerful supporters in distant East Timor had their own agenda, and clearly resented Habibie's decision. Moreover, they were getting to be aware of the President's diminishing ability to impose his writ on this far-flung outpost.

I recalled an observation made many years ago by the English history teacher at my school. Talking about King James II and King Charles II, he said that one monarch could if he would, while the other would if he could. It seemed that this would apply, mutatis mutandis, to Presidents Suharto and Habibie, as far as East Timor was concerned.

14

Agreement Between the Republic of Indonesia and the Portuguese Republic
NEW YORK: APRIL AND MAY 1999

> This is a historic moment
> —*Secretary-General Kofi Annan,* at a
> Press Conference, United Nations,
> New York, May 5, 1999

By mid-April we had completed our work at UN headquarters on the preparations for the Ministerial meeting, for which purpose I had engaged in intensive consultations with the US, UK, Australian, Japanese, and New Zealand delegations in New York, as well as with Stanley Roth in Washington. I thought that the best format would be to prepare three draft agreements.

The first was a main Basic Agreement, which covered the broad political issues, and this was to be supplemented by two additional agreements, one entitled the "Agreement Regarding the Popular Consultation of the East Timorese Through a Direct Ballot," and the other entitled "East Timor Popular Consultations: Agreement Regarding Security." Each of the three agreements was to be signed by the Foreign Ministers of Indonesia and Portugal, and by the Secretary-General.

The three drafts were presented by the Secretary-General to the Foreign Ministers at a Tripartite Meeting in New York on April 22 and 23, 1999 and, as expected, were the subject of extensive discussion. The two days of negotiations were amongst the most intensive that I have known,

At a lively press conference at UN Headquarters, New York, on 23 April 1999, the Secretary-General expresses optimism. Left to right: J.M.; Ali Alatas, the Foreign Minister of Indonesia; UN Secretary-General Kofi Annan; and Jaime Gama, the Foreign Minister of Portugal. UN/DPI Photograph by Milton Grant.

and revealed a fascinating array of temperament, skill, and tenacity, all coupled with admirable statesmanship. Kofi Annan deftly directed the process as he prodded and coaxed Alatas and Gama, each in turn, into making concessions and accepting compromises, and gently urging and easing them on to a solution which had been the intrinsic desire and objective of both ministers.

The Main Agreement, in its preambular, took note of the position of each side, and went on to express their agreement to ascertain the wishes of the people of East Timor by subjecting the autonomy proposal to a "popular consultation." The Secretary-General was requested to "devise the method and procedures for the popular consultation through a direct, secret, and universal ballot."

Article 2 of the Main Agreement requested the Secretary-General to establish a UN Mission in East Timor to "enable him to effectively cant out the popular consultation," while Article 4 requested the Secretary-General "to report the result of the popular consultation to the Security Council, the General Assembly, as well as to inform the Governments of Indonesia and Portugal, and the East Timorese people."

Articles 5 and 6 defined the actions that the governments of Indonesia and Portugal were required to take upon the basis of the Secretary-General's report of the results of the popular consultation. In the event of the acceptance of the autonomy proposal by the East Timorese people, the Indonesian government would take the constitutional measures necessary for integration, and the Portuguese government would initiate measures to remove the "Question of East Timor" from the Agenda of the General Assembly of the United Nations.

In the event of the rejection of the autonomy proposal (Article 6), "the Government of Indonesia shall take the constitutional steps necessary to terminate its links with East Timor, thus restoring under Indonesian law the status East Timor held prior to July 17, 1976, and the Governments of Indonesia and Portugal and the Secretary-General shall agree on arrangements for a peaceful and orderly transfer of authority in East Timor to the United Nations. The Secretary-General shall, subject to the appropriate legislative mandate, initiate the procedure enabling East Timor to begin a process of transition toward independence."

Article 7 requested the Secretary-General to maintain an adequate presence in East Timor in the period between the ballot and the implementation of its result. Article 3 of the Main Agreement was brief, concise, and explicit. It stated that "the Government of Indonesia will be responsible for maintaining peace and security in East Timor in order to ensure that the popular consultation is carried out in a fair and peaceful way in an atmosphere free from intimidation, violence, or interference from any side."

There was no ambiguity in the text, and yet it gave us the greatest concern, was the most vexatious in negotiations, and became the subject of greatest contention in the days, months, and perhaps years, to come.

It may be noted that the Agreement terminated any possibility of an interim period of autonomy, an option that had been under serious consideration in the negotiation process until now, and which had in fact found favor with Xanana Gusmao as well as with Bishops Belo and Nasciemento. I was told by Alatas in quite unequivocal terms, which were later endorsed by Habibie in an equally frank manner, that the East Timorese had to come to an immediate decision, one way or another.

Indonesia was in no mood to continue to bear the economic burden of maintaining East Timor for another five or ten years, only to be then told "Thank you, and good-bye." This attitude was not a surprise, since the definitive nature of the proposal was the essence of Habibie's abrupt decision. Moreover, Jakarta had always maintained that East Timor's domestic resources were incapable of generating more than 7 percent of its budgetary needs, and that it was dependent upon the center for the overwhelming requirements of its finances. After making every allowance for statistical exaggeration, there can be no doubt that East Timor would continue to need massive external economic support.

The first supplementary agreement, entitled "Agreement Regarding the Modalities for the Popular Consultation of the East Timorese Through a Direct Ballot," set the date for the ballot for August 8, 1999. Our original proposal for the ballot date was September 9 and it was based upon a prudent estimate that took into account the time needed to meet the minimum security as well as logistical requirements.

However, the September 9 date was shot down in flames by Alatas the moment I proposed it at the ministerial meeting. He indignantly stated that this was the very date on which the MPR was scheduled to convene, and that the question of East Timor was among the first on its agenda. It was absolutely essential, therefore, that President Habibie carry in his dossier the UN report on the East Timor ballot well before the scheduled meeting of the MPR. Alatas summarily dismissed our apprehensions about the security situation, and assured us that the Indonesian authorities would soon restore calm and order in East Timor.

As for logistics, that was the UN's problem, and he urged that the Secretariat ginger up its complacent bureaucracy and devise creative measures to respond to this unique challenge posed within a limited window of opportunity. I had not realized, until Alatas told us so, that September 9 was the projected date for the MPR session, and therefore immediately appreciated Alatas' point and his concern.

Habibie's decision had left the government precariously poised amidst the turmoil and political uncertainty that was prevalent in Indonesia, and they therefore badly needed an immediate UN commitment as a fait accompli that would enable them to hold the line on East Timor. Although Alex can be quite masterful at feigning indignation during negotiations, this time I was convinced that his concerns were genuine. He was trying to gain support in Jakarta not only for his President, but also for the survival of a brittle peace process, which was in a particularly vulnerable phase. On the other hand, we too had our problems, which were by no means inconsiderable.

It was not easy for me to discard the time frame assessments of my UN colleagues, who were experienced experts in the field, and were much better aware of the administrative and logistical problems than I was, particularly when the tenor of reports on security conditions in East Timor had shifted from the disquieting to the alarming. Just as discussions in the Ministerial Meeting began to veer from agitation to acrimony, the Secretary-General made his soothing intervention and accepted, in principle, the date of August 8, 1999.

Having sensed and understood the implications of the larger political situation, he coolly prepared to work for the August 8 deadline. It was not for the first time, and perhaps also not for the last, that the courageous Kofi would commence operations under a Damocles' sword. His personal initiatives, attention, and interest were the main reasons why UNAMET got going in such short record time.

Paragraph B of the Modalities Agreement contained the carefully negotiated form and text of the question that would be put to the East Timorese voters:

> "Do you ACCEPT the proposed special autonomy for East Timor within the Unitary State of the Republic of Indonesia?" ACCEPT
> OR
> "Do you REJECT the proposed autonomy for East Timor, leading to East Timor's separation from Indonesia?" REJECT

The United Nations logo would appear on the ballot paper, which would also bear symbols to facilitate voting by illiterate persons.

Paragraph C of the Modalities Agreement concerned voting entitlement. The minimum age was fixed at seventeen years, and eligibility was extended to those born in East Timor, those born outside East Timor but with at least one parent born in East Timor, or those whose spouses fell into either of these two categories.

We felt that we had negotiated a pretty watertight qualification requirement, until we received reports from Lisbon on polling day indicating that a number of obviously European Portuguese had ingeniously discovered that their ancestral or other connections had conferred voting qualifications, and had accordingly cast their votes. Fortunately, their numbers were very few, and Ambassador Neves told me, with obvious sincerity and regret, that their action, though legally permissible, was morally unacceptable.

Paragraph D of the Modalities Agreement drew up a schedule of the consultation process, and set up dates for the procedure, commencing with Operation/Planning on May 15 and concluding with the Polling Day on August 8. For reasons beyond our control, as will subsequently become evident, there was considerable slippage in these dates.

An elaborate Information Campaign was devised, with the UN making available the text of the Main Agreement and the Autonomy Document in four languages—Tetun, Bahasa Indonesia, English, and Portuguese —and arranging for it to be widely disseminated and explained to the voters, and utilizing all outlets, including radio stations. Two hundred registration centers were to be established by the UN in East Timor, as well as a number in selected cities in Indonesia, Portugal, Australia, Mozambique, and Macau.

Registration would take place over a continuous twenty-day period,

The crux of freedom: voter education. Posters illustrate and instruct.

and the usual provisions were made for the display of registration lists, and challenges thereto. As for the ballot, it was specified that voting would take place simultaneously, in 700 polling stations located in 200 centers in East Timor, and in the designated centers elsewhere.

A Code of Conduct for the campaign was devised, and it was agreed that Observers from Indonesia and Portugal, in equal numbers, as well as from various international NGOs would be present. In a significant departure from normal practice for such an exercise, the Secretary-General appointed an Electoral Commission, consisting of three eminent international jurists with experience of political conflict.

They were Judge Johann Kreigler of South Africa (Chairman of the Electoral Commission), Judge Pat Bradley (former Chief Electoral Officer for Northern Ireland), and Judge Bong-Seuk Sonh (Commissioner of the National Electoral Commission of the Republic of South Korea).

The Electoral Commission was a totally independent body and was to function as the final authority on all electoral matters, including complaints, challenges, and any other disputes. It was also the certifying body for each stage of the electoral process, and was responsible for conveying the final certified results of the popular consultation to the Secretary-General. The Electoral Commission's functions were to be fully independent of both UNAMET and New York.

Finally, paragraph G of the Modalities Agreement stipulated that "the Indonesian authorities will ensure a secure environment for a free and fair popular consultation process and will be responsible for the security of the United Nations personnel. A number of United Nations security guards will be deployed to ensure the security and safety of United Nations personnel and property. A number of international civilian police will be available in East Timor to advise the Indonesian Police during the operational phases of the popular consultation and, at the time of the consultation, to supervise the escort of ballot papers and boxes to and from the polling sites."

The second supplementary Agreement related exclusively to the security aspect, and is quoted below in full, since it had such an important bearing on subsequent events

> The Governments of Indonesia and Portugal and the Secretary-General of the United Nations agree as follows:
> 1. A secure environment devoid of violence and other forms of intimidation is a prerequisite for the holding of a free and fair ballot in East Timor. Responsibility to ensure such an environment as well for the general maintenance of law and order rests with the appropriate Indonesian security authorities. The absolute neutrality of the TNI (Indonesian Armed Forces) and the Indonesian Police is essential in this regard.

2. The Commission on Peace and Stability established in Dili on April 21, 1999 should become operational without delay. The Commission, in cooperation with the United Nations, will elaborate a code of conduct, by which all parties should abide, for the period prior to and following the consultation, ensure the laying down of arms, and take the necessary steps to achieve disarmament

3. Prior to the start of the registration the Secretary-General shall ascertain, based on the objective evaluation of the UN mission, that the necessary security situation exists for the peaceful implementation of the consultation process.

4. The police will be solely responsible for maintenance of law and order. The Secretary-General, after obtaining the necessary mandate, will make available a number of civilian police officers to act as advisers to the Indonesian police in the discharge of their duties and, at the time of consultation, to supervise the escort of ballot papers and boxes to and from the polling sites."

The issue of security had been a paramount consideration during the negotiations, for the obvious reason that the UN would need an environment of peace and tranquility if it were to conduct a credible ballot. The foregoing draft agreement did not, in my view, secure the requisite guarantees, and left a great deal to be desired. But even if we had obtained a more cast iron document at that time, it would have been extremely doubtful whether Jakarta would have been able to implement its commitments on the ground. The violent events in Liquica and Dili earlier in April were ominous portents, the consequences of which were by no means assuaged by the newly formed Peace Commission, which had been organized by Wiranto.

After the Ministers left New York on April 23, carrying with them the texts of the three Agreements for final clearance at their capitals, we held an interdepartmental meeting to review the situation. We took account of the fact that the Indonesians had insisted on deletion to references to the following items in our draft:

A. The disarmament of pro-Indonesian militias by ABRI.

B. The need for an early and substantial withdrawal of Indonesian forces.

C. The cantonment of both remaining Indonesian armed forces and FALANTIL one month before the ballot.

D. The training role to be played by UN civilian police.

Nevertheless, we felt that our concerns should be emphasized that, whether or not they were specifically included in the Security Agreement, the above measures were vital to creating the conditions which would allow the consultations to move into the operational phase, especially in view of the threats being issued by pro-integration militia leaders.

We further decided that it would be necessary to enumerate these to the Indonesian leadership, and that it should be done in a letter before May 5. Accordingly, the Secretary-General wrote to President Habibie on April 30, 1999:

> I have the honor to write to you on the eve of what we all hope will be a fruitful culmination of our long effort to find a just, comprehensive, and internationally acceptable solution to the question of East Timor, which owes so much to your personal courage and vision.
>
> I would like to share with you at this time some elements that are usual requirements in United Nations operations of the kind which we are about to initiate, particularly with the Agreement Regarding Security Arrangements, which will be signed on May 5 together with the other two agreements. I refer, in particular, to the provision contained in that Agreement which states that a secure environment devoid of violence or other forms of intimidation is a pre-requisite for the holding of a free and fair ballot in East Timor. While, under the terms of that Agreement, it is Indonesia's responsibility to ensure such an environment, I am being entrusted with a number of tasks relating to the popular consultation, including ascertaining that the necessary security situation exists for the peaceful implementation of the consultation process. This requirement also has a direct bearing on the safety of United Nations personnel, including those to be contributed by Member States, for whom obviously this would be a prerequisite.
>
> It is in this connection that I wish to convey to Your Excellency my understanding of the main elements that will have to be in place in order for me to decide (as provided for in paragraph 3 of that Agreement) whether or not the necessary security conditions exist for the start of the operational phases of the consultation process. These include:
>
> 1. As an urgent first step, the bringing of armed civilian groups under strict control and discipline;
>
> 2. An immediate ban on rallies by armed groups while ensuring the freedom of all political groups and tendencies, including both pro-integration elements and also the CNRT and other pro-independence forces, to organize and conduct peaceful political activities;
>
> 3. The prompt arrest and prosecution of those who incite or threaten to use violence against others. In this connection, I have noted with concern public threats already issued to the United Nations by certain individuals;
>
> 4. Assumption by the Indonesian Police of sole responsibility for the maintenance of law and order;
>
> 5. Redeployment of Indonesian military forces to designated areas one month before the vote;
>
> 6. Free access to the mass media for the United Nations as well as both sides of the political divide in East Timor;
>
> 7. Full participation of the United Nations in the Commission on Peace and Stability, which should provide a forum for all par-

ties to address security issues effectively during the consultative process and for resolving disputes and frictions on the ground.

I also regard as vital to the process the disarming of all armed groups, including FALANTIL, well in advance of the holding of the ballot."

The receipt of this letter from the Secretary-General was not formally acknowledged by President Habibie, and Alatas informed me verbally that its contents were not acceptable to his government. This was not very satisfactory from our point of view, but even though we obviously had no way of forcing the epistle down the throat of the Indonesian Government, we knew, at least, that our concerns had been conveyed in unmistakable fashion, to serve as our implicit guidelines for assessing security needs.

By the last week in April we were in the final stretch of the negotiating process, with the Australian, US, and UK Governments taking the lead in this flurry of diplomatic activity. On April 27, following a meeting in Bali between Australian Prime Minister Howard and President Habibie, we were informed by Ambassador Penny Wensley that Habibie had accepted, in toto, the three draft agreements that Alatas had brought from New York.

This oral communication was followed up by a substantive aide memoire, which, after expressing concern over Portugal's tentative suggestion of revisiting the security issue, suggested a number of measures. It acknowledged that the agreement as it stood had significant shortcomings, but warned that reopening the security annex at this juncture could unravel the entire process by inviting obvious Indonesian rejection, thereby risking increased volatility in East Timor.

On the issue of military observers, the Australians felt that since the question was not taken up during the trilateral discussions, the Indonesians would be "expected to respond with some indignation that the UN has moved the goal posts." The aide memoire then went on to convey the cautionary advice that "we know from the Prime Minister's discussions at the Bali summit that there is very strong resistance within the Indonesian Government to any UN military deployment to East Timor before the consultation process." It suggested, therefore, that the UN should "outline in clear terms to Indonesia a set of clear expectations in terms of the signature of the agreement."

The Australian aide memoire also indicated that Howard had persuaded Habibie to bump up the UN civilian police component (CIVPOL) from thirty to three hundred police officers, and that Australia was prepared to make "a significant contribution to this force." Finally, after issuing one last warning about the perils of a delay in the proposed ballot date of August 8, the Australians sugarcoated the document with the welcome offer of a contribution of ten million Australian dollars to the UN Trust Fund for East Timor.

The Australian Government was not alone in its apprehension that a further emphasis on security arrangements at this stage could unravel the agreement. At a meeting in New York on April 29, US Assistant Secretary of State Stanley Roth expressed his concern regarding the language of the Secretary-General's letter to Habibie on the issue of disarmament and security, and was assured that the letter would stress the importance of disarmament without laying down conditions.

Roth then made a forceful representation to us about putting anything, either specific or conditional, to the Indonesians that could make President Habibie, whom Roth described as being at the end of his tether as regards East Timor, balk at the last fence. Roth also warned against our making any specific references to disarmament or the deployment of military observers.

The last week of April found us in countdown mode for the final agreements. I sensed, for the first time since the commencement of the negotiations, that the "Question of East Timor" was nearing a solution, and that the end result might just mean freedom for the East Timorese. I also knew that the path ahead would certainly be difficult, and probably bloody. But none of this would happen unless we first had the agreements signed, sealed, and delivered. It was therefore vital that we kept things on an even keel over the next few weeks.

As already stated, the Secretary-General's letter of April 30 to President Habibie had evoked indignation in Jakarta, and Alatas had informed us of his intent to withhold its delivery to the President for the time being. We decided to play it cool, knowing that the contents of the missive had been communicated and its intent noted, even though not acknowledged, and that our concerns had, in fact, been conveyed. I accordingly prepared a Summary for the Secretary-General on May 4, 1999, just prior to his meeting with the two Foreign Ministers, and also presented on May 4, a Memorandum to Alatas and Gama.

In my Summary to the Secretary-General, I stated that the lack of specificity in the Security Agreement remained a matter of concern, especially in view of the escalating violence in East Timor, and the negative reaction of Foreign Minister Alatas to the Secretary-General's letter to President Habibie enumerating the specific arrangements that would constitute the minimum security conditions. Our assessment of the strategy being pursued by those elements in Indonesia which were opposed to Habibie's policy consisted of:

A. Avoidance of any commitment to disarm the militia or redeploy the army units;

B. Insistence on holding the ballot on August 8th irrespective of the prevailing situation on the ground;

C. Use of all available resources to mount a massive campaign in favor of autonomy, while restricting the activities of CNRT and pro-independence groups.

We recommended that the Secretary-General call Alatas' attention to the above, and also urge the release of Xanana Gusmao so that he could participate in the campaign. I also briefed the Secretary-General on the precarious position in which Habibie was now placed, and reported the concerns of the Australian and US Governments—concerns which I fully shared—that we not push Habibie over the edge. Once again, Kofi would be obliged to play a delicate balancing act when he had his bilateral with Alatas the next morning.

As later events were to show, he did it in his usual consummate fashion. He also handed over to Ministers Gama and Alatas a memorandum in which he wished "to share with the two Governments some elements which are the usual requirements in United Nations operations," such as the task to conduct popular consultations, which are entrusted to the Secretary-General under the three East Timor Agreements.

He went on, in the memorandum, to outline "the main elements that will need to be in place in order to enable him to determine that the necessary security conditions exist for the start of the operational phases of the consultation process." These included the bringing of armed civilian groups under firm control; a ban on armed demonstrations, while permitting peaceful political activities by all political groups; the arrest and prosecution of all individuals who threaten or use violence; the assumption by the Indonesian police of sole responsibility for law and order, coupled with the redeployment of Indonesian military forces; free access to the mass media by all sides; full and effective participation of United Nations representatives in the Peace and Stability Commission; and finally, the immediate institution of a process of laying down of arms, to be completed well before the holding of the ballot. The memorandum thus outlined a list of requirements, which were by no means either unreasonable or unattainable, but in actual fact, and as subsequent events would reveal, it remained little more than a wish list.

The Tripartite Ministerial Meetings on May 4 and 5, 1999 were as intensive as expected. The Secretary-General received the Foreign Ministers of Indonesia and Portugal individually on the morning of May 4 and used these sessions to prepare the ground, not to mention the positive atmosphere, for the formal Tripartite, which he chaired that after-

Secretary-General Kofi Annan (center) and Foreign Ministers Ali Alatas of Indonesia (left) and Jaime Gama of Portugal sign the New York Agreements on 5 May 1999. UN/DPI Photograph by Eskinder Debebe.

noon and the following morning, by which time agreement was reached on the texts of all three Agreements.

This was only to be expected, since there was already a basic accord on the drafts. Nevertheless, we did have a further discussion on the security issue. Alatas continued his fierce resistance to any specificity with regard to troop dispositions, and even audaciously proposed the inclusion of a definitive date by which the Secretary-General commit to the commencement of the electoral process. But we remained firm in our insistence on flexibility, and on the Secretary-General's right to take the final decision based upon his assessment of the prevailing security considerations.

The formal documents were then drawn up, and the three Agreements were signed, at a simple ceremony at the UN Press Center, by Foreign Ministers Gama and Alatas, and by the Secretary-General, who then made a brief statement:

> This is a historic moment. I am delighted to tell you that we have just signed three Agreements on East Timor between the Republic of Indonesia and the Republic of Portugal.
>
> There is a Basic Agreement and two supplementary ones: one covering the security arrangements for the peaceful implementation of the popular consultation, and the other the modalities for this consultation.
>
> As they have done throughout the negotiations, my good friends Ali Alatas and Jaime Gama have shown an exemplary spirit of cooperation and statesmanship. I am very grateful to them both, as I believe the whole international community should be, and in particular the people of East Timor itself.

We are now moving immediately on to the next phase. United Nations staff are already on their way to the region to begin preparing for the popular consultation. All of us are determined to ensure that it is free, fair, and thorough.

If we are to fulfill that pledge, the United Nations must be able to work freely and in an atmosphere of security.

Security in East Timor is the responsibility of the Indonesian Government. I welcome the assurance given by President Habibie that his government will fulfill effectively its responsibility for law and order and the protection of civilians.

I am gravely concerned about the recent increase in violence in East Timor. I strongly urge all elements and political tendencies in East Timor to refrain from any resort to force, and to cooperate with the United Nations in fulfilling its vital tasks.

I cannot stress too strongly that the success of the process on which we have embarked depends upon the ability of the United Nations to conduct its work in an atmosphere of calm and security. I hope and trust that the United Nations will receive the full cooperation of all concerned.

I should like, once again, to thank the two Foreign Ministers, and through them their governments, for the excellent and constructive role that they have played in bringing this long drawn-out negotiation to such a promising conclusion.

It is my earnest hope that today's signature will open a new and more peaceful chapter in the history of this troubled territory. Thank you very much.

Ali Alatas and Jaime Gama next made brief statements acknowledging the historic importance of the occasion, and assuring full support of their respective governments for the implementation of the Agreements. They were also kind enough to express their appreciation for the efforts of the Secretary-General and his staff. During the press conference that followed, there were some expressions of apprehension that the vital issue of security had been entrusted solely to the Indonesian government. Alatas responded with the indignant assertion that the government of Indonesia was serious about the responsibility that it assumed, and would ensure a situation of peace and tranquility.

On May 6, I reported first to the Security Council, and then to the Secretary-General's Support Group on East Timor, in more or less the same terms, on the details and implications of the May 5 Agreements. To the Security Council, I said:

"The Security Council is today seized of an issue which has been on its agenda for some twenty-three years, and which over the past sixteen years had been the subject of discussion between the Governments of Indonesia and Portugal through the good offices of the Secretary-General.

Mr. President, I am pleased to be able to report to the Council that a major step forward in the efforts of the two Governments and the Secretary-General was accomplished yesterday with the signature of an overall agreement and of two additional agreements, which you have before you. Under the main Agreement the Secretary-General has been requested to organize and conduct a popular consultation in order to ascertain whether the majority of the East Timorese people accept or reject a proposed constitutional framework for providing for East Timor within Indonesia. He has also been requested to establish immediately a United Nations mission in East Timor for the purpose of conducting the popular consultation, which has been scheduled for August 8, 1999.

Under the terms of those agreements, the Indonesian authorities have the responsibility to ensure a secure environment devoid of violence or other forms of intimidation, since the establishment of such an environment is an obvious prerequisite for the holding of a free and fair popular consultation. It will be for the Secretary-General to determine that such an environment exists and he will be reporting on this and other aspects of the consultation process at the appropriate time.

I will not conceal from the Council that both the Secretary-General and I harbor serious concerns about the serious security situation in the Territory. The arming of the militia and the paramilitary groups and the incidents of violence and intimidation that have occurred in the past month lead one to the conclusion that a major effort needs to be made by the Indonesian authorities to bring these forces to heel. The Secretary-General discussed this matter at some length with the two Foreign Ministers on Wednesday and pointed out that a series of elements would need to be in place in order to enable him to determine that conditions exist for the start of the operational phases of the consultation process. (Some of these elements are spelled out in paragraph 6 of the Secretary-General's report).

Members of the Council will have noted that there is barely three months available between now and the date of the consultation. Given the magnitude of the task, the Secretary-General has already sent an assessment team and a preliminary mission to East Timor, and he intends to start the deployment of civilian personnel by next week. This has inevitably required him to make use of a Trust Fund established for this purpose without waiting for assessed contributions.

Given the urgency of the situation and the necessity for early action, it would be most helpful if the Council were to signify its welcome of the Agreements and its support for the effort of the Secretary-General in order to enable him to get the operation off the ground as soon as possible. Thank you.

The Security Council immediately commenced work on drafting a resolution, which would formally establish the United Nations Mission in East Timor (UNAMET), and after satisfying the United States requirement to consult Congress, adopted the resolution on June 11, 1999.

Meanwhile, we had commenced work on the establishment of UNAMET, starting with the nomination of its chief. The Secretary-General chose Ian Martin, a Briton who combined intellectual brilliance with able administrative talent and skills.

Added to this was a deep humanitarian motivation, which had been manifest in his several years' stint as the Secretary-General of Amnesty International. Martin had also served as Deputy High Representative for human rights in Bosnia, and therefore brought with him a formidable combination of international experience and expertise. After the mere formality of my meeting with Ian on May 7, I telephoned Alatas and Gama to obtain their clearance for Martin's appointment as Special Representative of the Secretary-General (SRSG) for East Timor. As subsequent events would soon reveal, the choice could not have been more fortuitous and felicitous.

With the UN Trust Fund for East Timor already cashed up with contributions from Portugal, Australia, Japan, and the United Kingdom, we were able start operations and assemble a team in anticipation of the Security Council mandate. The numbers originally envisaged were 400 UN volunteers who would be recruited to serve under the Chief Electoral Officer as District Electoral Officers at 200 registration and polling centers. In addition, there would be 300 civilian police officers (CIVPOLS) to liase with the Indonesian police.

At UN headquarters in New York, the East Timor project had suddenly assumed high priority, extending beyond its original Department of Political Affairs to cover most of the Departments that constituted the United Nations Secretariat—electoral affairs, humanitarian affairs, legal affairs, administrative, security and communications, and later to the Department of Peacekeeping Operations, and the High Commissions for Refugees and Human Rights.

In those early days of May 1999, I was privileged to observe, closely and at first hand, the efficient and purposeful manner in which the various agencies and departments that constitute the UN moved into action over East Timor. It was, in its own fashion, an inspiring and revealing spectacle.

So this was it. In February 1997, East Timor was a tiny speck in the UN constellation, with a three-man component of Francesc Vendrell, Tamrat Samuel, and myself reporting directly to a benign Secretary-General. The May 1999 Agreements, with their attendant requirements, had now inevitably blown it into a major United Nations enterprise incorporating, apart from the Secretary-General, the Security Council and several key departments of the UN.

Equally important, also, was the active and formidable involvement of a number of governments. Moving from the early days of February 1997 to the hectic excitement of May 1999 was, I mused, a bit like Don Basilio's delightful aria "La calunnia è un venticello" in Rossini's *Il Barbiere di Siviglia*. Starting in a soft and low tremolo, "piano piano, terra terra, sotto voce," it vibrantly builds up to a great crescendo, "come un calpo di cannone, un tremuoto, un temporale, un tumulto generale."

15

UNAMET and the Arduous Path to the Ballot

NEW YORK, JAKARTA, DILI, SYDNEY, AND CANBERRA: MAY TO JULY 1999

> Peace is not only better than war, but infinitely more arduous.
> — *George Bernard Shaw*

As the United Nations rapidly moved into the implementation phase immediately following the signature of the East Timor Agreements, we were faced with three priority issues: the first was the matter of administration and logistics, the second was the requirement of compliance with an extremely tight time schedule, and the third was the perpetual matter of security.

The nature and extent of these problems had been brought to the attention of the Security Council by the Secretary-General in his report on the Agreements. A follow-up report to the Council on May 22 also by the Secretary-General, outlined the requirements for the establishment of the United Nations Mission in East Timor (UNAMET) which, in its initial phase, envisaged fifteen political officers, and an electoral component of twenty-eight officers who would be supplemented by four hundred UN volunteers who would serve as district electoral officers and would be stationed at headquarters and in eight electoral offices.

In addition, UNAMET would have two hundred and seventy-five CIVPOLS, two hundred and seventy-one administrative and technical staff, including its own security officers, and a medical unit. The Office of the High Commissioner for Human Rights (OHCHR) and the Office for the Coordination of Humanitarian Affairs (OCHA) also nominated officers who worked with the political officers of UNAMET.

In addition, we opened a UNAMET office in Jakarta, headed by the experienced Tamrat Samuel, for the delicate purpose of liaising both with the Indonesian Government and Xanana Gusmao, who remained in detention. Arrangements were made with the International Organization for Migration and with the Australian Electoral Commission for the conduct of the ballots in the overseas posts. Last but not least, we commenced the recruitment of the first component of the four thousand local staff whom we would need at the peak time of the polling.

As already indicated, the United States Congress requirement for prior consultation meant that the Security Council could not formally mandate UNAMET, and thus obtain budgetary authorization, until June 11, 1999, a date which was absurdly close to our timetable of opening voter registration on June 22.

The Secretary-General had, with usual foresight, anticipated this budgetary delay and had finessed it by establishing the East Timor Trust Fund, which received immediate contributions from Portugal, Australia, Japan, the US, and the European Union, and thus enabled us to commence operations without waiting for the authorization of assessed contributions. In point of fact, of the eventual overall UNAMET expenditure of approximately $80 million, an amount of about $50 million was met through voluntary contributions in cash and kind.

The security issue, which was always a dominant concern, now assumed a different complexion. An increasingly strong view had begun to prevail, both within the UN Secretariat as well as amongst the member states participating in UNAMET, that some form of UN military presence was essential in East Timor. The argument was reinforced by the correct apprehension that the Indonesian police, to whom the Agreement had allocated responsibility for security, would not be able to take effective action against the militias, who were receiving active support from the military (TNI).

I was therefore urged, both by my colleagues in the Secretariat as well as by some of the government representatives in the Core Group, to prevail upon the Indonesians to accept a military component within UNAMET. As we already knew only too well, the Indonesian reaction to any foreign military presence in East Timor had been antagonistic in the extreme, and they had just provided further proof of this by turning down my request to establish a military field hospital in Dili for the exclusive use of UNAMET personnel.

The problem here was that civilian field hospitals simply did not exist, and the only field hospitals available anywhere in the world were military units. I was extremely concerned about leaving the dedicated UNAMET personnel without adequate medical cover. Evacuation to Darwin was an alternative, but not an answer, to the problem.

In spite of all my urging, Jakarta did not make an immediate exception and it was not till several anxious weeks later that we were able to get an agreement for our field hospital. The omens for obtaining military observers for UNAMET were not, therefore, very propitious, especially since the East Timor Agreements contained no reference to their inclusion. Nevertheless, I decided to raise the matter with Jakarta, and started with a delicate probe, suggesting the desirability of establishing a direct line of communication between UNAMET and TNI, on the basis "of soldier to soldier," in order to maintain and improve liaison.

Following a series of importuning meetings and telephone calls to Alatas and Wiranto, the Indonesians generously overcame their neuralgic aversion to the issue, and we were able to hammer out an agreement for the appointment of fifty "Military Liaison Officers" (MLOs) to the staff of UNAMET, who would work directly with their counterparts in the TNI.

The designation "Military Liaison Officer," instead of the conventional "Military Observer," was the diplomatic face-saver that enabled us to get the project going. The Chief Military Liaison Officer (CMLO), was Brigadier Rezaqul Haider of Bangladesh, a tough, forthright, resourceful, and courageous officer, who did a truly splendid job, under the most trying and demanding conditions. I considered myself honored and fortunate to have known him as a friend and colleague.

UNAMET was established with a rapidity that was unprecedented in United Nations annals. As I said before, this was in large part due to the interest and encouragement displayed by Kofi Annan personally, and now backed by the formidable organizational talents and brusque initiatives of Louise Frechette, the Deputy Secretary-General. The whirlwind staff meetings that she chaired at UN headquarters in New York triggered a flood of personnel and equipment from all parts of the globe to the tiny island of East Timor.

The Australians were the first to jump in with aircraft, helicopters, and jeeps. From the UN's logistical base in Brindisi, Italy, a fleet of giant Russian Antonov aircraft ferried vast quantities of technical equipment, transport, and supplies. And the Japanese sent in trucks, vehicles, and communications material, including a large number of transistor radios for carrying UNAMET's message throughout the island.

In addition to the personnel for staff and headquarters duties, UNAMET rapidly recruited, under the UN Volunteer Program, the four hundred District Electoral Officers (DEOs) that were so urgently needed. Most of these remarkable women and men, coming from seventy-three different countries, already possessed previous UN electoral experience, and readily adapted to the spartan living conditions in the districts of East Timor. Most importantly, UNAMET set up an office and staging post in Darwin, Australia, which was used for pre-deployment training of personnel, as well as a base for storage and back up facilities.

On June 4, 1999, Ian Martin raised the United Nations flag at UN headquarters in Dili, and our staff took up office in the very suitable premises provided by the Indonesian authorities. Ian's extremely competent team of senior advisers consisted of Chief Military Liaison Officer Brigadier Rezaqul Haider (Bangladesh), Police Commissioner Alan Mills (Australia), Chief Electoral Officer Jeff Fischer (US), Chief Political Officer Beng Yong Chew (Singapore), Chief Administrative Officer Johannes Wortel (Netherlands), and Chief of Public Information David Wimhurst (Canada). In addition, there was Tamrat Samuel (Eritrea), as head of the UNAMET office in Jakarta.

The Indonesian government, in a move that quietly and sensibly circumvented Governor Abilio Suares and his incompetent administration, established its own high powered team in Dili, "The Indonesian Task Force for the Implementation of the Popular Consultation in East Timor," which was the operating arm of the impressive Special Ministerial Task Force that had just been set up in Jakarta. The latter comprised the Coordinating Minister for Political Affairs, the Ministers for Foreign Affairs, Home Affairs, Justice and Defense, and the Chiefs of the Armed Forces, the National Police, and the National Intelligence Coordinating Agency.

The Dili Task Force was headed by Ambassador Agus Tarmidzi, a most able diplomat and former Indonesian Ambassador to the United Nations in Geneva, and included Major General Zaki Anwar Makarim, the former Director of Military Intelligence. Others were officers from the Indonesian Foreign Ministry, Police, and TNI, who were deputed to liase in the districts with their UNAMET counterparts.

Initial reports from Dili indicated that the Indonesian authorities were being most helpful and cooperative, but the honeymoon was soon tempered by irritants. Alatas telephoned me to express his dismay and displeasure at some of the statements issued by David Wimhurst, UNAMET's

Chief Spokesman. Although I did not say it to Alatas, I too thought they were a bit intemperate, and we urged Wimhurst to show more discretion, while at the same time tightening up our clearance procedures for public pronouncements of a political nature.

But the damage was done, and this unfortunate misunderstanding that developed early in UNAMET's relations with the Indonesian authorities persisted, in some form or the other, till the very end. Another deleterious matter related to the issue of East Timorese recruitment to the local staff of UNAMET, and the charge that preference had been given to pro-independence elements in the selection process. In this case, I saw very little substance to the allegations, because we had done everything possible to display and demonstrate the UN's total neutrality, including demanding written declarations of neutrality from all applicants, and ascertaining their veracity as far as possible.

There was certainly no deliberate bias in the recruitment process, but since the vast majority of East Timorese were pro-independence, (as later events were to prove), it was reasonably likely that these proportions would be reflected in the composition of UNAMET's local staff.

By the first half of June, thanks to the superb effort by all concerned within the UN system, the build up and deployment of UNAMET was in full swing. But the good news from East Timor was, as always, tempered by the bad. A marked increase in the activity of the militias, coupled with compelling evidence of encouragement and support from the TNI, had resulted in an alarming new situation, the creation of a huge number of internally displaced persons (IDPs), figures for which varied in estimates from 40,000 to 100,000.

This was an unexpected and dangerous complication: not only could it destabilize the whole process of consultations, but it was a situation that in itself was beyond our capacity to cope with or handle. Following a series of emergency meetings with the Indonesian and Portuguese Ambassadors in New York, as well as with the representatives of the Secretary-General's Core Group in New York, I departed for the region on June 17. It was already quite clear that for both logistical as well as security reasons, we would not be able to meet the June 22 deadline for the commencement of the registration process, and I felt it necessary to make a personal assessment of the situation on the ground before submitting any recommendations to the Secretary-General with regard to revised dates.

I knew also that these dates would have to be both realistic, in terms of the window of opportunity provided by the current Indonesian political situation, and firm, in terms of our capability to deliver: any slippage would cause moral, political, psychological, and administrative damage of unacceptable proportions.

A little prior to these events, on May 11, 1999, Mary Robinson, the United Nations High Commissioner for Human Rights, announced in Geneva that she would send a Personal Envoy to East Timor, nominating Mr. Soli Sorabjee, the Attorney General of India, and an eminent jurist who had previously served as the UN Special Investigator for the human rights situation in Nigeria.

Sorabjee visited the region from May 14 to the 25, 1999, and met all the key personalities, including President Habibie, Ministers Alatas and Muladi, as well as Xanana Gusmao and other East Timorese leaders. His report contained perfectly valid apprehensions about the security situation, the plethora of weapons, and about the inability of the Indonesian authorities to control the militia. His attempts to secure the release of Xanana Gusmao were not successful, but Sorabjee's presence in the region proved to be valuable since it called international as well as domestic attention, in a timely and important manner, to the deplorable human rights situation in East Timor.

I arrived in Jakarta to find, as always, that things had changed since my last visit. The Indonesian general elections, which were held on June 7, 1999, were the first free and fair elections in the country's history. Contrary to the grim forecasts and expectations of most foreign observers, the elections had been conducted in a relatively free and orderly fashion. This was no mean feat, considering the geography and history of Indonesia: forty years of dictatorship in a country composed of over sixteen thousand islands, a population of over two hundred million people of diverse religious and ethnic groups, and staggering under the massive blows of a major political and economic crisis. As I congratulated my Indonesian friends on an achievement of which they could be justly proud, I was aware, too, that their euphoria over the present was considerably tempered by a sense of uncertainty about the future. Although the final results were not announced until mid-July, it was already apparent that Megawati Sukarnoputri had obtained 33.7 percent of the popular vote, and secured 154 seats in the Peoples Consultative Assembly (MPR), while Habibie's Golkar Party had secured 22 percent of the popular vote and 120 seats.

The MPR consisted of 700 members, of whom only 462 were elected representatives. Of the rest, 38 seats were reserved for the military, while 200 members were to be appointed by regional and special interest groups. The new President of Indonesia would be elected by the MPR at its next session, which though scheduled for early September, eventually met in early October.

Thus, I now found myself in Jakarta, which, in its political atmosphere, was a veritable corral for some lucrative horse trading, with the Army and especially General Wiranto being the particular centers of attraction. This air of wheeling and dealing was certain to impinge on the East Timor issue and to that extent make my life correspondingly more interesting.

My first appointment was, as usual, with Alatas at the Foreign Ministry, and it was not terribly pleasant. He started by complaining about the attitude of UNAMET (and David Wimhurst, in particular), and worked himself into a state of high indignation about the prospect of a delay in the timetable for the popular consultation process. I ignored the former complaint but responded quite sharply to the latter, and brought to Alatas' attention the deplorable security situation, as well as the numerous acts of unchecked violence that had occurred in East Timor.

I told him it was clear, under the present circumstances, that there was no way in which we could commence registration on the originally envisaged date of June 22 and that this postponement would inevitably effect the August 8 date for the polls. Alatas said that this would not go down at all well with the President and General Wiranto, and that a decision of this nature would obviously have to be taken by "higher authorities." He cautioned that any announcement of a delay would have to cite logistical reasons and not security concerns.

Our discussions then assumed a much more pleasant and workmanlike atmosphere as we took up the matter of UNAMET deployment, and Alatas proved most helpful in sorting out some of the administrative problems that we inevitably encountered in East Timor. From the Foreign Ministry I went to the Defense Ministry for a meeting with General Wiranto and his staff.

We discussed the security situation in some detail, and I conveyed the serious concerns that would now certainly compel a delay in the consultation process. Wiranto received this observation without comment, and described to me in some detail the measures which were being taken to restore law and order, emphasizing that in many cases the Indonesian security forces had been compelled to react to provocations by the pro-independence elements.

That afternoon, Ian Martin and I were received at the Presidential Palace by Habibie, who had lined up for the meeting an impressive array of Ministers, including Alatas, Wiranto, Justice Minister Muladi, and his Presidential Adviser, the vivacious and intelligent Devi Fortuna Anwar. President Habibie had by now been fully briefed on our suggestion for a delay in the consultation process, so there was little discussion when I raised the issue.

He imperiously summoned an aide who arrived with a calendar ready in hand, and after leafing through the pages Habibie dramatically signaled his acceptance of a two-week postponement of the ballot date, subject to two conditions. The first was that the delay should be attributed solely to logistical, and not to security, reasons. The second condition was that the ballot, originally scheduled under the Agreement for Sunday August 8 should now be held on a Saturday instead of a Sunday, the reason cited being Jakarta's respect for the religious susceptibilities of the East Timorese Christians.

I expressed my reservations to both conditions, but told President Habibie that I would convey them to the Secretary-General. While it was obvious that postponement was inevitable, we had managed to get an agreement on it without any acrimony: the conditions suggested by Habibie could be worked out over time.

The East Timor negotiations are occasionally dotted with episodes that spring out of nowhere, assume sudden dramatic importance, and then quietly disappear by themselves. The designation of the polling day is one such example. Under the May 5 Agreement it was fixed for Sunday August 8, 1999. The Portuguese, who had somewhat reluctantly accepted the delay in the balloting date, resisted the change from Sunday to Saturday, for the same obvious reasons that the Indonesians had proposed it: the prospect of the influence of the church if the people went straight from Sunday mass to the polling booths.

Bishops Belo and Nasciemento, when I discussed this issue with them, were quite unaffected, and even quietly amused: they serenely observed that it would make no difference either way, since Christian sensibilities would not be offended by a Sunday ballot, nor was the Church's influence on its parishioners limited to Sunday. So we decided to keep the issue in suspense for a while, and eventually settled on August 30, 1999 as the date for the polls: it was a Monday, which was the same day of the week on which the recent Indonesian general elections had taken place.

As for Habibie's first condition, it was clearly unacceptable that the United Nations should assume all blame for the delay, and the Secretary-General, correctly presenting the situation, conveyed his decision to the Security Council on June 22, 1999. His report stated, inter alia, "in many areas, pro-integration militias, believed by many observers to be operating with the acquiescence of elements of the army, carry out acts of violence against the population and exert an intimidating influence over it ... I would be unable to certify that the necessary conditions exist to begin the operational phases of the consultation process, given the security situation and the absence of a level playing field. I would also wish to allow

UNAMET sufficient time to reach the strength necessary to begin registration successfully.

"It is therefore my intention that UNAMET not begin the operational phases until it is fully deployed, which would also give the Indonesian authorities time to address the pending security concerns." The result of this decision was that the Secretary-General's determination was postponed for three weeks, registration was to open on July 13 and the ballot date was to be postponed by two weeks.

The next item on my agenda for the meeting with Habibie was the issue of the release of Xanana Gusmao from house arrest. The violence unleashed by the militias in East Timor was clearly on the increase, and was equally clearly compounded by the failure, and in some cases the ominous complicity, of the authorities to bring it under control. The pro-independence elements had hitherto displayed admirable restraint, largely in response to Xanana's instructions from his confinement in distant Jakarta.

But patience was wearing thin, and the situation could well explode if the Falantil were to react violently to the increasing provocations of the militias. I therefore felt it essential that Xanana be allowed to return to East Timor and actively participate in the political process. Not only would his presence provide a calming effect, especially on the pro-independence groups, but it would also help UNAMET in the extensive campaign that we had just begun to explain and "socialize" the ballot process and procedures.

Habibie's response to my request was a flat and unequivocal denial. Xanana would only be released after the ballot had been concluded and the East Timorese had arrived at a decision. The argument advanced, both at the official meeting in the President's office and in subsequent informal talks with Alatas, Devi Fortuna Anwar, and Muladi, was that there was a real danger to Xanana's life and that an assassination at this juncture would not only be blamed on the government but would also throw the whole consultation process into turmoil.

Habibie had made a considerable political investment in the East Timor proposal and could not afford an upset at this delicate point in time. At first, I rejected these arguments as being somewhat specious, and went on hammering at the demand for Xanana's release. But as time went on, I discerned the merit in this precautionary policy, however unacceptable it seemed in outward appearance.

It was based, I sensed, on the assessment of Habibie and his close advisers of a combination of two factors: the political and symbolic importance of Xanana himself, and Habibie's inability to ensure the security of the former from recalcitrant elements in the armed forces operating in

East Timor. The elimination of Xanana at this stage of the game would be fatal to Habibie's bold East Timor initiative, and would have disastrous consequences for all of us.

Subsequent events were to reveal that the threat to Xanana's life was clearly substantial, and that even when he was subsequently released from house arrest in Jakarta, he was first obliged to seek asylum in the British Embassy before going on to East Timor by way of Australia.

My next two days were spent in a busy round of meetings with some of my usual kind and helpful ambassador friends, and with a number of the leaders of the Indonesian political parties. The most important of the latter were, of course, Abdurrahman Wahid and Megawati Sukarnoputri, with both of whom I had dealt before and had kept briefed on the East Timor negotiating process. My meeting with Megawati this time took place at her home, situated in the suburbs of Jakarta, and was reached after a long drive past crowded, shop-lined streets, eventually leading into a leafy, rural enclave.

The home itself was simple and modest, tastefully decorated with Indonesian art and artifacts, and not surprisingly displaying mementoes of her illustrious father's life and activities. The garden had a rustic, unkempt simplicity, attractively adorned by the presence of a tethered cow, and some dogs and chickens that roamed about in nonchalant contentment. After the initial pleasantries of our greetings, I congratulated Megawati on her electoral success, and asked if I could continue with my earlier reports on the progress of the East Timor negotiations.

Megawati cut me off and said to me in person what she had already proclaimed in public, that Habibie as an unelected, interim President had no right and no business to make such an important and far-reaching commitment on behalf of Indonesia. She thought that when she came to power she and her party would probably revisit the entire issue. She was convinced that East Timor should remain a part of Indonesia (she was, after all, Sukarno's daughter, I thought to myself), and that the East Timorese would opt for integration once they were assured that the threat of military repression had been removed.

I responded by saying, very politely, that while the wishes and desires of the people of East Timor could still be a matter of speculation and conjecture, there could be no debate about the finality of the New York May 5 Agreements. This was a solemn international obligation entered into by two sovereign states and the United Nations. Agreements of this nature were made between nations, and not governments which, even if changed, are committed to fulfill obligations entered into by its predecessors.

I added that the Habibie Government had made a number of agreements with the World Bank and the International Monetary Fund, resulting in a considerable easing of Indonesia's serious financial crisis. Did Megawati propose to revisit these agreements also? And would these agreements not be effected if Megawati unilaterally chose to review the East Timor Agreements? Finally, I said, the East Timor Agreements were not imposed upon any party. They were devised, by mutual consent, to ascertain, in a free, transparent and democratic manner, the will of a people.

It would be highly contradictory for Megawati, who had struggled so hard and finally succeeded in bringing democracy to Indonesia so that the people of the country could freely exercise their vote, to deny the same freedoms to the East Timorese people. The final argument was obviously the clincher, and after a long and thoughtful pause Megawati said that she now accepted the situation, and would endorse whatever result emerged from the East Timor ballot. But she did not give up the fight entirely, and suggested that the ballot be postponed for some time.

She thought that there would be much violence and bloodshed if we went ahead at the present moment, and warned against this. I responded that there were now binding international agreements, with dates specific, for the consultation process, and it was therefore impossible to bring about an indefinite postponement at this stage. There was a window of opportunity that we would clearly have to seize, and we relied on the solemn undertaking of the government of Indonesia to fulfill its obligation and commitment to maintain law and order.

I assured Megawati that once the period of campaigning commenced, she would be free to visit East Timor and present her views to the people. Our meeting then concluded on a very cordial note. History would record that this pleasant, modest, and courageous lady remained true to her word, accepting with good grace the result of the ballot, despite all her reservations. She has certainly earned my respect and affection, and I should like to believe that these sentiments are, in some small measure, also reciprocated.

Another important visit, once again in the distant shady suburbs of Jakarta, was with Abdurrahman Wahid "Gus Dur." This time, his review of the political situation in Indonesia tended to be Delphic rather than analytic, and it was quite apparent that as a key figure in the nation's uncertain, murky, and evolving post election climate, Gus Dur had decided to exercise an element of reticence.

On East Timor, however, he remained consistent to his position, and reiterated that although he would prefer integration to independence, the final choice should rest with the East Timorese people. This was satisfactory, from my point of view, especially as I was by now convinced that Gus Dur had his sights on the Presidency, and was skillfully manipulating his way into that office.

On arrival in Dili on June 24, I immediately went to UNAMET headquarters for a series of intensive briefings by Ian Martin and his senior colleagues. They had hit the deck running, and the enthusiasm and energy with which they assumed their multifarious duties was an exhilarating spectacle. We then went on to a meeting with the Members of the Task Force, led by Ambassador Tarmedzi. Here, a sense of reality replaced some of the euphoria generated at the earlier session at UNAMET headquarters.

These meetings between UNAMET and the Task Force, which became a regular feature of our activity in East Timor, formed an important institution for our contact with the Indonesian authorities at the all-important working level. The atmosphere was friendly but purposeful, and we discussed not only methods for creating a level playing field for the campaign, but also the problem of a volatile security situation resulting from the recent vicious militia activities.

I also repeated to the Task Force the strong protest, which I had already conveyed to Jakarta, over Governor Soares' recent outrageous declaration threatening dismissal to any East Timorese civil servant who opted for independence. For the Task Force, which operated independently of the Governor, this was a matter of embarrassment rather than guilt.

The next day I went on a helicopter inspection of the UNAMET facilities that were being established in other parts of the island, and visited Baucau and Liquicia. The impression was extremely positive as far as UNAMET activities were concerned, and its relationship with the local population could not have been more heart-warming. We were surrounded by cheering crowds of men, women, and children whose delight at the UN presence was joyously manifest.

On the other hand, we also saw evidence of the brutalities committed by the militia, and more ominously, received credible reports of either inaction or encouragement by the TNI and police. I subsequently took up this matter on my return to Jakarta, but it was only after considerable persuasion, pressure, and the international outrage that followed foreign news reports from Dili that President Habibie decided to send a Ministerial mission under General Wiranto, which did not take place till as late as July 12, 1999.

I held a meeting with the entire staff of UNAMET and expressed to them the thanks and the appreciation of the Secretary-General for the splendid work that they had done. This was followed by a press conference, during the course of which I expressed satisfaction at the progress made by UNAMET, and went on to state my frank concern at the deplorable security situation and at the Indonesian authorities' failure to bring it under control.

At this stage it may be relevant to enumerate the immediate objectives of UNAMET. These were (a) registration and preparation for the ballot, (b) dissemination of voting procedures to the electorate, (c) supervising the electoral campaign including preparation of a code of conduct, (d) reconciliation, and the laying down of arms, (e) organization of the ballot and its attendant procedures, (f) counting the ballot, and conveying its results to the Secretary-General, and (f) fixing the dates for each of these activities.

The registration was carried out with remarkable speed, efficiency, and accuracy by UN volunteers working under the leadership of Jeff Fischer, the Chief Electoral officer, and of the lively and dynamic Carina Perelli, who led a team of specialists from the Electoral Assistance Division, seconded from headquarters in New York. The registration was computerized in Sydney, Australia, to which base the data collected in Dili was transmitted on a regular basis. Lists of voters for each polling station were displayed over a five-day period (August 19 to 23), and challenges were attended to by the Electoral Commission.

On August 25, at the end of the twenty-day registration period, the Electoral Commission issued its formal determination, indicating a total of 451,792 voters: 438,517 were from East Timor, and 13,296 were from overseas centers. By contrast, 400,000 had registered during the Indonesian general elections, a figure which also included Indonesian residents in East Timor. The Electoral Commission expressed its approval of "the calm and reassuring atmosphere of competence and determination manifested at registration centers." Similar reports of approval were issued by a number of Observer NGOs, including the Carter Center.

While the registration process was under way, UNAMET continued a vigorous campaign of information and education with regard to the ballot process. This was conducted in Tetun, Bhasa Indonesia, English, and Portuguese, and was disseminated through the press, TV, and radio: a Japanese government contribution of several thousand transistor sets proved particularly helpful in this regard.

The Public Information section, which never lacks creative talent, had composed a catchy and cheerful little ditty, urging people to go out and vote. The result was that the "UNAMET Song," played by a young local pop group, soon hit the top of the East Timor charts, and stayed there. Apart from instructing the voters on the technicalities of the procedure, I was particularly keen that they be assured of the total security and secrecy of the ballot, and that the UN would do everything possible to prevent any form of pressure or intimidation.

A Code of Conduct for the participants had been prepared, after consultation with the political parties of both groups, and it was formally presented to the leaders by the Special Representative of the Secretary-General at a ceremony on August 9. The document was signed by representatives of UNIF and CNRT, and witnessed by Bishop Belo, the Chief of Police, and representatives from the Indonesian and Portuguese Observer Missions as well as the Indonesian Task Force. The format for the ballot paper, complete with symbols, was also adopted.

The issue of reconciliation and the laying down of arms remained as difficult and vexatious as ever. In spite of our concerted efforts, in several different approaches and directions, the results were never satisfactory. An earlier meeting at Dare convened by Bishops Belo and Nasciemento in September 1998 had been an attempt to bring the different groups together, but had not achieved much success. They tried again, this time with UNAMET support, and a Dare II Peace and Reconciliation Meeting was held in Jakarta from 25 to 30 of June 1999.

The Indonesian Government, in a welcome and far-sighted act of statesmanship, rendered active support and cooperation to the meeting, permitted Xanana Gusmao to participate in the proceedings, and issued visas to CNRT exiles, including Ramos Horta. The atmosphere in the conference was very good—better than anything I had seen in the old AIETD days—and we were treated to the unusual spectacle of Alatas and Ramos Horta not only meeting, smiling, and shaking hands, but actually saying some quite nice things about each other.

But these pleasantries, acceptable and positive in themselves, did not lead to any substantive action or results, and even a modest measure, such as the creation of a Joint Commission, failed to obtain support from the pro-integration groups. Nevertheless, we in the UN wished to keep the ball rolling, and, taking advantage of the presence of the East Timorese leaders in Jakarta, as well as the goodwill and momentum generated by Dare II, we decided to step in with a new initiative.

We organized a meeting of the East Timorese leaders, including Xanana Gusmao, at the UN Mission's office in Jakarta, where Ian Martin, Vendrell, and Tamrat Samuel conducted the negotiations. The Indonesian government, who was informed of the meeting, gave us their support. Xanana set the tone of the discussions with the observation that the result of the ballot should be seen as the desire of the East Timorese people, and that "there should be no winners and no losers, no heroes and no traitors."

It was decided that an East Timorese Council would be established immediately after the ballot, and would be responsible for encouraging reconciliation and stability, while at the same time assisting in the work of transition. The body was officially designated the East Timorese Consultative Council, and would consist of twenty-five members, ten to be nominated by each of the pro-integration and pro-independence groups, and five to be nominated by the Secretary-General in consultation with the two groups and the Governments of Indonesia and Portugal.

The establishment of the Consultative Commission was obviously a good idea, and showed considerable promise at the time it was set up, but the violence that erupted after the ballot destroyed any possibility of its implementation.

The issue of "the laying down of arms" was, of course, critical to the whole process of the Popular Consultation, and our failure to solve this problem resulted in the devastation that followed the ballot. But this failure needs to be viewed in the overall context of the negotiations, and not judged simply in terms of the efforts that were made on the ground just prior to the ballot.

The fierce Indonesian insistence on retaining responsibility for security and law and order has already been indicated, as has been the Indonesian Government's assertion of its commitment to see through a process that bears the imprimatur of President Habibie. Our attempts to push the envelope on this issue were therefore constantly circumscribed by the realistic threat of a deal breaker. The possibility of a general disarmament was discussed, but rejected as being too impractical, and was certainly beyond the very limited resources and time available to the UN at that moment.

Alatas then suggested that the expression "laying down of arms" would be an appropriate term, both as a means of conveying intention, as well as a matter of practical application. Accordingly, the May 5, Agreements, while expressing the view that security for the popular consultation necessitated "the laying down of arms" by all groups, and the redeployment of the TNI, decided to entrust the operational responsibility of this exercise to the newly formed Commission on Peace and Stability (KPS).

It stated that "the Commission, in cooperation with the United Nations, will elaborate a code of conduct, by which all parties should abide, for the period prior to and following the consultation, ensure the laying down of arms, and take necessary steps to achieve disarmament."

Unfortunately, as a result of a preemptive move by Wiranto, the KPS never became an impartial body, and therefore lacked both institutional as well as operational credibility. Xanana Gusmao insisted, with good reason, that FALANTIL was, and had been for over twenty years, in conflict with the TNI: the militias were merely a recent adjunct of the TNI.

On the other hand, the TNI insisted that the process of the laying down of arms should be restricted to FALANTIL and the militias, and should not affect the TNI. This impasse was never solved. The nearest we got to a solution was to persuade Xanana to agree to the unilateral cantonment of FALANTIL forces: an action, which he took, with typical foresight and courage.

To return to the chronological narrative, the second half of July had seen the full deployment of UNAMET and the purposeful execution of its multifarious duties. At the same time there had been an increase in violence in East Timor, forcing us into a perpetual, tension-filled balancing act whereby we were required to judge between the time frame for registration and the minimum requirements for security.

We mobilized friendly governments to exercise pressure on the Indonesian authorities, pointing out that July 16 was the last possible date on which registration could commence if we were to conduct the ballot at the end of August. We monitored the situation very carefully, and after taking into account all the factors, including the Ministerial visit to Dili led by Wiranto on July 12, the Secretary-General informed the Security Council that he proposed to start registration on July 16, 1999: "The requisite certification of security conditions and the opening of registration would be confirmed if concrete progress is made on improving the security situation in East Timor as defined in the criteria."

UNAMET's preference in Dili was for a further postponement, to allow for a better evaluation of the results of the action taken by the Indonesian authorities in response to our pressures. But at the same time, I wished to firmly counter any impression that the United Nations could be swayed from its course by the hoodlum actions of the militias: the ballot should not be allowed to slip beyond its end August deadline. I conveyed this view to the Secretary-General, and after we had carefully and thoroughly reviewed all aspects of the problem, he decided to go ahead with the process.

Accordingly, on July 14, he reverted to the Security Council, indicating that while he was still unable to certify that the necessary security conditions, as stipulated in the Agreement, existed, he had nevertheless decided to commence registration "based on positive assurances by the Indonesian authorities, on the condition that meaningful, visible improve-

ments in the security situation will be observed in the immediate future."
The Secretary-General added that there would be a further assessment
of the security situation halfway through the registration process.

These decisions on the timing of the registration process were taken
while I was shuttling between Dili, Jakarta, Singapore, Canberra, and
New York, all the while maintaining communications between headquarters and the region. As far as UNAMET was concerned, the obvious
course for me was to eschew micromanagement, and to leave matters in
the competent hands of Ian Martin and his splendid team. My inborn
abhorrence of driving from the backseat, coupled with the obvious
efficiency of the UNAMET operations, made this decision an easy one.

I concluded that henceforth my presence in Dili would be restricted
to essential moments, and would remain as unobtrusive as possible. I
therefore spent the last days of June in Jakarta, maintaining contact with
a large number of Indonesian officials and political leaders, as well as
diplomats, members of the media, and, of course, Xanana Gusmao. The
latter had by now become something of a cult figure, receiving visitors
from near and far in his house of detention, which was by now under
siege by a large posse of reporters and cameramen. So much so that Alatas
was provoked into making to me the observation, partly in jest, that
"Xanana now sees more VIPs than I do!"

On July 1, I left Jakarta for a brief visit to Australia and Singapore.
Way back in March 1997, just after I had assumed the East Timor assignment, the Australian Government had invited me to visit Canberra for
consultations on an issue to which they obviously attached the highest
priority.

I could not earlier avail of this offer, partly because I had first wished
to get the negotiating process under way, but more so because we were in
substantive contact with the thinking in Canberra, thanks to the very productive, close, and friendly relations that we had developed with Ambassador Penny Wensley and the Australian Mission in New York.

However, the time had now come when developments in East Timor
necessitated a visit to Canberra for consultations over what was obviously
going to be a very close and important relationship with UNAMET, and
one that was going to enhance, in major fashion, the already considerable
key role played by Australia in the region. We spent a delightful week-
end in Sydney, guided and befriended by Juan Carlos Brandt, the Chief
of the United Nations Information Center in Australia.

Dynamic and resourceful, Juan Carlos exudes enthusiasm and a lively
wit, which he combines with organizational and administrative ability of
a high order. His wide-ranging contacts in Australia were most helpful

during our visit, and his valuable services were always unhesitatingly placed at the disposal of UNAMET during his frequent trips to Darwin.

This was our first visit to Sydney, which must surely be one of the loveliest and most friendly cities in the world. Nature's bountiful gifts of sea, sand, sun, green hills, and blue skies have clearly been lovingly nurtured by the inhabitants, who have crafted onto this enchanting base an architectural necklace of wondrous beauty, ranging from the majesty of the Harbor Bridge and the graceful Opera House to the fairy-tale charm of the dwellings that scatter the surrounding bays and hillsides. Added to this was the pleasure of an encounter with a warm, hospitable, and carefree people, zestfully enjoying the good things of life, as we saw when we took in a concert at the Opera House, and dined at the hearty chop houses.

Canberra, like contrived capitals in other countries, was broad of boulevard and a little antiseptic, with an austere town-planned beauty, which seemed to have not quite got off the drawing board and into real life. But there was no lack of reality as far as our work was concerned. The Australians had organized a series of meetings and discussions, both at the policy level with the Deputy Prime Minister and the Ministers of External Affairs and Defense, and at the working level with the Heads of Departments, all of which proved to be extremely valuable.

I was escorted at these meetings by Brigadier (now Major General) Mike Smith, who also gave me an extremely useful working paper containing his thoughts and views on the East Timor situation. I have yet to see a more persuasive and analytical document on the subject. Mike is one of the rare breed of soldier scholars who combine intellectual curiosity and capability with sound professional military practice. He is as impressive, deploying with his troops in military camouflage uniform, as he is when seated around a conference table in a sober civilian suit, quietly making an effective point.

Foreign Minister Alexander Downer, whom I had frequently met in New York, epitomized the new aggressive Australian approach to the East Timor problem. While conscious of the dynamics of maintaining an equilibrium in terms of his country's relations with Indonesia, Downer appeared prepared to assume a leadership role in any coalition that may be required to deal with a rapidly and dangerously evolving situation in the region.

When in Canberra, I received further disquieting reports of increasing activity by the militias in East Timor, this time escalating into an attack on a United Nations post and on a UN convoy. The Secretary-General expressed "grave concern," and the Security Council warned that

Jakarta would be held accountable for any violence against UN personnel. I issued a strong statement deploring the attack and reiterating the determination of the UN to continue with the consultation process: Alexander Downer firmly expressed his Government's support of our decision "not to be bullied by hoodlums and thugs."

The volatile situation in East Timor induced an increased sense of urgency and realism into our discussions in Canberra. The Australians had already provided a large contingent of CIVPOLS to UNAMET, and the Commissioner of Police, who provided a succinct briefing and assessment, added to its value by a generous offer to increase the number of police officers.

My next meeting at the Australian Electoral Commission brought glad tidings in terms of the preparatory work, and that the computerization and printout of electoral lists in Sydney was going well, despite the very tight schedule. It was a matter of relief and satisfaction that this important aspect of our task remained on track.

At the political level, I had two reassuring meetings with Defense Minister John Moore and Paul Barrat, the Permanent Secretary for Defense. I was informed that the Australians had placed a ready deployment force in Darwin, consisting of the 1st and 3rd brigades (each composed of about 2,600 troops, plus equipment which included armor and helicopters), together with the "Jervis Bay," an impressive troop-carrying catamaran.

These deployments were officially described as comprising "a higher level of readiness," but I was informed that they could be used as part of a peacekeeping force in a post ballot situation, if the UN so desired. As later events were to prove, this force deployment was neither premature nor unnecessary, and its rapid presence could not have been more vital or timely.

My final brief meeting in Canberra was with Deputy Prime Minister Tim Fischer, with whom I ran over most of the topics that had already been discussed with his colleagues, and who expressed his hearty support of the UN effort. A quintessential Australian, Fischer had just announced his retirement from politics for personal reasons, a decision which appeared to have been received with a great deal of public regret. Nevertheless, Fischer did make a visit to East Timor shortly thereafter, when his sturdy presence and robust counsel did much for the morale of UNAMET.

I left Canberra for Singapore on July 7 for a short visit and meetings with the Foreign Minister and Senior Minister Lee Kuan Yew. I briefed them on developments in East Timor and on the progress of the consultation process, and obtained some very friendly and pertinent advice, especially from the latter. Obviously, no one who meets Lee Kuan Yew can fail to be impressed by his personality, but any awe that lesser mortals may feel in the presence of a living legend are quickly put to rest by his easy, nonchalant simplicity.

A tart but by no means unkind humor emanated from Lee's sparkling mind, and found reflection in the brilliance of his eyes. Lee thought that the East Timor situation seemed to be on its way to a solution, and applauded Habibie's courageous and wise decision to hold a ballot. His greater concern, however, was over Indonesia itself, and of the impact that developments in that vast archipelago might have over the entire South East Asia region.

I returned to New York for the next session of the Ministerial Tri-lateral and the Senior Officials' Meeting, during the course of which we hoped to provide positive directions to a process that was now well under way, lurching and thrashing toward its next objective, the ballot box.

16

The Popular Consultation in East Timor: The Ballot

NEW YORK, JAKARTA, AND DILI: JULY AND AUGUST 1999

Deep in the Siberian mine
Keep your patience proud;
The bitter toil shall not be lost,
The rebel thought unbowed.
The heavy, hanging chains will fall,
The walls will crumble at a word,
And freedom greet you in the night
And brothers, give you back the sword.

—Alexander Pushkin

A Senior Officials' Meeting was held in New York on July 15 and 16, 1999, to review the current state of the popular consultation process, and to make an assessment of the post consultation issues. As for the former, apart from the usual discussion on security, we also prepared a Code of Conduct for the Official Observers (Indonesia and Portugal), and the other Observers, such as NGOs and journalists.

The post ballot scenario, for which we prepared a working paper, focused on Phase II, the interregnum between the announcement of the results of the ballot and the convening of the Indonesian National Assembly (MPR), which would legislate on the result of the ballot. Anticipating that this would be a period of tension, we had prepared a series of measures to ensure tranquility. But, as later events were to prove, this was an exercise in futility, because the extent of the post election violence exceeded our worst expectations, and required measures far more stringent than those contained in our modest proposals.

Meanwhile, as has already been indicated, we had decided to start the registration process, and the Secretary-General accordingly addressed a letter to the Security Council on July 14:

> It is not, however, possible for me to conclude at present that the necessary security conditions exist for the peaceful implementation of the popular consultation process throughout the Territory.... As I noted in my letter of July 10, the security situation in the whole of the Territory remains serious, and there has not been time to properly assess how far recent steps taken by the government will result in an improvement. In particular, as I have previously reported to the Council, violence and intimidation have been permitted to be carried out with impunity by pro-autonomy militias. Nevertheless, determined as I believe we should be to go ahead, undeterred by the intimidation, and in view of the need to adhere to the shortest possible time frame, I have decided to begin the registration, based on positive assurances by the Indonesian authorities, on the condition that meaningful, visible improvements in the security situation will be observed in the immediate future. UNAMET will continue to keep the security situation constantly under review, and I intend to make another assessment of conditions based on its objective evaluation, halfway through the registration period. At that time, I will determine whether there has been enough significant progress to continue registration on the basis that the people of East Timor are able to participate in the popular consultation safely and free of intimidation.

I followed this up with a brief to the Security Council, in which I reported on the encouraging progress in the deployment of UNAMET as well as the less encouraging nature of militia violence. I thanked the Members of Council for their support, and informed them that I would shortly visit Jakarta and East Timor for an assessment of the situation, after which I would report to the Secretary-General in order to enable him to decide on "how to proceed in the light of current and foreseeable future security conditions."

On my arrival in East Timor, I discovered to my delight that the registration process, which had commenced on July 16 had assumed a truly astonishing momentum. There could be no more convincing justification for our decision to go ahead with our plans. Despite the manifest voter intimidation and the militia activity that continued unabated, the people of East Timor presented themselves, in enthusiastic but orderly fashion, at the registration booths.

Even the over 60,000 internally displaced persons (IDPs) managed to get to the registration centers before disappearing back into their hideouts in the forests and hills. At the end of the stipulated period, UNAMET had registered 451,792 people, of which 433,576 were in East Timor, while the rest were from the various other centers. The wondrous people of East Timor had demonstrated a collective act of courage and spontaneous democratic motivation that filled us with admiration.

It was truly a bold gesture of quiet majesty that defied the bullies and the cynics, and humbled the rest of us. The registration card, a simple scrap of paper issued in a rustic UNAMET polling station, had suddenly become the most proud, fiercely guarded, and valued possession of over 400,000 people. It was carefully preserved, concealed, and guarded, until the day that its possessor could redeem it in the vote, in exercise of a freedom so long awaited and so implacably contested.

However, my satisfaction at the success of the registration process was tempered by a sense of the awesome responsibility that now devolved upon us. I was determined to do everything possible to ensure that the United Nations would justify the faith and trust that the people of East Timor had so vividly placed in us. They had done their magnificent bit, and now it was up to us.

The delay in the registration automatically delayed the date for the ballot. The convoluted post-election process in Indonesia itself had by now made it quite clear that there was no possibility of the MPR being convened by the end of August deadline, as originally envisaged. This, in turn, not only eased the pressure on us, but also gave the Indonesian authorities more time to bring the security situation under control.

After intensive discussions with UNAMET in Dili, and careful consideration at headquarters in New York, the Secretary-General decided to fix the new and final date for the popular consultation ballot on Monday, August 30, 1999. He conveyed this decision to the Security Council in a letter on July 28.

It may be noticed that we had finessed our way out of the conflicting demands of the Indonesian and Portuguese governments over the day of the ballot (Saturday said the Indonesians, Sunday said the Portuguese) by choosing a Monday, which was also, incidentally, the day on which the Indonesian government had conducted its recent national elections.

The die was now cast, and following the end of registration the period of campaigning commenced on August 14. It was by no means peaceful and intimidation by the militias continued, with the newly opened CNRT offices being particular targets. Earlier, US Assistant Secretary Stanley Roth had visited Jakarta and East Timor. Outraged by the inability or unwillingness of the security forces to contain the militia, Ross had issued a stern warning to Habibie stating that any delay in the ballot caused by security concerns would have a very adverse impact on US and Indonesian relations.

I returned to Indonesia in early August and found, despite my short absence, a noticeable change in the atmosphere. The economic and political turmoil had taken their toll, and Jakarta now had the look of an impecunious nobleman who had known better times: forlorn, a little down at the mouth, and clothed in a former finery which was now unkempt and fraying at the cuffs.

As usual, my first meeting was with Alatas, followed by one with Wiranto, and our discussions were obviously concerned with the ongoing consultation process and the security situation in East Timor. The Indonesians, while conceding that more needed to be done to ensure law and order, refused to place all the blame on the militias, and insisted that violence had also been committed by pro-independence elements.

The next day we held a meeting of the Senior Officials, hosted this time by the Indonesian Ministry of Foreign Affairs, and continued the agenda of our earlier New York meeting. We also reviewed the Dare 11 process and the work of the East Timor Consultative Commission, which by now was running into difficulties.

After the Senior Officials Meeting, Ian Martin and I were received by President Habibie, who greeted us warmly and had the full panoply of Ministers in attendance. I told Habibie that the United Nations was determined to continue our program with regard to the process of popular consultation, and looked forward to his cooperation to ensure that the bold initiative that the President had proclaimed in January would be carried to its logical successful conclusion.

However, the security situation in East Timor was still a matter of great concern, and was a major impediment to the processes of registration and campaigning. I conceded that while there had been a marginal improvement in recent days, there was still a great deal to be done. Habibie and his Ministers reiterated their commitment to the process, thought that our view of the security situation was unduly alarmist, and assured us that normalcy would soon be restored. Ian and I were much less sanguine.

Nevertheless, our meeting concluded with the understanding that while the UN would continue with the consultation process, it would do so on the basis of a watchful and ongoing assessment of the security situation. I reported this to the Secretary-General who, in turn, informed the Security Council of his decision in a letter dated July 26, 1999.

"Feelings." The soldier and the diplomat in harmony. General Wiranto (left) and J.M. at President Habibie's dinner. Photograph: Ministry of Foreign Affairs, Indonesia.

> The people of East Timor are showing laudable determination to participate in the popular consultation despite continuing intimidation. I therefore intend to continue registration on the understanding that the Indonesian authorities will work with UNAMET to achieve the further necessary improvements in the security situation and urgently address the problem of internal displacement. The completion of registration and the continuation of the popular consultation process will depend on my being satisfied that these improvements are achieved and sustained.

That night President and Madame Habibie graciously hosted a dinner in honor of Arnaz and myself at their magnificent personal residence. The other guests were Foreign Minister and Madame Alatas, General Wiranto, Justice Minister Muladi, and Ian Martin. A sumptuous Japanese style dinner was served, to the strains of live music consisting of Indonesian and Western popular melodies, creating a congenial atmosphere of warmth and relaxed friendship.

Just as desert was being served, Habibie jumped out of his chair, seized a microphone, and began singing a series of Western pop songs of fifties and sixties vintage, moving around the dinner table as he crooned away to his guests. I am quite certain that this was the first and last time that Arnaz, Ian, and I would be serenaded by a Head of State.

Bizarre as the episode may sound in its retelling, there was an unpretentious charm, grace, and spontaneity in Habibie's gesture that will always remain delightfully memorable. But the show did not end there, and in due course each of the men in the party had to take the mike, pick a song from a book that Habibie had unearthed, and sing for his supper.

By popular demand, Wiranto had to give a number of encores to his rendition of "Feelings," and we were treated to the implausible spectacle of the stern, sphinx-like Commander of the Indonesian Armed Forces in a near professional performance as a crooner. It is fascinating and delightful incongruities of this kind that make the Indonesians such a remarkable and lovable people.

The next morning it was back to business, and I had a long and very productive meeting with Xanana Gusmao. We discussed the impasse that had now appeared in the Committee on Peace and Stability (KPS). Not only was the participation of the CNRT (and also the UN), becoming marginalized, but there were also serious differences in basic perceptions. As already mentioned, for the Indonesian military (TNI), the process of disarmament would apply only to the militias and FALANTIL (the military component of the CNRT), leaving the TNI unaffected.

Xanana's argument, which had considerable merit, was that the twenty-five year struggle had been between the TNI and FALANTIL, and that the process of disarmament required reciprocity between the two. In order to get out of this dilemma, I suggested to Xanana that he should place the bulk of the FALANTIL forces into a cantonment, and I would work on the TNI to withdraw into their barracks.

In any event, I thought it most important that at this late stage in the negotiations it was imperative that FALANTIL should hold its fire and not get provoked into large-scale retaliation. This could only result in a civil war, and a setback to the consultation process. Xanana needed little convincing on this score, and in a remarkable display of far-sighted leadership and discipline, kept the FALANTIL in its cantonments despite the devastating provocations of the militias that were soon to occur.

I left for Dili on August 14, for a three-day stay, during the course of which I was briefed on UNAMET's activities, met with the representatives of both the pro-independence and pro-integration groups, and had useful discussions with Bishops Belo and Nasciemento. I also attended a meeting with the Indonesian Task Force, during the course of which the security situation was discussed intensively and with some acrimony.

In an otherwise tense and apprehensive atmosphere in Dili, there was one positive and encouraging element. This was the continued splendid dedication and morale of the UNAMET staff members. Carina Perelli, who headed the Electoral Assistance Division in New York, was now, in her own remarkable and energetic manner, engaged in the electoral process on the ground, and was supervising activities in close collaboration with Jeff Fischer. Despite intimidation and threats, which were now becoming an almost daily occurrence, the courageous UNAMET staff remained enthusiastic, poised, and ready to go.

The Portuguese Government were anxious to have a further round of the Senior Officials' Meeting prior to the ballot date, and since the last round had just been held in Jakarta, our rules of reciprocity demanded that the next one be held in Lisbon on August 25 and 26. Our talks took place amidst a backdrop of messages from East Timor conveying both increased tension as well as advanced preparations for the ballot.

I hurried back to Dili on August 28 for consultations with Ian Martin and the Senior Officers of UNAMET. This was followed by a meeting with the Indonesian Task Force, at which it was agreed that all political and paramilitary groups would keep their supporters off the streets during the polling.

For our part, I had instructed all UNAMET staff to maintain a high profile during the ballot process, and to make quite sure that the UN presence was active and visible all over the island. It was important that our gestures convey a degree of reassurance to the voters at the time of the ballot. Also, as part of our continued effort to counter the intimidation of voters, we issued a final, strong reiteration of what had been the main theme of UNAMET's public information campaign.

We stressed that under the May 5 Agreements, (a) there would be complete secrecy of the ballot, and no one would know how any individual or any region had voted, and (b) that UNAMET would remain in East Timor, regardless of the outcome of the ballot, whether it was in favor of autonomy or of transition to independence.

On the evening before the ballot I received two quiet signals, each of which had a significance of its own. The first was at the conclusion of our meeting with the Indonesian Task Force, when Major General Zaky Anwar, with whom I had by now established something of a personal accord, came over to me and said with quiet assurance, "Mr. Ambassador, you have my personal assurance that the ballot will go peacefully." I thanked him, and wished him good luck.

Shortly thereafter, Arnaz and I dined with Ambassador Lopez da Cruz and his wife at their home in Dili. It may be recalled that Lopez da Cruz was an East Timorese who served in the Indonesian Foreign Ministry as an Ambassador with Special Duties for East Timor, and Arnaz and I had, over the years, developed an agreeable personal friendship with this modest, charming couple. Over conversation at dinner, which naturally centered on the next day's referendum, I was astonished to be told by Lopez da Cruz that according to their intelligence estimates, the ballot results would show over sixty per cent support for integration.

So sure were they of success that Lopez da Cruz had planned a large victory celebration party at his residence the next evening. Since there were only the four of us at dinner, and our conversation had been pretty free and uninhibited, there was no need for Lopez da Cruz to show any bravado. I was therefore convinced that he believed the estimates that had been fed to the administration by its intelligence sources. Since our own impression indicated an overwhelming support for independence, I was hard put to conceal my unspoken astonishment at Lopez da Cruz's sanguine assumption. I left the dinner thinking that once again the spooks had misled their masters, and this time appeared to have done so right royally.

Preparations for polling day were now complete. There were over two thousand accredited observers, comprising one hundred official Portuguese and Indonesian observers, four hundred and ninety international observers from Governments and NGOs from the European Union, Australia, Brazil, Canada, Chile, Ireland, New Zealand, and Spain, and about seventeen hundred Indonesian and East Timorese non-government observers.

Arrangements for the ballot procedures involved the close cooperation between the UNAMET Civpols under Commissioner Alan Mills and the Indonesian Police under Chief Silaen. There would be one UNAMET Civpol officer at each of the 200 polling centers, and they would each be assisted by at least two armed Indonesian Police officers, their joint responsibilities and duties being the sealing, collection, transport, and security of the ballot boxes.

On polling day I would visit the various polling booths by helicopter, accompanied by the CMLA. Police Commissioners Mills and Silaen, together with Jeff Fischer, would use the second helicopter for the same purpose, and the third helicopter would remain on stand-by for any emergency requirements. Ian Martin would remain at headquarters in Dili and hold the fort.

We were up early on August 30, and spent the entire day in a helicopter, moving from one polling booth to another. Everywhere we were greeted with joy and enthusiasm, with tears, embraces, and the kissing of hands, and with thousands of pairs of hope-filled eyes. The voters could not have been more orderly and disciplined, and yet it was entirely self-imposed, as our CIVPOLS did little other than act as guides and observers at the polling stations.

As we hopped from post to post, we saw the same scenes of enthusiasm coupled with an innate sense of orderly cooperation. From the air,

Discussing polling arrangements with UN field staff. Brigadier Rezaqul Haider, Chief Military Liaison Officer (CMLO), has his back to camera. Photograph: author's collection.

too, we were able to see the occasional trail of people heading from the hills to the polling stations and vice versa. That evening, as we returned to UNAMET headquarters, I felt that I had lived through one of the most productive and emotionally satisfying days of my life.

We made a hurried review of the day's events. Violence had been minimal. One East Timorese UN worker had been stabbed to death after the polls closed in Ermera; seven out of the two hundred polling stations had been temporarily closed under threat of violence, but had been quickly reopened.

We estimated the turnout to be about 80 percent of the 439,000 registered voters, but in this we were wrong, because the final tally put the figure at an astonishing 98.6 percent! Ian Martin and I met a number of international observers and found them to be universally appreciative of UNAMET's conduct of the ballot. The Irish Foreign Minister, Mr. David Andrews, who represented the European Union, commended "the professional, effective, and dedicated way in which UNAMET staff conducted the poll."

From Jakarta, too, came positive comments on the way the polls had been carried out. Alatas appreciated the fair conduct of the polls, and believed that when the results were announced they would be regarded as free and fair, and General Wiranto also said that "on the whole" UNAMET had done a commendable job.

Top: My standard mode of transport in East Timor. Photograph: author's collection.

   Bottom: Enthusiastic voters lined up in orderly fashion at a polling booth. Photograph: author's collection.

Arnaz with some cheerful young East Timorese citizens who thronged the polling booths, despite their obvious lack of voter qualification. Photograph: author's collection.

On the evening of August 30, I informed a crowded press conference in Dili of the day's events, of the massive voter turn out, and of the efficient and generally peaceful manner in which the polls had been conducted. I ended by paying a humble personal tribute to the people of East Timor:

> One thing is manifestly clear. Whatever the outcome of the ballot, today the eagle of liberty has spread its proud wings over the people of East Timor. Many of the people who went to the polling stations today did so under conditions of considerable hardship. They defied poverty, distance, climate, terrain, and in some cases dark intimidation, in order to exercise their God-given right to vote in freedom.

17

The Aftermath of the Ballot
DILI, JAKARTA, AND NEW YORK:
AUGUST 31 TO OCTOBER 31, 1999

> This was not only a crime, Sire. It was also a mistake.
> —*Talleyrand's comment to Napoleon,* after the
> Emperor had arranged to have the Duke of
> Enghien kidnapped in Germany, and then shot

I left Dili for Jakarta the day following the ballot, and shortly there-after received reports of trouble, both in the outlying districts of East Timor and in Dili itself, where the militia had attacked pro-independence supporters as well as foreign journalists, some of whom were compelled to seek shelter in the UNAMET compound.

I made the strongest protests to Alatas and Wiranto, pointing out that not only was the whole consultation process in jeopardy, but that Indonesia's position and prestige in the international community was now very much on the line. The excesses in East Timor and Jakarta's inability to control them were a serious breach of the solemn international obligation that the Republic of Indonesia had assumed under the New York Agreements of May 5, 1999.

Already there were calls for an international peacekeeping force to be deployed in East Timor, and matters were not helped by the brusque response of a government spokesman: "Just for everyone who has not got the message, Australia will *not* be invading Indonesia." Such defiant and intemperate words only served to act as a tacit encouragement to the militias to continue their rampage.

My hectic activities in Jakarta were concentrated on three issues.

The first was to get the Indonesian government to stop the rampage by the militia in East Timor. The second was to ensure the security of the UNAMET premises in Dili and above all of the museum building near the airport, where the ballot boxes had been stored and where the ballots were being counted.

My greatest apprehension was that the militia might attack the museum premises and destroy the ballot papers, thus frustrating our work at the very last moment. I put the utmost pressure on Wiranto over this matter, and did not leave his office until I was satisfied that he had ordered additional security personnel to guard the UNAMET Electoral Center at the Dili museum. My third priority was to urge Xanana Gusmao to continue to exercise restraint by the FALANTIL forces, despite the fierce attacks and provocations to which they, and the East Timorese civilians, were being exposed.

We were now confronted with the matter of the timing of the announcement of the results of the ballot. The problem was exacerbated by the upsurge of violence on September 1, when hundreds of militia converged on Dili and unleashed a campaign of terror, burning, and looting, attacking the pro-independence supporters as well as foreign news correspondents.

In New York, the Security Council issued a strong statement of condemnation, and in Jakarta I had stormy meetings with Alatas and Wiranto, demanding that they take more effective action against the militia. I also strongly urged Wiranto to be present in Dili on the date of the announcement of the results of the ballot, a request that he had earlier declined. However, the escalation of violence in East Timor compelled me to reiterate my demand.

I told him that an American CIVPOL officer had been shot and seriously wounded by the militia the previous day, and that attacks on UNAMET personnel and offices were not only on the increase, but remained unchecked by the TNI. Accordingly, Wiranto and Justice-Minister Muladi flew to Dili for a one-day visit on September 5.

At an airport meeting, Ian Martin briefed them on the deplorable nature of the situation (no gesture could be more incriminating than the Ministers' reluctance to go into the town), but the Indonesians responded with the disturbingly unsatisfactory comment that the security forces were "using persuasion" to get the militia to exercise restraint: if they were to use force, then there would be war.

Wiranto also said that FALANTIL had received new weapons, and this was a matter of concern. UNAMET had no evidence of this, and all our reports indicated that the FALANTIL commanders, with whom our MLOs maintained constant liaison, were exercising admirable restraint.

Much to my relief, the increasing mayhem in Dili had not so far effected UNAMET's counting center at the museum, and the electoral staff, in a final burst of the superhuman efforts that had characterized their entire work, completed the count on the night of September 3 and early morning of the 4. We had earlier announced, as a matter of due caution, that the results of the ballot would be declared "within seven days" of the voting.

However, now that the count had been completed, and the Electoral Commission had also been able to certify its authenticity, we felt that it was necessary to make an early announcement. Jakarta had suggested some delay, but after speaking to Alatas, who also saw the danger of any leakage if we did so, it was agreed that the announcement would be made by the Secretary-General in New York on the evening of September 3, with a simultaneous announcement being made by Ian Martin in Dili on the morning of September 4.

This procedure allowed for the legitimate preference of the Indonesian administration for a daylight announcement, which would put it in a better position to contain any violent reaction. The Electoral Commission submitted their final determination to the Secretary-General: "The Commission was able to conclude that the popular consultation had been procedurally fair, and in accordance with the New York Agreements, and consequently provided an accurate reflection of the will of the people of East Timor. There can be no doubt that the people of this troubled land wish to separate from the Republic of Indonesia."

The results of the ballot, as simultaneously announced by the Secretary-General in New York on the evening of Friday, September 3, and by Ian Martin in Dili on the morning of Saturday, September 4 was that 446,953 East Timorese (98.6 percent of the registered voters) had cast their ballots, both within and outside East Timor.

Of these, 94,388 (21.5 percent) of East Timorese voted in favor of the autonomy proposal, and 344,580 (78.5 percent) voted against it. The Secretary-General called upon the government of Indonesia to implement the results of the ballot, and to maintain law and order in East Timor.

Shortly after this announcement, the pro-integration militia, in a massive escalation of violence, unleashed a campaign of terror and destruction that led to the devastation of a large part of the island and left the charming little town of Dili in smoldering ruins. It was a criminal act of vengeful, cruel, senseless destruction that defied description or explanation.

It may be appropriate at this point to deviate from the chronological narrative and follow the destiny of UNAMET through the next inspiring phase of its activity under the courageous and dedicated leadership of Ian Martin, CMLO Brigadier Rezaqul Haider, CIVPOL Chief Commissioner Alan Mills, and their senior colleagues.

On September 5, as their activity gained momentum, the militia attacked the premises of the International Committee of the Red Cross in Dili, and went on to destroy the Bishopric, where 3,000 refugees had taken shelter, and forced the evacuation of Bishop Belo to Baucau. As the rampage and destruction continued, I received confirmed reports of active TNI collaboration with the militia, and even more ominously of the herding of East Timorese onto the docks in Dili for forcible expulsion to West Timor.

In the meanwhile, on September 4 UNAMET had been obliged to declare "Security Phase Three" which, under UN rules, requires the evacuation of non-essential staff. It commenced by closing its outlying posts, gradually withdrawing the staff into its perimeter at headquarters in Dili, and airlifting surplus personnel to Darwin. But soon the situation within the UNAMET premises itself became untenable, when some 2,000 terrified internal displaced persons (IDPs) were attacked by the militia and jumped over the barbed wire fences into the UNAMET compound for safety, adding to the hundreds of local and international staff who were already there.

Ian Martin was then faced with a series of difficult and heartbreaking choices, which included the question of the continuation of the UNAMET presence, the security of international personnel, and the fate of the internally displaced persons who were now in UNAMET's protection. Martin carried out a hectic schedule of negotiations with the Indonesian authorities, with headquarters in New York, with the IDPs, and with his own indomitable staff, during these difficult days.

At the same time, as will be revealed subsequently, there was mounting international pressure on Jakarta, a pressure that eventually compelled the Indonesians to accept an international peacekeeping force. But until that happened, there were a series of dramatic events in Dili, events that testified to the courage, dedication, and humanity of the illustrious staff of UNAMET and their dedicated East Timorese charges and colleagues.

These dramatic events are best left to be described by Ian Martin and any others who actually lived through them in Dili. For me, the conduct and dedication of the UNAMET staff restored one's faith in mankind, especially when contrasted with the gross inhumanity and violence that had been unleashed by the militia. This was truly a real life demonstration of both the good and the evil in human nature.

When the UNAMET compound was finally closed on September 14, the international staff had completed their assignment, the internally displaced persons had been duly cared for, and a small group of twelve brave and dedicated staff, under Brigadier Rezaqul Haider, moved to the Australian mission compound to await the arrival of the international peacekeeping force, INTERFET.

To return to the narrative, I remained in Jakarta from September 4 onwards, and was in constant touch with the Secretary-General in New York as we monitored the rapidly deteriorating situation in East Timor. I was also on the phone to Stanley Roth, keeping him informed of the situation as he powerfully weighed in with Jakarta.

On September 6, I had a round of meetings with Alatas, Wiranto, and finally President Habibie. These were difficult and tense sessions, at which I pointed out that the crass failure of the Indonesian authorities to maintain security in East Timor, coupled with the increased attacks on the United Nations, were making it imperative that we induct an international peacekeeping force.

I added in quite unambiguous terms that the actions of the militia, supported by the TNI, could well warrant and trigger a War Crimes Tribunal. Habibie was by now visibly agitated, and told me that he intended to impose martial law in East Timor the next day: he was confident that this would bring the situation under control.

I expressed frank skepticism, pointing out that since the troops charged with enforcing martial law were the same ones that were committing the atrocities, it all sounded to me a bit like putting the fox into the chicken coop. Wiranto interjected to say that new units were being flown in from Sumatra, but I remained unconvinced and told him so. Meanwhile, we discerned the first glimpse of flexibility on the part of the Indonesians, occasioned no doubt by the demarches that were being made to Jakarta from various world capitals, and by the Secretary-General in particular.

In a telephone conversation with the latter at this time, Habibie said that if martial law failed to restore order then "we will say that the UN is coming in as a friend." Kofi Annan's response, just as the Indonesians imposed martial law on September 7 was to call Habibie and give him forty-eight hours to improve the security situation in East Timor.

At the same time, a five-member Ambassadorial mission from the Security Council arrived in Jakarta. It was a strong and unmistakable gesture of concern on the part of the international community, and a demand that the Indonesians fulfill their solemn obligations. There was by now a quite palpable sense of urgency and high drama in the Indonesian capital, stimulated as it was by the violence in East Timor and the compulsions on UNAMET to close its posts, one by one, and retreat into the beleaguered compound in Dili.

It now became absolutely necessary to bring to bear every form of pressure on the Indonesian Government, and over the next few days the international community acted in a powerful and measured manner. The most important factor was the presence of the Security Council delegation's presence in Jakarta and Dili, where the members not only saw for themselves the devastation that had taken place, but more importantly conveyed in the strongest terms to the Indonesian leadership the feelings of revulsion of the international community, and their demands for the induction of a peacekeeping force.

The United States added its considerable weight to the effort through the unusual process of a series of direct telephone conversations between Clinton, Albright, and Cohen, each with their Indonesian counterparts, Habibie, Alatas, and Wiranto. In addition, there was a meeting of the Asia Pacific Economic Cooperation group (APEC) leaders in Auckland, New Zealand, from September 9 to 12 which was attended by the Prime Ministers and Foreign Ministers of the member states, as well as by Madeleine Albright of the United States, Lloyd Axworthy of Canada, and Robin Cook representing the European Union.

Habibie and Alatas absented themselves from the meeting, but the message they received from Don McKinnon of New Zealand was unequivocal. The members, who between them possessed over three quarters of the world's GDP, deplored the events in East Timor and were prepared to support an international presence in the island in order to ensure security and the compliance of the results of the ballot. Indonesia's economic condition had by now deteriorated from the parlous to the perilous, and the country's dependence on foreign assistance was desperate.

Further pressure in this direction came from Jim Wolfensohn, the World Bank President, who wrote to Habibie on September 8: "For the international financial community to be able to continue its full support it is critical that you act swiftly to restore order, and that your government come through on its public commitment to honor the referendum outcome."

Michel Camdessus, the Managing Director of the International Monetary Fund, issued successive warning statements, and followed this up on September 9 with a decision to defer the planned visit to Jakarta of a mission which was scheduled to discuss the resumption of a desperately needed credit trance from an IMF loan.

On that same fateful day of September 7, the Indonesian Govern-

ment freed Xanana Gusmao from house arrest, but this tardy gesture was
of no help to Xanana in the prevalent situation. He accepted the timely
and generous offer of hospitality made by Robin Christopher, the British
Ambassador, and after a short stay in the Embassy left for Australia.

It was not until October 22 that this heroic figure, the remarkable
and undisputed leader of the East Timorese people, was able to return to
his beloved homeland. The previous day, just prior to his release and just
after my acrimonious session at the President's office in Jakarta, I met
Xanana in his residence of detention.

The visit was both painful and emotional, to say the least. In the first
place, there had been widespread rumors that Xanana's father had been
killed by the militia in the course of their rampage; fortunately this information proved to be false, but we were not to know it at the time. When
I expressed my sympathies to Xanana, he was quite stoic over the news
about his father, but broke down and wept openly about the killings and
sufferings of his people.

What went wrong? Had he erred in agreeing to go ahead with the
ballot? Had he been wrong in restraining the FALANTIL? And finally,
although he was too much of a gentleman to say so, his eyes were an inter-
rogation: could he trust the United Nations any longer?

I urged Xanana not to lose heart, and assured him that we would put
things right. His brave people had expressed their will to the world in
unequivocal terms, and the world had taken note of this with admiration.
We would ensure that their will prevails. I left him with a hug and a
thumbs-up signal, but it was a tense parting.

On September 7, the Spokesman for the Secretary-General, United
Nations, in New York issued a statement warning the Indonesian Government that it had forty-eight hours in which to restore law and order
in East Timor. Alatas responded with the somewhat defiant counter warning "not to issue ultimatums," and added that any peacekeeping force
"would have to shoot its way" into East Timor.

In private, however, there were signs of softening and change, as the
Secretary-General told me he had detected, in a further lengthy, frank,
and straightforward telephone conversation with Habibie. As in so much
else, Kofi has no equal in the art of long distance telephone diplomacy.

On September 11, the Secretary-General in his report to the Security Council reiterated that the militia actions in East Timor might well
be categorized as international crime, and urged Indonesia to immediately agree to the presence of an international peacekeeping force. "If it
refuses to do so it cannot escape responsibility for what could amount,
according to reports reaching us, to crimes against humanity."

The Secretary-General went on to add, in terms of consummate tact, that "the international community is asking for Indonesia's consent to the deployment of such a force. But I hope it is clear, Mr. President, that it does so out of deference to Indonesia's position as a respected member of the community of states. Regrettably, that position is now being placed in jeopardy by the tragedy that has engulfed the people of East Timor."

The debate in the Security Council lasted throughout the day of September 11 with the participation of fifty nations, the overwhelming majority of which called on Indonesia to accept an international peace-keeping force. The Council decided to delay consideration of a resolution until it had received a report from its delegation on return from Jakarta.

While dealing with the Security Council in New York, the Secretary-General had also been in constant contact with Habibie in Jakarta, and had finally secured the latter's agreement to accept a peacekeeping force in East Timor. On September 12, after a meeting with his cabinet, Habibie informed the Security Council delegation that he would accept a UN peacekeeping force in East Timor.

There were no conditions to this acceptance, and Alatas would fly to work out the implementation details. That night Habibie announced his decision to the Indonesian nation on radio and television, stating that Indonesia had invited a UN peacekeeping force in East Timor in order "to protect the people and to implement the result of the ballot of 30 August."

The decision came too late, of course, to save many innocent lives and to prevent the virtual destruction of Dili, as well as many other towns and villages in East Timor. On September 20 an Australian-led UN peacekeeping force, under the command of Major General Peter Cosgrove, landed in Dili and was rapidly deployed all over the Territory. The International Force East Timor (INTERFET) would eventually comprise 7,500 troops from twenty-two nations, including most of Indonesia's ASEAN neighbors: Thailand, the Philippines, Malaysia, and Singapore.

It was a thoroughly professional outfit, well-armed and-well trained, and very quickly and vigorously established its authority. Above all, INTERFET operated under the robust mandate of a Chapter VII Security Council resolution, which enabled it to use its military muscle whenever it was felt necessary. The cowardly militia hoodlums, who had hitherto roamed unchecked killing defenseless men, women, and children, showed little inclination to take on a disciplined military force, and were soon brought under control. UNAMET, which had been forced to withdraw from Dili on September 14, returned to re-establish its headquarters on September 28 and commenced its cooperation with INTERFET.

The week beginning September 13, 1999 was devoted to a series of meetings in New York, which was now once again the focus of activities. The Security Council, after considering the report of its Five Member delegation to Indonesia, rapidly passed Resolution No.1264 on September 15.

Acting under Chapter VII of the UN Charter, commonly known as the enforcement chapter, the Council authorized the establishment a multinational force, INTERFET, with powers to use "ail necessary measures" to restore peace and security in East Timor. It was also mandated to assist in the massive rehabilitation program that was now being mobilized.

Following the Security Council resolution, we held a Ministerial Trilateral Meeting at which the Secretary-General and Ministers Alatas and Gama worked out the modalities for the launching of a large scale humanitarian relief effort, as well as arrangements for the repatriation of over 250,000 East Timorese who had been forcibly removed to West Timor.

It was also agreed that Indonesian troops and police would begin a withdrawal from East Timor, coordinating this exercise with the deployment of INTERFET forces. There was therefore a veritable flurry of diplomatic activity in New York that week; this was spiced by the lively presence of two key players in the East Timor saga—Foreign Minister Alexander Downer of Australia and Jose Ramos Horta of East Timor.

The following week I chaired a Senior Officials Meeting, at which we prepared and presented to the Ministerial Trilateral Meeting proposals for the ad hoc measures that would be required to fill the vacuum created by the early departure of the Indonesian authorities. The proposals were approved by the Secretary-General and the two Foreign Ministers, who then formally reiterated the agreement of the governments of Indonesia and Portugal for the transfer of authority in East Timor to the United Nations.

On October 19 the Indonesian Peoples Consultative Assembly (MPR) formally recognized the results of the Popular Consultation, and enacted the requisite legislation. On October 25, the Security Council, by its Resolution 1272 (1999), established the United Nations Transitional Authority in East Timor (UNTAET) which took over authority from INTERFET.

On October 31, 1999, the last Indonesian troops left East Timor, thus ending a period of foreign occupation that had covered over four centuries. The last few weeks of these were particularly gruesome, and mostly unnecessary. It reflected, very aptly, Talleyrand's observation that not only was the action a crime, it was also a mistake.

One of the persons present at Dili's Comoro airport on that October day, who attended the departure of the last of the Indonesian military and administrative officers, was Xanana Gusmao. He had seen them invade his land in 1975, had carried out a fierce and determined resistance, had been captured and sentenced to life imprisonment, yet continued to organize and direct this resistance from his prison cell, and had returned to his devastated home just eight days prior to this dramatic and historic moment.

His presence at Dili airport, to bid farewell to his former adversaries and enemies, was the chivalrous gesture of a civilized man. As I was to discover in later conversations with him, Xanana remained remarkably free from bitterness.

18

A Review, and Some Reflections

Just outside the city of St. Petersburg, Russia, at the famous Pis-karevsky Cemetery, a million victims of the siege of Leningrad in World War II lie buried amongst surroundings of somber beauty. The War Memorial carries a poem by the Leningrad poet and diarist, Olga Bergolts, who had herself endured those dark days of war and siege. The poem ends with the words:

"Let no one forget;
Let nothing be forgotten..."

As Xanana Gusmao saw off the last of the Indonesian officials at Dili's Comoro airport on October 31, 1999, he found himself the leader of a new and free country, a country that had for too long endured sufferings in the past, was materially devastated in the present, and faced a future in which hardship was the only certainty. A Security Council resolution had established a United Nations mandate, the United Nations Transitional Authority in East Timor (UNTAET). This was placed under the dynamic leadership of a Brazilian diplomat and senior United Nations official, Under Secretary-General Sergio Vieira de Mello, who was designated as the Special Representative of the Secretary-General (SRSG), and whose responsibility it was to commence the immense task of nation building, in collaboration with the representatives of the East Timorese people. It was a daunting but exciting and worthwhile challenge.

First the rubble of physical destruction had to be cleared, and at the same time the emotional scars of deaths and disappearance in the long, widespread conflict had to be healed. A series of international donors' conferences, organized by the United Nations, provided the resources, in cash and kind, for the reconstruction of East Timor. At the same time, the task of rebuilding or creating institutions was commenced, so that national requirements—as diverse as education, legal systems, sanitation, power supplies, agriculture, trade, and other economic activities—could be put into effect.

Just as important, the issue of the examination of human rights violations was addressed. This, in turn, was coupled with the gradual induction of political institutions and the political process was set in motion, with East Timorese participation in administration and legislation.

This is a most satisfactory outcome, judged by any standards. But the independence of East Timor was not achieved without cost, particularly to its own people, and it is obvious that some form of balance sheet needs to be drawn up. The final verdict will, as always, be left to history, but an active participant in the United Nations process and efforts may be permitted to record some observations.

In the first place, it seems to me, we need to examine the historical context of the East Timorese struggle against Indonesia, which commenced in 1975. This is particularly relevant as far as the issue of casualties is concerned. Figures are difficult to quantify with accuracy, but it is generally believed that between 1975 and 1997, as a result of the civil war, the Indonesian invasion, and the subsequent long guerrilla struggle, there were approximately 250,000 East Timorese killed.

This is about a quarter of the entire population, and when I first commenced the negotiation process I was horrified by the knowledge that there was hardly an East Timorese citizen who had not lost a friend or a family member in violence over the past twenty years. To this large figure must be added the casualties on the Indonesian side which, though far less numerous, nevertheless add to the gruesome total of the toll of human lives that were sacrificed in this long running conflict.

At the time when the pro-integration militia unleashed their murderous assaults, from August to November 1999, we had the impression that there had been a tremendous blood bath. Subsequent events have revealed that although the destruction of property, particularly in the urban areas of East Timor, was almost complete, the loss of life had been mercifully far less than I had originally feared, and current estimates put the figure at between one and two thousand.

This was probably because most people fled to the hills, and thus escaped massacre. While the loss of even *one* life is to be strongly deplored, it would not be unreasonable to assert that the final spurt of bloodletting, just before independence, was a tiny fraction of the casualties that had occurred over the previous twenty-five years.

The Question of East Timor remained largely dormant on the agenda of the United Nations until Kofi Annan assumed the office of Secretary-General in January 1997, and the course of the action that he then initiated forms the content of this account. Kofi's personal initiative and involvement on East Timor was the *Schwerpunkt* and remains so throughout this saga, as it provides both constancy and momentum to the process.

The second momentum was provided by the events in Indonesia that led to the fall of President Suharto. This in turn led to the third factor, which was his successor, President Habibie's dramatic announcement of the referendum, and the fourth and last was the implementation of that decision, with the complicated choices—moral, political, and pragmatic—that emerged from this opportunity.

Thinking back on this sequence of events, I am reaffirmed in my conviction that without Kofi's initial decision to activate a negotiating process on East Timor and to not only keep it alive but to vigorously push it at all times, the United Nations would not have been in a position to seize the opportunities offered by the devolution of political events in Indonesia. In other words, we kept the ball in our possession, and ran with it as soon as we got the chance.

A few personal thoughts in elaboration of this contention may be relevant. By January of 1999, we had an ongoing process of negotiations that was firmly in place, and which appeared to be quite promising. The unexpected Habibie announcement suddenly provided us with an exciting window of opportunity, which we were determined to seize, especially as our negotiating institution was now in such substantive form and position.

It also soon became clear to us that the Habibie initiative was largely personal, and that far from enjoying broad-based support it was, in fact, opposed by powerful elements, both civilian as well as military, within Indonesia. Hence our acceptance of the difficult time constraints demanded by the Habibie administration, since we wished to do what we could to help it to prepare and present the package to the MPR for its August meeting.

The issue of security was, of course, a matter of major concern and consideration, and any fool could see that the ideal solution would have been to prepare and induct an international peace keeping force into East Timor. But the prevalent realities ruled out such a possibility, and rendered equally foolish any idea of the possibility of its implementation.

In the first place, the lack of time and the high improbability of obtaining troop contributors would have made it impossible to obtain an enabling Security Council resolution for this purpose. Secondly, the Government of Indonesia was profoundly, and quite rightly, jealous of guarding its sovereignty: it vehemently opposed the presence of peacekeeping forces in East Timor, which it regarded as Indonesian soil. In the third place, Foreign Minister Alatas, in his usual persuasive fashion, made the irrefutable argument that since the proposal for popular consultation, complete with an urgent time frame, emanated from President Habibie himself, it was axiomatic that he would do everything to ensure its implementation in peace and good order.

These, then, were some of the major considerations on which we proceeded to the May 5 Agreements. But even so, we managed to insert a number of supplementary safeguards on security. It was quite clear, from my own assessment as well as those of the US, UK, Australian, New Zealand, and Japanese Governments, that we had pushed the envelope as far as it could go. Any further insistence on the deployment of international peacekeepers would have been a deal breaker.

Alatas was frankly and publicly adamant on this issue: "We do not regard ourselves as an occupying power in East Timor, and we will never allow foreign troops in to oversee the vote." He added, "For us, this is an absolute matter of national sovereignty."

Our next critical and decisive moment came during the period of voter registration and campaigning. The security situation was far from satisfactory, but the modalities for the popular consultation were progressing in encouraging fashion, and UNAMET was carrying out its duties in enthusiastic and efficient fashion. We decided, therefore, that although there was no green light, we could carry out a carefully calibrated progress on a red and amber light basis, until we reached the time of registration.

And when registration day arrived, we faced our next critical moment. The magnitude and enthusiasm with which the brave citizens of East Timor responded to the registration process became for me the decisive factor. I was determined to go ahead with the ballot, doing in the meanwhile whatever we could, through pleas, pressures, threats, and imprecations to the Indonesian authorities, to minimize the fury of the militia.

It was clear to me that for the purposes of the campaign we were nowhere near the level playing field as decreed by the May 5 Agreements, but it was also equally clear to me that if we were to wait for this to happen, we would never reach the day for the ballot.

I put this situation frankly to Xanana Gusmao, and he fully concurred with our decision to stay on course, adding that the CNRT had been campaigning for twenty-five years and did not now need the formality of the level playing field arrangements envisaged in the Agreement. In this connection, there is a revealing report from *The Asian Wall Street Journal* in its October 22/23, 1999 issue:

> In early August, Megawati Sukarnoputri, then the presidential front-runner, made the last of her many appeals to delay East Timor's referendum on independence from Indonesia.
>
> Sitting beneath a portrait of her father—Indonesia's founding president Sukarno—at her suburban Jakarta estate, Ms. Megawati warned Jamsheed Marker, a United Nations special envoy, that the risk of bloodshed was simply too high.
>
> Mr. Marker's response was equally blunt. "I told her it had to go ahead," he says. "It was the UN's solemn duty to go ahead with the vote."

The next critical phase came on Monday, August 30, 1999, the day of the ballot. Here again a comment from the same piece in *The Asian Wall Street Journal* is relevant:

> Despite misgivings about leaving security to the Indonesian military, the meeting led Mr. Annan and his aides to determine that pushing for an international peacekeeping force would be a deal breaker. Diplomats from the US, Australia, and other key allies, who weren't at the meeting, soon also came to the same conclusion: Either Indonesia would take care of security, or the vote wouldn't happen.
>
> Pushing Jakarta too hard made little sense to the US, in any event. Indonesia was still struggling to emerge from the political chaos that followed the end of President Suharto's 32-year old rule last year. Inside the White House, fears ran high that the world's fourth-most-populous country might splinter or slip into anarchy. East Timor seemed important, administration officials say, but the vote wasn't important enough to undermine Indonesia's stability. As a result, US officials walked a political tightrope.

The post ballot violence obviously provoked a great deal of international outrage at the time. Not surprisingly, it also evoked considerable Monday morning quarterbacking and, equally without surprise, it was once again open season on the United Nations. But even in those dark, hectic days I knew that we had done the right thing. It was clear to me that the people of East Timor, even though they knew that they were likely to be the victims of intimidation and violence, wanted the ballot to go ahead, and participated in it with courage and determination.

Xanana Gusmao was also quite clear on this issue, although he later confided to me that he had underestimated the scale and nature of the pro-integration reaction. From the political aspect, a postponement or delay of the ballot would have had disastrous and unpredictable consequences for the consultation process, and thrown into jeopardy the May 5 Agreements.

And the people of East Timor, who had so courageously conducted themselves and placed such implicit trust in the United Nations, would have found themselves facing an uncertain future, abandoned at the last critical moment, in the most cruel and unconscionable fashion. Lastly, all the evidence strongly suggests that violence and killings would have increased, and not decreased, if the ballot had been postponed.

It is my firm conviction, profoundly reinforced after the registration results, that the United Nations *had* to stay on course for the rest of the consultation process. There is also one final matter for speculation: as subsequent events would shortly reveal, President Habibie, who was the strongest proponent in Jakarta for an East Timor referendum, soon found himself out of office. Would his bold East Timor policy not have also followed him into the wilderness?

The member states who were most closely involved in the East Timor negotiations—Australia, New Zealand, Japan, the United Kingdom, and the United States—always remained fully convinced that the United Nations should proceed with the consultation process and the ballot. It is this conviction that motivated the political pressure that each brought to bear, at the highest level, on Jakarta, and which finally persuaded Habibie to accept an international peacekeeping force in East Timor.

The final sterling contribution of this group of Friends of the Secretary-General was the rapid and efficient deployment of the peacekeeping force, which arrived at unprecedented speed, a mere sixteen days after the ballot, and effectively contained the widespread deaths that would have occurred.

The last word must rest, as always, with the East Timorese people. When Secretary-General Kofi Annan made his first visit to East Timor on February 17, 2000, he was accorded a vast, spontaneous greeting that was both emotional and overwhelming. He received, of course, the profuse and deeply felt thanks of the leaders, such as Xanana Gusmao, Jose Ramos Horta, and Bishops Belo and Nasciemento.

But more than that he received the thanks, the blessings, and the embraces of thousands of enthusiastic East Timorese citizens. And he was told by these same people, in words, in tears, in joyous gestures, and roaring accolades, that they would always be grateful to him for what the United Nations had done in East Timor. Many of them told him this even as they showed him their destroyed homesteads and the graves of their loved ones.

East Timor had endured three centuries of colonialism, followed by a quarter century of occupation. Now, the United Nations had negotiated, and I stress the word negotiated, its long awaited freedom and inde-

Secretary-General Kofi Annan (left) and President Abdurrahman Wahid at a press conference, Jakarta, 16 February 2000. UN/DPI Photograph by Eskinder Debebe.

pendence. In a conflict that has lasted as long as the one in East Timor, there are always many heroes and a not inconsiderable number of villains. But there are many whose motives and motivations have been unexceptionable, even though their actions may be questionable.

This applies, in particular, to a large number of Indonesians whose attitude toward East Timor was founded on considerations of patriotism and national unity, and not on aggrandizement or oppression. It is a tribute, therefore, to their moral integrity that they willingly entered into negotiations to ascertain the will of the East Timorese people, and an even greater tribute to their moral courage when, overcoming a quarter century of emotional attachment, they accepted the outcome of the referen-

Top: Secretary-General Kofi Annan meets Bishop Belo (left) and Bishop Nasciemento in Dili, 17 February 2000. The Bishops, whose tasks could not have been more exacting, played a key role in the political process. Their counsel and guidance were vital during negotiations.

Bottom: East Timor's Kofi Annan thanks the United Nations. Xanana Gusmao in the left foreground, unidentified man behind Gusmao, Kofi Annan, Sergio Viera de Mello in background to right of Annan and a unidentified camerman.

dum. This applies, of course, to the overwhelming mass of the Indonesian people, and not the brutal few militia (most of whom were East Timorese, anyway) who committed the outrageous acts of violence in the post-referendum period.

Above all, the problem of East Timor was solved through a process of negotiations in which the United Nations was constantly and intimately involved at all stages, from initiation to completion. Prince von Bulow once defined diplomacy as "a first class stall seat at the theater of life," and it was my privilege and good fortune to have occupied one such seat as the saga of East Timor was played out.

What it revealed was the extent and nature of the crucial role played by three great statesmen—Kofi Annan, Ali Alatas, and Jaime Gama. Guided by principles and motivations of the highest moral and humanitarian nature, Alatas and Gama overcame the difficulties and obstacles posed by narrow personality interests or domestic political compulsions. They worked with the wise Kofi, as he quietly encouraged, prodded, persuaded, and suggested ways to move out of a dilemma and into progress.

Concessions were made by both Alatas and Gama for the purpose of securing overall progress, and this, in its own fashion, led to an atmosphere of mutual respect and understanding. For the United Nations, East Timor is a success story which was brought about by three wise men, who negotiated and worked on the basis of Edmund Burke's profound exhortation, "our patience will achieve more than our force."

Epilogue

All the forces in the world are not so powerful as an idea whose time has come.

Victor Hugo

On Monday 20 May 2002 the United Nations Security Council, meeting in New York under the presidency of Singapore's Foreign Minister, by appropriate coincidence an ASEAN member, declared: "The Security Council looks forward to the day in the near future when East Timor will join us as a member of the United Nations, and to working closely with its representatives."

In Dili, half a world away and twelve time zones earlier, the people of East Timor had enthusiastically celebrated their independence at a mass gathering where speeches, songs and dances, and a burst of fireworks mingled in ecstatic fashion. At the stroke of midnight as 20 May commenced, in a solemn and moving ceremony, UN personnel under the approving gaze of Secretary-General Kofi Annan lowered the United Nations flag; Xanana Gusmao supervised, in its stead, the hoisting of the flag of East Timor, which fluttered for the first time over the independent land of which it was the symbol. The latter half of the Twentieth Century has witnessed the creation of more new states than ever before in human history, and in many cases their independence was nurtured to a considerable extend by the United Nations. Nevertheless, the emergence of a new nation is not a daily occurrence, and East Timor has the dual distinction of being the first newly independent nation in the 21st century as well as the one hundred and ninetieth member of the United Nations. The midnight independence celebrations in Dili included the speeches of Secretary-General Kofi Annan as well President Xanana Gusmao, punctuated by traditional folk songs and dances. It also included a

Secretary-General Kofi Annan and Xanana Gusmao address a joyful gathering of
East Timorese, Dili, 18 February 2000.

dramatic welcome by Xanana to Megawati Sukarnoputri, the latter's short
flying visit to Dili being not without considerable controversy in Jakarta.
Xanana received the Indonesian President at the airport, drove with her
first to a military cemetery in Dili where both leaders rendered homage
to the graves of Indonesian soldiers killed in East Timor (a gesture obviously designed to placate Megawati's domestic opposition), and then
brought her to the site of the independence celebrations. Here Xanana
paid a generous public tribute to Megawati and assured Indonesia of East
Timor's friendship and co-operation.

The next morning, at a public ceremony, East Timor's first President,
Prime Minister and Cabinet Ministers took their oath of office, after
which they proceeded to a meeting of the Constituent Assembly, where
the newly elected members passed their first resolution, seeking East
Timor's membership of the United Nations: a copy of this document was
then handed over to Secretary-General Kofi Annan. Next, the Secretary-
General inaugurated the new UN premises in Dili, henceforth designated
as the United Nations Mission of Support in East Timor (UNMISET).
Scheduled to remain for two years, with a Security Council mandate to
assist the fledgling government of East Timor, UNMISET has an initial
strength of 5,000 peacekeeping troops, 1,200 police officers and about 100
civilian experts.

Xanana Gusmao, in his inaugural address, described East Timor as

"Viva!" A greeting from Xanana Gusmao (left) to J.M. (center) and the crowd at a celebration meeting in Dili, 18 February 2000. Arnaz Marker at right. Photograph: Tamrat Samuel, author's collection.

Kofi Annan and his wife, Nane, with some of the orphans who survived the militia terror.

"the poorest country in Asia". Whilst this was true under prevalent circumstances, fortunately it is not likely to remain so for long, as there are several factors which provide grounds of optimism. In the first instance, contributions from the international community in terms of funds and technical assistance would enable the country to establish its basic economic and administrative structures over the first few years of its existence. By that time the generation of revenues from lucrative Timor Sea oil and gas resources should commence. Current budget projections estimate that the taxes from oil and gas revenues will cover most government expenditure until 2006, with an anticipation of earnings estimated at $7 billion in the first seventeen years. To this could be added the later earnings from the even richer Sunrise seabed sector, estimated to be about three times the size of the current Bagu Udam fields. Considering that the population of East Timor is less than a million people, the availability of these revenues is most reassuring.

Just as reassuring is the commitment of East Timor's present leadership to the concepts of freedom, democracy, egalitarianism, human rights and the rule of law. The long and bitter freedom struggle has created a cadre of dedicated leadership that promises "good governance," an essential requirement of stability and statehood that is more lasting and valuable than natural wealth, which can be so easily squandered through irresponsible public profligacy. In this respect, the vision, ideas and dedication of Xanana Gusmao and his colleagues are perhaps just as important for East Timor as the Bagu Udam and Sunrise oilfields on the bed of the Timor Sea. Now, Timor Loresae is both a reality and "an idea whose time has come."

Index

African National Congress (ANC) 52
Alatas, Ali "Alex" 26–27, 33, 45, 48–
49, 66–68, 75, 84, 86–91, 93, 99, 103,
107, 109, 117, 119–121, 123, 125, 132,
134–135, 137–139, 141–142, 145, 147,
153–157, 159, 163–167, 169, 184–185,
189, 192–194, 196–200, 205, 210
Albright, Madeleine 141, 197
Alexander, David 51
Alkateri, Mari 63
All Inclusive East Timorese Dialogue
(AIETD) 16–17, 22, 27, 35, 50, 53,
62–65, 80–84, 88, 90, 93, 98, 101–
104, 106, 111, 174
Andrews, David 141, 189
Annan, Kofi 4–5, 7, 10–12, 46, 59, 65,
75, 79, 124, 132, 144–145, 155, 163,
196, 198, 204, 206–207, 210–212, 214
Annan, Nane 214
Anwar, Devi Fortuna 167, 169
Armed East Timorese Resistance
(FALANTIL) 110, 151, 176, 186,
193, 198
Asia Pacific Economic Cooperation
group (APEC) 197
The Asian Wall Street Journal 206
Association of Southeast Asian
Nations (ASEAN) 8–9, 21, 74–75,
78, 199
Aurelius, Marcus 18
Axworthy, Lloyd 197

Bacon, Francis 86, 92
Barrat, Paul 179
Bay, Kam Ranh 9

Belo, Ximenese 10, 19, 21, 38, 40–42,
47, 63, 71, 88, 91, 97, 99, 102, 105, 112,
115, 135, 146, 168, 174, 186, 195, 207,
209
Bergolts, Olga 202
Bhagat, Mohinder 36
Boutros-Ghali, Boutros 4
Bradley, Pat 150
Brandt, Juan Carlos 177
Brazael, Aurelia de 50
Burke, Edmund 210

Camdessus, Michel 67, 197
Caralascalao, Mario 110
Carascalao, Joao 63
Carascalao, Manuel 71, 114
Cavafy, C. P. 7
Ceauşescu, Elena 3
Ceauşescu, Nicolae 3
Charles II 143
Chew, Beng Yong 164
Chief Military Liaison Officer
(CMLO) 163, 195
Christopher, Robin 36, 198
Cipinang prison 34–35, 70, 92, 111,
120, 122
Civilian Police Component (CIVPOL)
153, 159, 162, 179, 188, 193, 195
Clinton, President Bill 141, 197
Cold War 1, 3, 9
Committee on Peace and Stability
(KPS) 175, 186
Confidence Building Measures
(CBMs) 62, 77, 80
Cook, Robin 64, 197

Cosgrove, Peter 199
Cruz, Lopez da 63, 111, 187–188

Damiri, Gen. Adam 38
Darusman, Marzuki 93
de Klerk, F. W. 61
Department of Political Affairs 12
Dhamiri, Adam 113
Dickens, Charles 132
Djalal, Dino Patti 116
Downer, Alexander 178–179, 200

Eldon, Stuart 14, 74

Fatchett, Derek 64
Feingold, Senator 51
Ferraro, Staatsekretarin Benita Walde-
   mar 64
Fischer, Jeff 164, 187
Fischer, Tim 179
Flecker, James Elroy 7
Frawley, Elizabeth 19
Frechette, Louise 163

Gama, Jaime 20–22, 48–49, 69, 73, 76,
   89, 103, 106–107, 124–125, 135, 145,
   154–157, 200, 210
Gandi, Mahatma 120
Gaulle, Charles de 130–131
Grant, Milton 145
Guiterrez, Antonio 21, 42, 73–76, 90
Gusmao, Xanana 10, 15, 33–35, 43,
   59–60, 66–71, 80, 82, 84–85, 87–88,
   90, 92–93, 96–100, 102, 104–105,
   109–113, 119–120, 122, 124, 135–136,
   146, 155, 166, 169–170, 174, 176–177,
   186, 193, 198, 201–202, 205–207, 209,
   211–213, 215

Habibie, Bacharuddin Jusuf "B. J." 72,
   75–76, 80, 85, 87–88, 94–98,
   117–120, 128–132, 134, 137–138,
   141–143, 146–147, 152–155, 157,
   166–172, 175, 180, 184–186, 196–199,
   204–205, 207
Haider, Rezaqul 163–164, 189, 195–196
Hamlet 17
Hanum, Hurst 84
Henry V 37, 44
Herodotus 72
Homer, The Odyssey: Book I 56

Horta, Jose Ramos 10, 15, 19, 21, 27,
   47, 63, 68, 82, 128, 174, 200, 207
Howard, John 128–129, 153
Hugo, Victor 211
Hutter, Joachim 36

Indonesian military (TNI) 176, 186, 196
Internally Displaced Persons (IDPs)
   165, 183, 195
International Committee of the Red
   Cross (ICRC) 57, 72
International Force East Timor
   (INTERFET) 196, 199–200
International Monetary Fund (I.M.F.)
   67, 76, 79–80
Isaac, Leandro 114

Jamall, Aban 109
James II 143
Jenie, Rezlan Ishar 34

Kennedy, Patrick 51
Khan, Aga 120
Koh, Siew Aing 109
Koh, Tommy Aing 109
Kohl, Helmut 33, 69
KOPASSUS 32, 69, 96, 110, 116
Kreigler, Johann 150
Krumbach, Schloss 62, 64, 103

Macaulay 24
Machel, Gracia 58
Machiavelli 101, 107
Macmillan, Harold 2
Makarim, Zacky Anwar 96, 109–111,
   164, 187
Makhota Hotel 39, 43, 114
Mandela, Nelson 35, 52, 57–61, 66–67,
   69–70
Marker, Arnaz 5, 45, 109, 117, 142, 185,
   187
Marker, Feroza 5
Marker, Niloufer 5
Marker, Sam 5
La Marseillaise 108
Martin, Ian 95, 159, 164, 167, 174, 184–
   185, 188, 193–195
McCarthy, John 36, 111, 128
McKinnon, Don 197
Mello, Sergio Vieira de 202
Military Liaison Officers (MLOs) 163

Mills, Alan 164, 188, 195
Ministry of Foreign Affairs (DEPLU) 26
Minty, Abdul 58–59
Monteiro, Antonio 14
Moore, John 179
Muladi, Justice Minister 117, 119, 166–167, 169, 185, 193

Nasciemento, Bishop Basilio de 38, 40–42, 92, 102, 109, 112, 115, 135, 168, 174, 186, 207, 209
National Council of East Timorese Resistance (CNRT) 82, 90, 152, 174, 183, 186, 205
Neves, Fernando 36, 53, 76, 81, 83, 101, 106
Nobel Peace Prize 10, 15
Nobel Prize Committee 9
Non Government Organizations (NGOs) 9, 19, 106, 181, 188
Nzo, Alfred 59

Office for the Coordination of Humanitarian Affairs (OCHA) 162
Office of the High Commissioner for Human Rights (OHCHR) 162

Parmenides 46
Peoples Consultative Assembly (MPR) 121–122, 128, 130, 134, 147, 166, 183, 200, 204
Perelli, Carina 186
Perez de Cuellar, Javier 4
Personal Representative of the Secretary-General (PRSG) 10, 12, 32, 49
Pfanner, Toni 111
Pickering, Tom 50–51
Powles, Michael 14, 74
Prendergast, Sir Kieran 13, 60
Pushkin, Alexander 181

Quarterman, Mark 95

Raies, Amien 35
Rajan, Ravi 36
Rivai, General 37–38, 42
Riza, Iqbal 12
Robinson, Mary 56, 166
La Rochefoucauld, François 121, 130
Roth, Stanley 50, 74, 78, 81, 87, 120, 141, 144, 183, 196

Roy, Stapleton 36, 111
Royal Indian Navy 1

Sampaio, Jorge 20–21, 68, 82
Samuel, Tamrat 13–14, 16, 18, 36, 58–60, 66, 103, 105, 108, 112, 136, 159, 162, 164, 174, 213
Santa Cruz massacre 9
Santos, Carlos dos 21
Schneider, Evan 125
Senior Officials Meeting (SOM) 50, 54–56, 62–63, 80–83, 105–107, 122
Shakespeare, William 37
Shattuck, John 50
Shaw, George Bernard 161
Silaen, Chief Timbul 188
Silva da Costa, Herminio da 114
Simbolon, Colonel 39
Smith, Mike 178
Soares, Abilio Osorio 39–40, 63, 91, 102, 164, 172
Soderberg, Nancy 14, 74
Sonh, Bong-Seuk 150
Sorabjee, Soli 166
Soto, Alvaro de 13, 55, 60
Special Autonomous Region of East Timor (SARET) 122
Subianto, Prabowo 32–33, 42, 69, 71
Sudrajat, Eddy 44
Suharto, President 29–32, 34, 42, 47, 52, 59–60, 66–68, 72, 74–76, 80, 87, 129, 143, 204
Sukarnoputri, Megawati 35, 93, 134, 170–171, 212
Suratnam, Tono 114, 116

Takasu, Yukio 14, 74
Tanjung, Feisal 44
Tarmidzi, Agus 164
Tocqueville, Alexis de 78

United Nations Mission in East Timor (UNAMET) 148, 150, 158, 161–165, 167, 169, 172–174, 176–179, 182–183, 186–189, 192–197, 205
United Nations Mission of Support in East Timor (UNMISET) 212
United Nations Transitional Authority in East Timor (UNTAET) 127, 200, 202

Vendrell, Francesc 13–14, 26, 36, 60,
  108, 111, 116–117, 159

Wahid, Abdurrahman "Gus Dur"
  35, 93, 112–113, 170–172,
  208
Wensley, Penny 14, 74, 153, 177
Westbrook, Roger 19, 74
Wibisono, Makarim 14
Wimhurst, David 164, 167
Wiranto, General 97, 117–120, 135, 141,
  163, 167, 172, 176, 184–186, 189, 192–
  193, 196–197
Wisnumurti, Nugroho 36, 53, 81, 83,
  101, 106, 111
Wolfensohn, Jim 197
World War II 1
Wortel, Johannes 164

Yew, Lee Kuan 69, 179–180
Yosfiah, Yunus 121
Yudono, Susilo Bambang 96, 110